The British Empire

The British Empire: Sunrise to Sunset is a broad survey of the history of the British Empire from its beginnings to its demise that offers a comprehensive analysis of what life was like under colonial rule, weaving the everyday stories of people living through the experience of colonialism into the bigger picture of empire.

The experience of the British Empire was not limited to what happened behind closed doors or on the floor of Parliament. It affected men, women and children across the globe, making a difference to what they ate and what kind of work they did, what languages and lessons they learned in school, and how they were able to live their lives. This new edition expands its coverage and discusses the relationship between Brexit and empire as well as the recent controversies connected to empire that have engulfed Britain: the Windrush scandal, the fight over the Chagos Islands and the Mau Mau lawsuits, bringing it up to date and engaging with key debates that govern the study of empire.

Painting a picture of life for all those affected by empire and supported by maps and illustrations, this is the perfect text for all students of imperial history.

Philippa Levine holds the Walter Prescott Webb Chair in History at the University of Texas at Austin, United States. A native of Britain, she is the author of a number of books about Britain and the Empire as well as the history of prostitution and of eugenics.

The British Empire
Sunrise to Sunset

Third edition

Philippa Levine

 Routledge
Taylor & Francis Group

LONDON AND NEW YORK

Third edition published 2020
by Routledge
2 Park Square, Milton Park, Abingdon, Oxon, OX14 4RN

and by Routledge
52 Vanderbilt Avenue, New York, NY 10017

Routledge is an imprint of the Taylor & Francis Group, an informa business

First edition published by Pearson Education Limited 2007
Second edition published by Pearson Education Limited 2013

British Library Cataloguing-in-Publication Data
A catalogue record for this book is available from the British Library

Library of Congress Cataloging-in-Publication Data
Names: Levine, Philippa, author.
Title: The British Empire : sunrise to sunset / Philippa Levine.
Description: Third edition. | New York : Routledge, 2020. |
Includes bibliographical references and index.
Identifiers: LCCN 2019033599 (print) | LCCN 2019033600 (ebook) |
ISBN 9780815366225 (hardback) | ISBN 9780815366232 (paperback) |
ISBN 9781351259682 (ebook)
Subjects: LCSH: Great Britain–Colonies–History. |
Commonwealth countries–History. | Imperialism–History. |
Decolonization–Great Britain–Colonies–History. |
Civilization, Modern–British influences. |
Great Britain–Foreign relations.
Classification: LCC DA16 .L48 2020 (print) |
LCC DA16 (ebook) | DDC 909/.0971241–dc23
LC record available at https://lccn.loc.gov/2019033599
LC ebook record available at https://lccn.loc.gov/2019033600

ISBN: 978-0-8153-6622-5 (hbk)
ISBN: 978-0-8153-6623-2 (pbk)
ISBN: 978-1-351-25968-2 (ebk)

Typeset in Sabon
by Newgen Publishing UK

Contents

List of figures   vi
List of maps   vii
Preface to the first edition   ix
Preface to the second edition   xi
Preface to the third edition   xiii
Acknowledgements   xv

1 Uniting the kingdom   1

2 Slaves, merchants and trade   13

3 Settling the 'New World'   31

4 After America   43

5 Britain in India   63

6 Global growth   83

7 Ruling an empire   102

8 Being ruled   122

9 Gender and sexuality   140

10 Contesting empire   162

11 Decolonisation   185

Chronology of British Empire   212
Index   258

Figures

2.1 Slaves ladle steaming juice from vat to vat, Antigua, 1823   19

2.2 Anti-slavery medallion created by the Wedgwood factory, 1787   22

3.1 *The horse America, throwing his master*, 1779   39

4.1 John Webber, *Poedua, daughter of Oreo, chief of Ulaietea, one of the Society Isles*, 1785   44

4.2 Thomas Watling, *A group on the North Shore of Port Jackson, New South Wales*   50

5.1 Brighton Pavilion   67

7.1 Golden Jubilee wallpaper, 1887   103

7.2 Thomas Joshua Alldridge, a district commissioner in Sierra Leone in the 1890s   105

7.3 The Empire on Whom the Sun Never Sets postcard   106

7.4 Craven tobacco advertisement, 'The Sun never sets'   107

7.5 'A Group of Hausa', 1901   114

7.6 Colonial troops of the British Empire in England for the Diamond Jubilee celebrations of Queen Victoria, 1897   116

8.1 An idealised depiction of the 'coolie' in the nineteenth century   132

8.2 Colonial authorities disinfecting the bedding of plague victims in India, 1897   134

8.3 George V Jubilee procession in Hong Kong   137

9.1 Missionary's wife and child seated on a hippopotamus, Africa, c.1910–20   154

9.2 Indian rebellion (1857) memorial at Cawnpore, India   156

10.1 Safe as the British Empire: War Savings Certificates, First World War poster   167

10.2 Advanced Australia! *Punch*, 25 April 1900   169

10.3 The King David Hotel, Jerusalem, after the bombing, 1946   176

11.1 The 1966 Royal tour of the West Indies   192

11.2 Strong words in Cyprus   197

11.3 Jamaican immigrants at Victoria Station, London, 1956   202

11.4 Mau Mau captives lined up prior to being transported to detention camps   208

Maps

0.1   Imperial Federation map, c.1886, by Captain J. C. Colombo   viii
2.1   The Empire in the West Indies   14
5.1   India in 1857   78
6.1   Britain's holdings in East and South-East Asia   84
6.2   Africa after the Boer War   94
10.1 The scope of the British Empire in the interwar years of the
      twentieth century   163

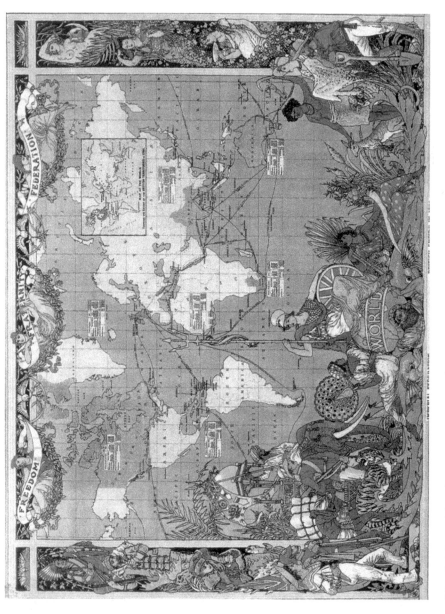

Map 0.1 Imperial Federation map, c.1886, by Captain J. C. Colombo

Source: World History Archive/Alamy Stock Photo

Preface to the first edition

In his autobiography, first published in 1936, the Indian nationalist leader, Jawaharlal Nehru, remarked rather bitterly that Indian nationalists were being chided for desiring national independence in an increasingly globalised world. 'It is curious', he pondered, 'how all roads in England – liberalism, pacifism, socialism, etc – lead to the maintenance of the Empire.'[1]

Contrast this view, which emphasises how central a concern empire was for the British, with that recently espoused by the historian Bernard Porter that the British were at best reluctant imperialists. As he puts it in the preface to his book, *The Absent-Minded Imperialists*, 'Imperial Britain was generally a *less* imperial society than is often assumed.'[2]

Porter's findings echo those more typically held in Britain, while Nehru's are more reflective of views held by those who experienced British colonial rule, and especially those jailed, censored and even tortured for their opposition to it.

This study leans in Nehru's direction, arguing that British history is incomplete without an understanding of its considerable imperial history, and that the British acquisition of an empire was by no means accidental or incidental. Whether one looks at the eighteenth century when wars with the European powers so often grew out of colonial disputes, at the nineteenth century when schoolchildren and exhibition-goers, novel readers and stamp collectors, all learned that Britain's greatness was in large part because of its imperial mission and its imperial possessions, or at the twentieth century when the effort to curb anti-colonial nationalism throughout the Empire was a policy shared by governments otherwise committed to significantly different political paths, imperialism mattered. It mattered to the British economy, it mattered to British definitions of national identity, and, above all, it mattered to those whose daily lives were affected by colonial rule, wherever they might live.

This study emphasises how both Britons and colonial peoples thought about, dealt with and lived in this vast and complex system. It foregrounds the experience of empire alongside the political fall-out that is so often the principal way in which imperialism is presented to us. As a result, the chapters of this book are themed in a number of different ways. For clarity the earlier chapters are geographical, each dealing with a particular site or region of imperialism and organised largely, though by no means exclusively, chronologically. Then come a series of chapters devoted to exploring how empire was lived and experienced: who ruled and how? How were men and women treated, regarded, shaped differently by and in the Empire? How did it feel to live under colonial rule, or to impose that rule? How were these experiences different in different kinds of colonies? Following these chapters, the study returns to the political arena to detail the disintegration of the Empire as protests against it grew and as the world stage changed especially in the years after the Second World War. Together these differently accented chapters offer a detailed view of the modern British Empire, from Ireland to India, from the West Indies to Hong Kong, from Africa to Malaysia and beyond.

Notes

1 Jawaharlal Nehru, *Autobiography* (Oxford: Oxford University Press, 1985; 1st edn, Delhi, 1936), p. 420.
2 Bernard Porter, *The Absent-Minded Imperialists. Empire, Society, and Culture in Britain* (Oxford: Oxford University Press, 2004), p. xv.

Preface to the second edition

In the few years between the first and second editions of this text, the scholarship on European imperialism generally, and on the British Empire specifically, has grown in both size and complexity. Keeping up with this burgeoning literature is no easy task, but it is a joy to see the range and diversity of analysis that is now not just commonplace but which accepts as routine the integration of British and British imperial history. Even five years ago, this was a contested claim, but the trend in books as well as in courses at universities around the world has been towards amalgamating these two once-disparate histories.

My own approach continues to believe that this is a fruitful course, and that neither the history of domestic Britain nor of its Empire can be fully appreciated without reference to the other. This revised and updated edition continues also to rely interpretatively on three more bolstering principles: that the British Empire was not a benign and kindly force when compared with its rivals, but a powerhouse always capable of attempting to impose its will through violence and coercion; that the British Empire was shaped by a deliberate set of policies and not acquired accidentally; and that the Empire was enormously important in and to Britain, and to the British people in many and varied ways.

In 2008, Paul Kennedy opined that 'I think it silly either to denounce or to rejoice in its existence. The empire happened. A small island state off the northwest shores of Europe ran a quarter of the globe for hundreds of years. This was no small thing. And it demands close study.'[1] Kennedy is right that this is a phenomenon that demands close study but my driving presuppositions necessarily question his belief that we are foolish to judge. The British Empire matters as much today, almost half a century after most of it rather rapidly disappeared. Why does it matter? In part because a good deal of the contemporary crises we face owe at least something to the activities and policies of the British, and solutions to problems are seldom hurt by the application of a historical perspective. But judging by the constant bubbling to the surface of both praise and longings for a return to the glory days of imperialism, it would seem that the Empire continues to have tremendous meaning certainly in the Anglo-American arena. Neo-imperialists in the United States regard the actions of the British Empire more favourably than some of its competitors, while in Britain imperial nostalgia continues to be a saleable commodity. Historians, surely then, are responding to current cultural and political positions; they cannot stand outside – aloof and objective, looking down from the Olympian heights – from the societies in which they live. Engaging with contemporary concerns is what keeps the discipline vital. Taking a position, whether favourable or opposed, on the phenomenon of imperialism does not strike me as 'silly' in the slightest.

Note

1 Paul Kennedy, 'The Imperial Mind: A Historian's Education in the Ways of Empire', *The Atlantic* (January/February 2008). www.theatlantic.com/magazine/archive/2008/01/the-imperial-mind/306566/, accessed 9 August 2012.

Preface to the third edition

On the face of it, the 2016 referendum that set in motion what was quickly dubbed Brexit, would seem to have scant connection to the British Empire. It was concerned, after all, with whether the United Kingdom should remain a member of the European Union, a body it managed to join only in the early 1970s after initial defeat and an increasingly desperate campaign to gain entry. But much of the debate and the sentiments surrounding this question, both before the vote and subsequently as Britain wrestles with how to effect its dissociation from Europe, stem from issues embedded in Britain's imperial history.[1]

Nostalgia for a powerful past and the argument for sovereignty are closely linked in the Brexit debate. The Leave campaign has emphatically argued that an independent sovereign Britain could once more be great, and it is clear that the 'greatness' it has in mind is akin to the power which the country wielded at the height of its imperial influence. Campaigning in 2016, the group Conservatives for Britain recommended exiting Europe 'so that we can control our borders, trade freely around the world and return power to Parliament to block harmful EU rules.'[2] Drier words, perhaps, than James Thomson's eighteenth-century lyrics for 'Rule Britannia' ('Rule, Britannia! Britannia, rule the waves! / Britons never, never, never shall be slaves') but reminiscent in sentiment, signifying that Britain does not take kindly to 'foreign' rule but is instead a 'natural' leader, the proof being its control of a vast Empire.

It was perhaps under Margaret Thatcher, prime minister from 1979 to 1990, that imperial nostalgia for this former greatness unencumbered by a European overlord began in earnest. Thatcher, initially a pro-European, increasingly came to see the EU as a European superstate trampling on local needs. Her ideas were increasingly rooted in a sentimental vision of Britain's former imperial greatness, and in the Falkland War of 1982 she revived a vision of glorious imperial Britain stamping out foreign despotism and corruption. It was a strategy that helped secure her re-election in 1983 despite her growing unpopularity (see Chapter 11).

Just as the Falklands incident was a canny diversion from Thatcher's less popular policies, Brexit has likewise proven a helpful distraction from the fact of the vast inequities in British society, offering the dream of a nationalism that unites all citizens under the flag whatever their economic status. In practice, neither Scotland nor Ireland see themselves as gaining from severing ties with Europe, reviving the colonial origins of their place in the British polity and likely risking violence in Ireland where the existing division between the Republic and Northern Ireland – a product of colonialism – poses nearly intractable border control issues.

The Brexit debate has also revived – or brought out of the shadows – a hostility to immigration that is on show in the immigration policies discussed in Chapter 11, themselves an outgrowth of the attitudes of British superiority that imperialism fostered in its heyday.

Mired in 'a fantasy of imperial-era strength and self-sufficiency', as Pankaj Mishra recently put it, Brexit may be the last gasp of an imperial nostalgia the British urgently need to shed.[3] Still, its tenacity in the national imagination speaks to just how large the Empire continues to loom and why it continues to matter as a topic of historical enquiry.

Notes

1 Stuart Ward and Astrid Rasch's collection of essays explore this theme: *Embers of Empire in Brexit Britain* (London: Bloomsbury, 2019).
2 https://digital.library.lse.ac.uk/objects/lse:jur367ber/read/single#page/1/mode/1up.
3 Pankaj Mishra, 'The Malign Incompetence of the British Ruling Class', *New York Times*, 7 January 2019. www.nytimes.com/2019/01/17/opinion/sunday/brexit-ireland-empire.html

Acknowledgements

When I first agreed to write this text, it never occurred to me that it would reach a second, let alone a third edition. Its longevity has kept me on my toes and helped me to stay current with an ever-growing literature on the British Empire, and most especially with the exciting new ideas that successive generations of scholars have produced. My greatest thanks, then, goes to those historians who have come after my cohort and who have transformed work in this field in innovative and stimulating ways.

I also thank those anonymous readers who took the time to review the previous edition and suggest changes, colleagues who assigned the book and let me know what did and did not work, and readers who, over the years, have contacted me to suggest corrections and changes. Knowing that there is still so much interest in this topic gives me hope in these turbulent times. Perhaps we might yet learn from the mistakes made.

Acknowledgements

1 Uniting the kingdom

Before the eighteenth century the colonial world was dominated by Spain and Portugal, and Britain's overseas activities in the sixteenth and even the seventeenth century were often focused on what could be wrested or gained from these powerful Iberian empires. The British Empire before the mid-seventeenth century was a highly local affair, and overseas activity was concentrated mostly on trading and exploration. The domination of Wales, Scotland and Ireland by England, which by the nineteenth century saw all these regions directly ruled from the Westminster parliament, is often dubbed 'internal colonialism'. Three Acts of Union – from the sixteenth to the very start of the nineteenth century – cemented the legal, political and economic relationships between dominant England and this so-called Celtic fringe. Bringing Wales, Scotland and Ireland within a broader British realm represents some of England's earliest forays into colonial rule, for though the formal statutes linking these countries take us through to the nineteenth century, English interest in, and often coercion of, these neighbouring regions has a much longer history.

The first of these lands to come directly under English control was Wales, brought formally into the English fold by a 1536 Act of Union that created 27 Welsh parliamentary constituencies. For at least a hundred years prior to this, conflicts between the Welsh and the English were common and, in the borderlands between the two especially, the English imposed discriminatory regulations and practices on the Welsh. The Welsh lacked many of the rights taken for granted by the English, a pattern of inequality and prejudice that would only grow after formal annexation.

Scotland's associations with England were more complicated, and its annexation more drawn out. It was under Stuart rule in 1603 that the union of the Scottish and English crowns was formalised, with the seat of government firmly located in England. The new king, James I (who was also James VI of Scotland), styled himself King of Great Britain, in which he included Wales, Scotland and England. Little more than a hundred years later, in 1707, an Act of Union robbed Scotland of its own parliament: 45 seats in the House of Commons and 16 in the House of Lords represented the new Scottish constituencies. Unlike Wales, however, and largely because it had been an identifiable sovereign state before unification, Scotland maintained even after union with England its own judicial system, its own national church (Presbyterian, unlike England's Episcopal Church of England) and a separate education system. And unlike the 1536 Act which had yoked Wales to England, the 1707 Act was a product of negotiation and not brute force. Scotland was in a position to sever its ties with England and the precise purpose of the 1707 legislation was to prevent that. The Act thus gave the Scots considerably more latitude than the 1536 Act had allowed the Welsh. Indeed, outside the wealthier segments of society, it probably made little difference to most Scottish men and women. Colin Kidd argues that, though always controversial, the Anglicisation of Scotland was welcomed by many Scots.[1] On the whole, the Union was reasonably harmonious and by no means wholly disruptive for Scotland.

The same could not be said for the 1800 Act of Union, which took effect on the first day of the new century, 1 January 1801. A number of critical political factors prompted this union with Ireland, largely related to Britain's vulnerability, perceived or real, to foreign invasion. Ireland's incorporation came at a time when Britain was almost constantly at war with the Catholic power of France, and sometimes with Catholic Spain, and shortly after a popular uprising in Ireland had been subdued. Ireland was, of course, a dominantly Catholic land. Wolfe Tone's 1798 Irish rebellion was a violent one, with almost 30,000 fatalities. The fact that the rebellion had been aided by the French (despite the fact that Tone was himself a Protestant) fuelled English fears, especially during the threatening years of Napoleon's rule when Britain's political and military strengths were severely tested.

With a far larger population than either Scotland or Wales, the 1800 Act granted Ireland 100 seats in the House of Commons and 32 in the House of Lords to represent its 5 million inhabitants. As with Scotland, this representation was premised on the dissolution of a separate Irish parliament, and though that all-Protestant body had long been under the English thumb, the symbolism of its abandonment was nonetheless potent in shaping the future of Irish politics.

Ireland's entanglements with England pre-date even those of Wales, and the Irish had experienced considerable erosion of their liberties over the years. English intrusions into Ireland date back to the thirteenth century, and by the sixteenth century England was actively engaged in a political, economic and religious subjugation of this neighbouring island. The dates are anything but coincidental, for the bloodshed over religion so characteristic of the Tudor years in England had deep and dangerous consequences for Catholic Ireland. By the late sixteenth century, there was some urgency to the policy of de-Catholicising Ireland through migration and plantation, as England became definitively Anglican. A greater and greater Protestant presence was imposed from the 1560s and for the next hundred years, with a corresponding dispossession and pauperisation of the Catholic Irish. When the Act of Union was passed in 1800 one promise upon which the old Irish parliament insisted before they would dissolve was that Catholics be allowed to vote and to hold public office. It was a promise that would remain unfulfilled for a further three decades. In March 1801, inability to keep that controversial promise prompted the prime minister, William Pitt, to resign his office.

After 1801, the kingdom – now consisting of Scotland, Wales, Ireland and England, together known as the United Kingdom – was governed as one polity from London. The state was more deeply centralised than ever before; the term Great Britain, already in use, now became the official designation of the nation. Some historians have argued that such centralisation was effective by 1640.[2] While this might be so in an informal sense, we can certainly point to 1801, the dawn of the nineteenth century, the moment when such centralising tendencies were fully and formally in place and when internal colonialism was complete. While Scotland retained a number of important local institutions, Britain had one parliament and a state religion secured by a Protestant succession to the monarchy.

It was fear of destabilising this Protestant sovereignty that prompted much of Britain's internal colonialism. Ireland as a predominantly Catholic region was the principal flashpoint for these religious debates within imperial policy, but religion was politically significant in Wales and Scotland too. In Scotland, Catholicism had largely given way by 1690 to a Calvinist-inspired Presbyterianism, under the influence of John Knox. It was distinctively different in character from English Episcopalian Christianity. The influence of Presbyterians among Protestant Irish groups, mostly centred in northern Ireland, was of considerable concern to English authorities in the eighteenth century. Presbyterianism in Scotland was acceptable, but its presence in Ireland added a complicating additional layer of religious discontent and dissent that could only add to England's problems there; the Protestant Irish strand was the origin of the Orange Movement, which quickly became deeply involved in political protests in Ireland. Meanwhile, in Wales the much-resented insistence by the Anglican Church that services be conducted solely in English secured a sturdy support for non-Anglican forms of Protestantism. The successful spread especially of Methodism and of Baptism owed much to the fact that these new Protestant movements conducted services in the local language. Likewise the translation of the Bible into Welsh, effected during the reign of Elizabeth I, ensured that virtually every household in Wales would continue to be exposed to Welsh even at a time when that language was under attack. The Welsh language remained alive in large part because of the actions of a monarch determined to impose Anglican conformity.

Non-Anglican Protestants and Catholics throughout the kingdom were barred from public office – local or national – by the Corporation Act of 1661 and the Test Acts of 1673 and 1678. These laws were part of the legal and political mechanism designed to protect a Protestant succession to the throne and to resist reinstatement of the Catholic Stuart dynasty. They also reflected a popular and growing sentiment that parliament – although hardly a representative institution at this time – was a specifically Protestant expression of liberty, what historian Linda Colley has called the 'Protestant inheritance'.[3] This celebration of Protestantism gave voice to a profound and long-standing anti-Catholicism in England, bolstered throughout the eighteenth century by the animosity between England and its most significant imperial and commercial rival, France. Ironically, after the defeat of France in the Seven Years' War in 1763, Britain's new colonial acquisitions made the Empire a far less identifiably Protestant one than it had formerly been. Catholics and non-Christians figured largely among those now subject to British imperial rule.

National stability and success depended on more, of course, than merely a continued adherence to Protestant Christianity. The needs of merchants and of bankers were vital, and the mercantilist economic principles of England in the seventeenth and eighteenth centuries meant that the state took a close interest in trade and commerce, actively regulating economic life as a way to pay government's expenses. In the early eighteenth century, for example, rarely a year passed in which a new law designed to regulate colonial trade in some fashion, or to control customs revenue (and its enemy, piracy) did not come before parliament. England kept a tight rein on colonial trade. Colonial goods were governed by strict regulations which gave a strong advantage to the English economy. Scots merchants and traders gained access to these lucrative colonial markets as a condition of the 1707 Act of Union. This meant that they were no longer required to route goods through England and pay duties on them, but could trade directly with other colonies within the British Empire. For Ireland, the wait was longer. An Act of 1696 had ruled that goods from the American plantations could not be landed in Ireland, a law that hindered the logical trade that might otherwise have flourished between America and Ireland, given their geographical proximity. Though this restriction was eliminated in 1731, Irish trade continued throughout the eighteenth century to be primarily with England, a situation that gave England as the dominant trading partner a considerable advantage.

Wales, like the often neglected Celtic region of Cornwall on England's south-west tip, was the site of active smuggling, both across the English–Welsh border and at the ports. The loss of government revenue that efficient smuggling represented made the control of contraband and of piracy a major component in England's desire to fold these 'peripheral' areas into the polity. The prospect of economic order in border areas – meaning a crackdown on smuggling and an organised customs agency pulling in significant revenue – was a key motive for internal colonialism.

This interest in potential revenues from the Celtic lands was seldom balanced by a corresponding commitment to investment in those regions. The Irish plantation schemes of the sixteenth and seventeenth centuries were more concerned with peopling the country with loyal Protestants than in giving economic aid to, or partnering with, the Irish. Centralisation, as it would do at a later stage of empire and in more distant lands, often worked to the advantage of the dominant and not the peripheral power. In the arena of banking, for example, London became more and more powerful at the expense of provincial centres, and the establishment of the Bank of England in London in the 1690s was some indication of the power lines in the fiscal world. While Scottish banks remained robust until the banking reorganisation of the 1840s, those in Wales and Ireland simply could not compete with their English rivals.

Economic competitiveness was crucial to political survival in this era, and here again it was English practices and activities which came to dominate, particularly from the eighteenth century. The landholding practices common in Celtic cultures were often incompatible with English ideas about inheritance, wealth creation and economic efficiency. The dominance of *gavelkind*, in which land was shared by all male heirs, contrasted with the typical practice of primogeniture in England, which concentrated wealth in eldest sons. In an era when the English economy was focusing increasingly on consolidating large tracts of land for more profitable and efficient cash-crop farming, the tendency in *gavelkind* for land plots to shrink to accommodate every son was regarded as a backward-looking and inefficient system. The clan system common in the Scottish Highlands was similarly regarded as hindering economic reform, with its sub-letting practices based on small farms and plots. English unwillingness to accommodate alternative practices and lifestyles led easily to a view of other cultures as barbarous, uncivilised and unproductive, an attitude that would re-emerge in relation to more distant cultures as imperialism grew, and which frequently became a justification for colonial rule or intervention.

This fear of the different and the alien also played heavily into another of the factors determining the course of internal colonialism, and that was Britain's European rivalries, most especially its enmity with France. Throughout the eighteenth century, France was England's most constant antagonist and tension between the two countries was frequently performed on the imperial stage. Between 1689 and 1815, the English and the French fought seven wars against one another. Furthermore, not only did the French aid the Americans in their quest for independence in the 1770s, but they helped the Catholic Stuart claimants in the 1715 and 1745 Jacobite uprisings in Scotland, which attempted to put a Catholic monarch back on the British throne. France and Britain fought one another in India, North America and the Caribbean. Rivalry between England and France would not die down until 1815, when the Napoleonic armies had been routed and their leader exiled. Britain also went to war with Spain and with Austria during the eighteenth century, and colonial trading rights were at the heart of these conflicts. These complex entanglements of religion, trade and expansionist rivalry directly affected the internal colonies of Scotland, Wales and Ireland. England's intent in annexing the Celtic lands had a lot to do with securing the borders to deter foreign invasion. Such fears were, of course, confirmed when Catholic France offered aid to the Stuart cause or in Ireland. When the 1798 rebellion in Ireland (which catalysed formal annexation in 1800) broke out, government feared that the resulting instability would allow a French invasion. This constant reading of the predatory hostility of France had powerful consequences; the marginality of the Welsh, Scottish and Irish was commonly transmuted into a potential disloyalty to the English state, a sentiment not always, of course, inaccurate given the resentments that colonialism invariably fostered. As a result, English control of these three regions grew, and the history of their relationship is one of increasing domination and supervision. England's close control of the Celtic regions was in part intended to stabilise rule at home and in part to secure the more distant outposts of empire so often under threat from rival European colonising powers.

This control made the Celtic lands more and more dependent, economically and politically, on England and, as a result, anxious to participate as much as possible in its complex, highly protected trading network. Even before formal annexation, the subjugation of Wales, Scotland and Ireland was high among English priorities. The 1720 Declaratory Act passed at Westminster was, in its own words, 'for the better securing the dependency of Ireland upon the crown of Great Britain'. The Act made laws passed at Westminster binding on Ireland and also ensured that appeals cases originating in Ireland were heard in England, formalising judicial control from the centre. This mechanism for asserting central authority was also applied in the American colonies in 1766, proclaiming parliament's right to legislate on behalf of the colonies in the wake of a slew of unpopular and vigorously resisted legislation. Unsurprisingly, neither the colonial assemblies in the Americas nor the Irish parliament welcomed such laws. The Irish Act of 1720 was repealed in 1782, and not insignificantly after the surrender of Lord Cornwallis' troops at Yorktown, the symbolically important colonial defeat for the English state that ended the American Revolution (see Chapter 3).

The Irish had made shrewd use of Britain's preoccupations in America. The American Revolution had wreaked havoc with the Irish economy, cutting off many of its markets. English merchants refused to relax any of the restrictions on Irish trade to help alleviate Ireland's crisis, and in the face of this intransigence the Irish retaliated by refusing to import British-manufactured goods. More pressingly, given how many of England's troops were deployed in America, Irish volunteer militia – Protestant and Catholic – began to drill and train all over the country, a move much feared by the English government which hastily moved to repeal the Declaratory Act. The Irish parliament was reconvened in an attempt to calm discontent, especially among Irish Protestants.

The victory of the Irish was, of course, short-lived, for within 20 years their parliament would once again be dissolved. And while Wolf Tone's rebellion in 1798 called for political representation for all Irish regardless of religious creed, the Irish parliament that had clawed back its existence in 1782 was an exclusively Protestant body with little interest in representing the Catholic majority. Internal tensions like these remind us that we should not classify the Celtic lands simply as victims of colonial aggression. Although they certainly experienced such aggression, the history of internal colonialism is far more complex; the Celtic regions were often also internally divided. They were also sometimes themselves anxious to colonise. In 1695, a Scottish expedition attempted to found a colony in Spanish Central America; the Darien project was a failure, but it certainly spurred the English to annex Scotland a decade later. The English were infuriated by this independent Scottish action, fearing its effects on English colonial trade and on relations with Spain. The Scots asserted their right to exercise an independent foreign policy, but the English threat to ban exports from Scotland to England subdued the Scots' protests. Scotland was clearly the weaker power in this exchange, yet it had attempted to colonise abroad despite its own experiences with a colonising power.

Further complicating any overly simple view is the tangible split between Lowland and Highland Scots. Urban Scotland in the eighteenth century was home to some of the most prominent thinkers of the era. Alongside such influential writers as David Hume, Adam Smith and Adam Ferguson, Scotland boasted sophisticated medical, scientific and legal establishments; medical and academic training in Scotland in the eighteenth century was far superior to that generally available to the south in England. In this intellectual climate, the poor and rural inhabitants of the Scottish Highlands were an alien people. The troops who defeated the 1745 Jacobite rebellion included many Lowland Scots as well as English soldiers. Highlanders were often regarded by the Lowland Scots as well as by the English as savages of little education and refinement. As a result, the destruction of Highland society after 1745, intended to discourage further rebellion, met with little opposition from influential Scottish politicians focused largely on the more economically developed southern regions of the country. Such divides suggest the dangers of over-simplifying, or indeed over-romanticising, colonial relationships.

In Wales, it was the English migrants who saw the Welsh as savages, for the Welsh population was small (half a million in 1801) and in some respects more homogeneous than the populations of Scotland and Ireland. English fear of intermingling with the Welsh had led, even before the Union, to regulations which, in a significant reversal of the typical status of men and women, classified as Welsh English men who married Welsh women. Wales, seen as backward, acquired such indices of modern development as universities and museums only towards the end of the nineteenth century, far later than the other Celtic regions.

Aside from the need to eradicate smuggling and to quell border raids, England's main interest in Wales was in its rich mineral possessions. Until the middle of the nineteenth century Wales was known mostly for the iron-working concentrated in Glamorganshire. After that, coal dominated. These raw materials spelled wealth and profit in the propertied echelons of society, but often ended up impoverishing the ordinary people of Wales. In many areas, there was no work other than in coal mining, and whole families worked at it, sons following their fathers into the mines, the women of the family providing domestic back-up and often working also at the coalface. Few opportunities to break this cycle were available, making Wales particularly vulnerable to economic depression. In the twentieth century especially, unemployment in the coal-mining valleys of Wales was among the most severe in the British Isles.

Ireland offers, in some respects, the most complicated of the various histories of internal colonialism. A separate island that remained overwhelmingly Catholic, its history of involvement with an aggressive expansionist England was lengthy. Historians have often regarded sixteenth-century Ireland as England's 'colonial laboratory', but the English yoke was felt far earlier. Poyning's Law, passed in 1494, forbade the Irish parliament from meeting without the approval of the English monarch. Finally repealed in 1782, it represented the beginning of direct rule over Ireland. Strict codes, collectively called the Penal Laws, regulated every aspect of the lives of Irish Catholics. Marrying into a Catholic family entailed a loss of civil rights. Harsh rules limited the type and amount of property Catholics might own, where they could work, who they could employ, where and what they might learn. They could not carry arms or practise law. While legal devices ensured that an independent Irish political structure could not develop, landholding practices there kept a large proportion of the population in penury. Land tenure in Ireland was highly unusual in that tenants and not owners were responsible for improvement and investment. Yet with no security of tenure, tenants had little incentive to invest in improvements. Absentee landlords, unwilling to spend money for improvements, were interested only in maximising profit and tenants had neither motive to improve the land nor, for the most part, the necessary finances. The plantation schemes of the sixteenth and seventeenth centuries, begun in the reign of Mary Tudor and significantly increasing in scope and size over time, only deepened existing inequalities, for the aim of these land-colonising schemes was to make Ireland more Protestant by granting tracts of land to the English. In this respect, the projects were in some manner successful: Irish Catholics owned 61 per cent of the land in 1641, 14 per cent in 1704 and a mere 5 per cent by the late 1770s. In almost every other way, the plantations were a failure, catalysing sporadic and bitter unrest, to which the English response was decidedly sectarian, deliberately wrecking the symbols and relics of the Catholic faith in retaliation.

Not surprisingly, given the discontent of a disenfranchised and increasingly dispossessed population, the English maintained a large military presence in Ireland, a tactic they would later use in many other colonies. It only added insult to injury that the Irish rather than the English were expected to finance these troops.

Brute force was by no means the only form of power that the English wielded, however. Throughout the Celtic lands, it was long-standing policy to discourage the use of local languages; English was the language of policy and law, of culture and perhaps most critically, of education. The Church of Wales lost ground because its services were routinely conducted in English, the language of annexation and power, while its Protestant rivals worshipped frequently in Welsh. This was particularly significant, for the use of the Welsh language was far more widespread than was the use of Scots or Gaelic. Despite the ban on teaching Welsh in elementary schools, not lifted until 1907, more than half the population of Wales still spoke Welsh in the 1890s. While smaller proportions of the Scottish and Irish populations used the local language, Gaelic too was deliberately excluded from the primary school curriculum, and instruction was conducted exclusively in English. The very existence of these bans sparked a revival of languages as a source of local pride, and in the nineteenth century in particular, organisations dedicated to restoring the Celtic languages flourished. The *Eisteddfod* poetry-reading competition established in Wales in the 1860s, and the 1876 Society for the Preservation of the Irish Language, are typical examples of the interest generated in the nineteenth century as both cultural and political nationalism grew stronger.

Not surprisingly, it was among the wealthy and the educated in Celtic populations that the use of English was most widespread. Language became one of the principal markers of privilege, an easily measured index of assimilation and of Anglicisation. It was critical, of course, for English rule to seek collaboration from within, as was the case in almost every colonial setting. And in an era in which marked inequalities of power, wealth, representation and rights were wholly unremarkable, looking to local elites for support was an obvious and a sensible strategy of colonisation, and largely successful. Wealthy Scots and Irish worked hard to fashion their lands and their lifestyles in accordance with English custom and aesthetics. They built their houses according to English style, affected English dress and speech and acted towards their tenants according to English practice. Prosperous Celts, like their English counterparts, saw the poor and the labouring classes as rough, uncivilised and often immoral. In Scotland, such divisions were also geographical, as we have seen. Lowland Scots tended to regard the more rural and isolated Highland regions as more primitive and unrefined, a throwback to earlier and ruder lifestyles, prejudices eerily reminiscent of how the English spoke of the Scots, the Welsh and the Irish. The Scottish scientist Robert Knox thought 'the Caledonian Celt of Scotland ... a race as distinct from the Lowland Saxon of the same country, as any two races can possibly be: as negro from American; Hottentot from Caffre; Esquimaux from Saxon.'[4] Similar discriminatory thinking would follow the huge Irish migration across the Atlantic to America, and around the globe to Australia.

The division along class lines that helped secure colonial rule was considerably strengthened by the passing of the 1832 Parliamentary Reform Act.

While this overhauling of the national electoral and parliamentary system of Britain did away with some of the more egregious inequities built into the voting system, the new constituencies it created clearly put English interests ahead of those of the Celtic regions. After 1832, one in five Englishmen was entitled to vote (women had everywhere been wholly disenfranchised by the Act), compared with one in eight Scots men and one in twenty Irish men. Furthermore, it was only with the Catholic Emancipation Act of 1829 that voting rights were extended to non-Protestant Christians, finally fulfilling the demand the Irish parliament had made before its dissolution in 1800.

Internal colonialism did little to alleviate the gap between the poor and the rich, instead exploiting that divide – as it would in more distant colonies – for colonial ends. What could the poor then do? In large numbers, they chose to migrate, further impoverishing depleted regions through depopulation. After the uniting of the kingdom, the Celtic population diminished relative to that of England, and even in earlier times migration was a solution, although not always an easy or a comfortable one, to the grind of poverty and hopelessness. Young Irish men and women figured prominently among indentured servants arriving in the American colonies in the seventeenth and eighteenth centuries, their labour a product of colonialism both at their place of departure and of arrival. The eighteenth- and nineteenth-century British Empire was a significantly Scottish enterprise; medical practitioners, military men and civil servants in the outposts of empire – hardly among the poorest segments of society – were disproportionately Scottish. For many, the disadvantages of being Scottish in an English environment diminished, for in far-flung colonial settings, the fact of being British rather than specifically English elevated one's status. In the Scottish Highlands, population control was cynically manipulated for economic ends in the nineteenth and twentieth centuries. The sinews of colonialism were thus at work inside Britain and beyond the waters surrounding it; internal colonialism, while different in some respects from the overseas enterprise, was nonetheless integral to the broader project of empire and constitutes some of its earliest episodes.

These developments and changes emanated from an expansionist and aggressive England intent on keeping intact its Protestant succession and its vigorous colonial trade. As we have seen, much of the military activity in which England engaged in the seventeenth and especially in the eighteenth century focused on keeping colonial trade and trade routes running smoothly and profitably. From about 1700, England's major trading interests shifted from Europe to the growing empire, and laws ensured that it was England's needs that took precedence in commercial arrangements. As far back as the 1650s, the Navigation Acts regulated all commercial shipping: British-built ships with British crews carried goods through British ports in British territory. Commerce was conducted as a form of 'closed shop' which privileged and protected the colonial centre as a matter of course, and though many restrictions were lifted over time, the protections for colonial trade and commerce always came first.

When George III came to the throne in 1760 he successfully pushed for more direct monarchical involvement in the running of the country. Aided by widespread anti-Catholic sentiment and the fears generated by the French Revolution, this monarchical revival culminated in the establishment of the Royal Jubilee in 1809. By the reign of Victoria, this cult of the monarch was a valuable colonial tool that imagined a harmonious unity between the disparate parts of Britain's Empire. The growth of royal visits to the colonies and the declaration of Victoria as Empress of India in 1876, along with the pomp and grandeur created for such occasions, pumped up a new populist loyalty in which the British Empire was the definitive symbol of British greatness. The emphasis on British unity so central to this rhetoric promoted a degree of amnesia about the brutalities that had accompanied internal annexation. As a result, it is all too easy to forget that the United Kingdom was a product of Britain's larger colonial enterprise, and never a 'natural' connection between the quite different groups that, as the Empire was consolidated, were brought together as Great Britain.

Notes

1 Colin Kidd, 'North Britishness and the Nature of Eighteenth-century British Patriotisms', *Historical Journal* 39, no. 2 (1996), pp. 361–82.
2 See, for example, Steven G. Ellis, '"Not mere English": The British Perspective, 1400–1650', *History Today* 38 (1998), p. 48. See also Ellis and Sarah Barber, eds. *Conquest and Union: Fashioning a British State 1485–1725* (London: Longman, 1995).
3 Linda Colley, *Britons: Forging the Nation, 1707–1837* (New Haven, CT: Yale University Press, 1992), p. 52.
4 Robert Knox, *The Races of Men. A Fragment* (London, 1850), p. 18.

Further reading

The literature on internal colonialism is surprisingly small. Michael Hechter's study, *Internal Colonialism: The Celtic Fringe in British National Development* (2nd edn, New Brunswick, NJ: Transaction Publishers, 1999), remains the major work in the field. R. R. Davies' *Domination and Conquest: The Experience of Ireland, Scotland and Wales, 1100–1300* (Cambridge: Cambridge University Press, 1990) is a helpful introduction to the earliest relations between England and the countries it colonised over time to create the United Kingdom. *A Union of Multiple Identities: The British Isles, c.1750–c.1850* (Laurence Brockliss and David Eastwood (eds), Manchester: Manchester University Press, 1997) takes as its premise a colonialism already in place. Murray Pittock's books, *Inventing and Resisting Britain: Cultural Identities in Britain and Ireland, 1685–1789* (Houndmills, Basingstoke: Macmillan, 1997) and *Celtic Identity and the British Image* (Manchester: Manchester University Press, 1999), are among the best studies that relate the different entities within the United Kingdom.

For good overviews of the history of Scotland, see Christopher T. Harvie, *Scotland and Nationalism: Scottish Society and Politics, 1707 to the Present* (4th edn,

London: Routledge, 2004) and Rosalind Mitchison's *A History of Scotland* (3rd edn, London: Routledge, 2002). Assessments of Scotland and empire are central to T. M. Devine, *Scotland's Empire 1600–1815* (London: Allen Lane, 2003), Michael Fry, *The Scottish Empire* (East Linton: Tuckwell Press, 2001) and *Scotland and the British Empire* (T. M. Devine and John Mackenzie (eds), Oxford: Oxford University Press, 2011). For the Scottish Highlands, see Colin G. Calloway *White People, Indians, and Highlanders: Tribal Peoples and Colonial Encounters in Scotland and America* (Oxford: Oxford University Press, 2008) and Eric Richards, *Debating the Highland Clearances* (Edinburgh: Edinburgh University Press, 2007). John McKendrick's *Darien: A Journey in Search of Empire* (Edinburgh: Birlinn, 2016) explores Scotland's failed attempt at colonisation on the Isthmus of Panama.

For Wales, John Davies' *A History of Wales* (London: Penguin, 1994) is a good general history, and would be well supplemented by the questions around nationalism posed in *Nation, Identity and Social Theory: Perspectives from Wales* (Ralph Fevre and Andrew Thompson (eds), Cardiff: University of Wales Press, 1999). For a lengthier sweep of chronology, readers might also profit from *Modern Wales: A Concise History, c.1485–1979* by Gareth Elwyn Jones (Cambridge: Cambridge University Press, 1984). Geraint H. Jenkins' *A Concise History of Wales* (Cambridge: Cambridge University Press, 2007) includes a number of relevant chapters.

Was Ireland a Colony? Economics, Politics, and Culture in Nineteenth-century Ireland (Terrence McDonough (ed.), Dublin: Irish Academic Press, 2005) speaks directly to the topic of this chapter, as does *The Making of Modern Irish History: Revisionism and the Revisionist Controversy* (D. George Boyce and Alan O'Day (eds), Abingdon: Routledge, 1996). In *Colonialism, Religion, and Nationalism in Ireland*, Liam Kennedy (Belfast: Institute of Irish Studies, Queen's University of Belfast, 1996) draws out the connections that link religious difference and colonial rule there. Standard texts include R. F. Foster, *Modern Ireland, 1600–1972* (London: Allen Lane, 1988) and S. J. Connolly, *Divided Kingdom: Ireland, 1630–1800* (Oxford: Oxford University Press, 2008). *Victoria's Ireland? Irishness and Britishness, 1837–1901* (Peter Gray (ed.), Dublin: Four Courts Press, 2004) examines the relationship between Irish and British identity in the years after the Union of 1800. Two edited collections – Kevin Kenny's *Ireland and the British Empire* (Oxford: Oxford University Press, 2004) and Keith Jeffery's *An Irish Empire? Aspects of Ireland and the British Empire* (Manchester: Manchester University Press, 1996) – explicitly connect Ireland to the rest of the Empire. Nicholas Canny's *Making Ireland British, 1580–1650* (Oxford: Oxford University Press, 2001) treats of an earlier period of Irish colonial experience, while *Britain and Ireland in the Eighteenth-century Crisis of Empire* by Martyn J. Powell (New York: Palgrave Macmillan, 2003) contextualises the Irish question during the period of the so-called First British Empire. In *Contesting Ireland: Irish Voices against England in the Eighteenth Century* (Dublin: Four Courts Press, 1999), T. O. McLoughlin examines early discontent with English incursions into Ireland.

2   Slaves, merchants and trade

By the eighteenth century Britain's powerful naval superiority was as much about colonial trade, shipping goods and peoples across the globe, as it was about the warfare so typical of the period. The visible growth in Britain's global activities, interests and profitability outside Europe led to a greater awareness, and often celebration, of the phenomenon of imperialism. Empire came, in the eighteenth century, more and more to connote British-held territories rather than merely British influence overseas. In parliament, imperial concerns took up an increasing amount of time; 29 Acts on colonial trade and related items were passed between 1714 and 1739 alone. Newspapers, magazines and journals in eighteenth-century Britain devoted considerable space to discussions of Britain's imperial possessions. More goods crisscrossed the globe, as did more people. Over the course of the century, the British Empire not only grew – in size, in stature, in profitability – but it also shifted in focus. For the most part, the eighteenth century was an era characterised by Atlantic domination, with North America and, more critically for British wealth, the West Indies at the imperial centre (see Map 2.1).

It was the Atlantic slave trade, without question, that secured much of the vital wealth and political success of the British Empire throughout the eighteenth century. Human enslavement had a long and a varied history by the time the Atlantic slave trade became profitable, but it was western European exploitation of existing slave practices in the Mediterranean and further south in sub-Saharan Africa that created the vast and distinctive trade associated with colonialism. Along the Gold Coast of West Africa, small fishing villages were transformed during the sixteenth and seventeenth centuries into bustling centres of commerce hosting European as well as African residents. Slaves were traded alongside spices, weapons and ivory in a lively and profitable economy, and for the greater part of the eighteenth century, few protested against its existence.

The imperial slave trade that supplied the Caribbean and North America was distinctive in a number of ways, however. This was a trade vast in scale, and it transported slaves much further away from their homelands than was routine in forms of slavery in which war captives and criminals comprised the bulk of slaves. Atlantic slavery was also unusual in being so racially

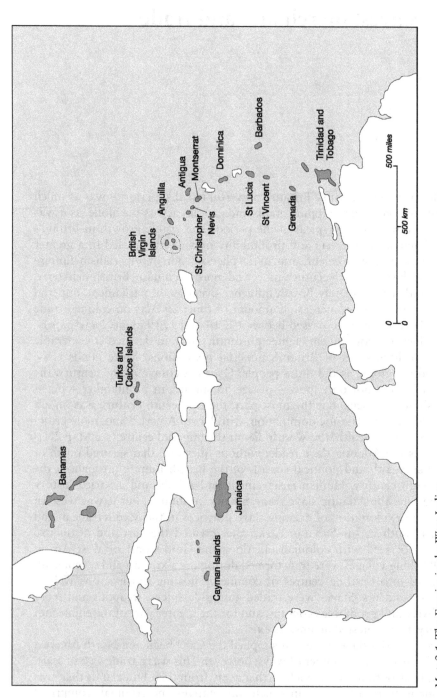

Map 2.1 The Empire in the West Indies

Source: *Cambridge Illustrated History of the British Empire*, Cambridge University Press (Marshall, Peter 1996), inset back cover map, © Cambridge University Press, Reproduced with permission of The Licensor through PLSclear

specific. Slaves in many societies would not have been that different from those around them; for those caught up in the Atlantic trade, their skin colour marked them as slaves. New World slavery was also distinct in being dominantly concerned with agricultural production. Slaves elsewhere fulfilled a far greater variety of duties and responsibilities, while in the Atlantic region they were put to work mainly in plantation agriculture. Plantation crops frequently arrived in the West Indies as a result of colonial exploration and travel. Both sugar and cotton were transplanted from other tropical regions, dramatically transforming the landscape, labour practices and social structure of the Caribbean. Joseph Banks, one of Britain's most celebrated naturalists, worked secretly for England's Board of Trade bringing Asian cotton varieties to the West Indies in the 1780s. Varieties of sugar native to the Pacific and the Indian Oceans helped improve sugar yields on West Indian plantations.

The bulk of those whose labour would prove so profitable for Europe's sugar, tobacco and cotton production were purchased along the West African coastline, and the majority of them were taken to the Atlantic region in the years between 1740 (although the trade had begun almost two hundred years earlier) and 1807, when the slave trade in the British Empire was abolished. With an average of 60,000 slaves shipped annually throughout most of the eighteenth century, the effect of slavery on Africa was just as great as it was on the Caribbean, on North America and on the imperial European powers. Slave-raiding, kidnapping and, inevitably, the extension of the tentacles of this trade to ever-wider areas transformed politics in Africa as well as the life of those bound for servitude. African elites did well out of the trade and understood the dynamics of trading with the European colonial powers whose access to their lands and goods they controlled shrewdly. African leaders, aware of their rivalry, played European merchants and trading companies against one another. Areas vulnerable to slave-raiding reorganised themselves for better protection, and this often led to the creation of more centralised states than had hitherto existed in West Africa.

Between the mid-fifteenth century and the late nineteenth century, some 12 million Africans were shipped in slavery to the Americas. Their experiences could differ drastically, according to where they found themselves landed, for slaves might find themselves on a sugar colony in the West Indies, on a tobacco plantation in Virginia, growing rice in the Carolinas, or even away from the life of the plantation further north in New England, New York or Canada. A few were brought to Britain where domestic service was the commonest form of labour allotted to African slaves. Early in the eighteenth century far more slaves were shipped to the British West Indies than to the colonies of North America; the reverse was the case by the end of the century.

Over the course of the seventeenth and eighteenth centuries, slave labour gradually replaced the earlier and widespread use of white labour, often Irish, in British colonies. Indentured labour had been widespread in the

West Indian and the American colonies before the eighteenth-century boom in the slave trade. White colonial labour had included a good number of convicts and a group known as 'redemptioners' who, if they failed within an agreed timeline to repay the captain of the ship in which they sailed, could be sold by him to pay off that debt. Convicts transported across the Atlantic consisted of both criminals (convicted largely of minor crimes such as pickpocketing, vagrancy and thieving) and political prisoners. Oliver Cromwell used transportation in the seventeenth century to rid himself of the Irish rebels who opposed his plantation policies. Religious dissenters who persistently defied the law could also find themselves aboard a convict transport bound for the colonies along the Atlantic seaboard. These groups were the least free among the poor whites in the Atlantic colonies. Indentured servants, by contrast, contracted with an employer for an agreed period, generally in return for a free passage to the colony where they would work. Some renewed their contracts. Some left the colonies. Some stayed on in non-indentured capacities. Their choices were often limited, but they did enjoy a degree of choice denied the enslaved. Throughout the eighteenth century, as slave labour came to dominate, African migration massively outstripped white migration to the region.

In the earliest years of West Indian settlement, slaves and indentured servants were often indistinguishable in the work they did and in how they were treated. On occasion slaves could even successfully sue for their freedom. As the slave trade grew and the economics of colonial slave plantations hardened, however, the line between indenture and slavery, between white and black, grew more visible and much harder to cross. The use of white labour in the plantation economy diminished radically and the importation of African slaves quickened.

Slaving was an expensive and risky business venture as well as labour intensive, but profits could be high so there were always entrepreneurs willing to risk disease, rebellion, shipwreck and piracy. Moreover, profit was not limited to those who sailed the slave trade routes and those who purchased their human cargo. The ship-building industry in English ports did very well out of the slave trade. By the late eighteenth century, around 21 ships, specially fitted for human cargo, were built each year in Liverpool, providing employment for a wide variety of workers. The metals industry churned out not just chains and fetters but goods used to barter for slaves in Africa.

Conditions aboard the slave ships were grim, with people jammed into small unhygienic spaces and locked down for large portions of the voyage. Those who refused to eat were force-fed. Communicable diseases ravaged these unwilling passengers: dysentery (known as the 'bloody flux'), smallpox and measles spread rapidly in these conditions and were greatly feared. The slave ship, *Arthur*, which sailed from West Africa in 1678 headed for Barbados, did not see a day go by without at least one African death. Altogether, 82 lives were lost on the two-month voyage out of some 350 boarded. Between 20 per cent and 40 per cent of those destined for slavery died during transport to the African coast for sale and shipping. Another 3 per cent to 10 per cent died before they could be transported, and a further 15 per cent or so died aboard the slave ships at more than twice the rate of unenslaved paying shipboard passengers in this era. More than a third of those transported as slaves died before reaching their destination, and yet more died once they reached the New World, mostly from diseases to which they had never previously been exposed. The death toll was simply appalling. In 1788 the British parliament passed the Dolben Act regulating conditions aboard slaving ships to mitigate the suffering and the losses, but mortality remained high among this human cargo.

Life was not much better when slaves arrived at their destinations. One in three slaves in the West Indies did not survive more than three years toiling in the fields of the Caribbean in the early years. Nothing in the life of a slave in a British colony was easy. Slaves mostly built their own accommodation, grew their own food staples and made their own clothes from the cloth rations given to them, and all this was in addition to the long hours of field work expected of them six days a week.

Yet slaves were not without the means to control at least some of their waking hours, and they quickly learned which forms of resistance were least likely to result in severe punishments and which were effective. Slaves pretended not to understand how to operate tools or follow instructions. They could slyly do substandard work and as they gained an intimate appreciation of the rhythms of agricultural production, their co-operation or lack of it could make a substantial difference to the quality and profitability of a crop.

Not surprisingly some found escape a greater temptation than these covert forms of resistance. Those who were not caught, punished and returned to work often banded together in what came to be called Maroon communities. Maroons lived in isolated, hard to reach areas to avoid capture, and they organised both raids on plantations and actual rebellions from time to time. The largest Maroon communities were in Jamaica where there were about 1,000 escaped slaves living mainly in two groups, one windward (east) and one leeward (west) on the island. Between 1729 and 1739 the Maroon War played havoc with Jamaica's economy. A treaty between the Maroons and the authorities in 1739 granted freedom to the Maroons in return for their agreeing to return runaway slaves to their owners. It was a curious alliance between those who had escaped and those from whom they had escaped, reached over the bodies of future escapees.

By the late eighteenth century, Britain had slave codes that laid out less the rights than the absence of rights endured by their slaves. These laws defined slaves as chattels (meaning they could be bought, sold and inherited), and made the prospect of manumission (freedom from slavery) almost impossible. They laid down punishments for slave misdeeds, and established pass laws severely restricting slave mobility. These Consolidated Slave Acts did provide an occasional concession: slaves were given one day a fortnight (except during the harvest) other than Sundays to tend their own crops, grown on small plots of land their owners found less amenable to profitable cultivation.

Over the course of the seventeenth century, Britain steadily increased its hold in the West Indies, consciously working to weaken Spanish power in the area and adding more and more colonies in order to rival and ultimately overtake Portuguese sugar production in Brazil. By the eighteenth century Britain was the dominant slave-trading nation, transporting more slaves than any other country; between the mid-1670s and 1800, over 40 per cent of slaves (some 930,000) destined for the Atlantic were transported by British ships. The acquisition of Jamaica in 1655 proved crucial: by the dawn of the eighteenth century, the island would be Britain's most important source of sugar, though still dwarfed by the French slave-sugar colony of St Domingue, destined to become modern Haiti after a major slave revolt in the early 1790s. While sugar was not the only crop cultivated by slave labour in the British Caribbean, it was indubitably the most important. By contrast, in the American colonies there was far more diversity of production and much less emphasis on monoculture. Fourteen of Britain's 19 colonies in the Caribbean were significant sugar producers. Tobacco, coconuts, coffee and other crops were grown too, but sugar yielded the greatest profit and required the most – as well as the most disciplined – labour. On average, sugar plantations in Jamaica by the early 1830s were worked by an average of 223 slaves compared with 128 in coffee production and 100 on livestock farms. The slave owners in Jamaica were, by the late eighteenth century, the wealthiest British subjects.

West Indian sugar production combined agricultural labour with modern factory practices. In order to ensure that the cane would not rot before it could be used, sugar was not only grown but partially processed in the West Indies and slaves worked not only in the fields but in the mills where a strict industrial schedule ensured the timely processing of the raw cane. This factory-style production, seen in Figure 2.1, was already operating in the colonies at a time when many workers in Britain were still tied to the land. Sugar was not, however, fully processed and refined in the West Indies. Strict laws governed the degree of processing that could be done prior to the cane reaching Britain. The bulk of refining was still done in Britain but the perishable nature of the crop made the colonies sites of early industrial production. The work was hard and unrelenting, though highly profitable for the plantation owners. Between 1770 and 1787, the British West Indian sugar colonies produced some 35 per cent of the sugar in the North Atlantic region, rising to about 55 per cent by the early years of the new century as slave revolts in French sugar colonies reduced production there. Since sugar was Britain's largest import between the 1750s and the 1820s, this was big business. The seemingly endless rise in British domestic sugar consumption – unmatched by any other European nation – boosted the value of this import

Figure 2.1 Slaves ladle steaming juice from vat to vat, Antigua, 1823 (print)
Source: Art Directors & TRIP/Alamy Stock Photo

throughout this period. The West Indian colonies in the second half of the eighteenth century were hugely important both to the British economy and the British palate. Like slaving, the establishment of a plantation was a costly business requiring a good deal of initial outlay, but the returns, if all went well, could be pleasingly high.

Slavery, unlike indentured labour, had the potential to provide the next generation of workers through reproduction. There was a clear economic incentive for ensuring that children born into a state of slavery could never exercise an option to leave the plantation. The children of slaves inherited their mother's status, and not their father's, in contrast to eighteenth-century British law in which women were minors, and children derived their status in life from their fathers. Without explicit laws, children born of slave mothers might under British law have avoided enslavement if their fathers (as was so often the case) were not slaves but white men who had impregnated slave women. It was Thomas Jefferson's opinion that a slave woman who bore a child every two years was more profitable in the long run than the strongest and fastest male slave because her fertility constantly replenished the work-force.[1] Nubile women were prized and often passed on as an inheritance in slave owners' wills as especially valuable property. Some slave owners, like Jefferson, realised the benefits of protecting slave women during their pregnancies since slave births in many places outpaced purchase of new slaves.

Such was the case on Barbados, a British colony since 1627, and a pioneer in producing the highly profitable commodity of sugar on large capital intensive plantations using slave labour. From the 1760s natural increase among the slave population was beginning to fulfil the island's labour requirements, but the island was not typical of the West Indian slave colonies. The conscious breeding of slaves was a practice more generally associated with American plantations where slave women were generally more fertile. The emphasis on sugar production in the West Indies, with its brutal and harsh work, adversely affected the fertility of women slaves. Male slaves were routinely assigned to the more skilled tasks associated with sugar cultivation and production, making women's labour vital to the field gangs. The heavy manual work of planting, weeding and pulling in gangs took its toll on women's health and fertility.

For some women slaves, pregnancy and early motherhood offered some respite from the hardships of slave labour. In some locations, though by no means universally, pregnant slave women enjoyed reduced workloads, a policy inspired by economic gain rather than sentiment. It was the lucky slave whose master implemented such policies. Richard Steckel's analysis of nineteenth-century plantation records in the United States suggests that some 54 per cent of slave pregnancies ended in stillbirth, infant mortality or early childhood mortality.[2] There is no reason to assume that the situation would have been any better at an earlier date or in British colonies. Although women might enjoy some benefits of this kind, they were always vulnerable to sexual abuse since they could not spurn the sexual advances of owners or overseers without potentially severe consequences. The widespread sexual contact between white men and slave women was the reason why laws determining the status of children born to slave mothers was so important to plantation owners. Such children, without that law, might be deemed white and free.

Violence was not limited, of course, to the sexual experiences of women. Violence began even before captives were boarded onto slave ships, as they were transported in fetters and forced onto ships where violence was routine. Nothing changed for those who survived the arduous voyage and found themselves far from home. Slave rebellions were common, and were invariably met with violence, although it did little to deter protest. Tobago saw repeated slave rioting in the 1770s as well as in the early nineteenth century. There were substantial uprisings in Antigua in 1736, in Barbados in 1675 and 1816, in Demerara in 1823, in Grenada in 1795, in Jamaica in 1760, 1776 and 1831 and in Trinidad in 1805. Slave revolts were in large part a reaction to the daily violence that defined plantation slavery. Slaves could be whipped and beaten, raped, assaulted – and even killed – with impunity. Their enslavement was a product of violence at every level. Coercion was central to the institution of slavery which rested ultimately on the lash, the gun and the boot. The violence slaves experienced nevertheless went well beyond the pain of physical abuse. These were men and women who had been forcibly removed from their communities and thrown together, often with strangers who spoke different languages. They were forced to go by names chosen for them by their owners, and to do any work their supervisors instructed them to do. Violence and coercion defined and dominated their existence.

Slave owning was widespread and widely accepted before the late eighteenth century. Queen Elizabeth I had invested in a number of the slave-trading voyages of John Hawkins in the sixteenth century, the first English ventures in slaving. In 1710 a Barbadian planter, Christopher Codrington, bequeathed his slave plantations to the Society for the Propagation of the Gospel in Foreign Parts, an Anglican missionary organisation, for the foundation of a college. He specified in his will that 'my desire is to have the Plantations Continued Intire and three hundred negros at Least Kept always thereon'.[3] Codrington College (which still exists) opened on the island in 1845, and the church managed the plantations and the slaves down to emancipation in 1838.

Towards the close of the eighteenth century anti-slavery sentiment began to emerge forcefully in Europe. Eighteenth-century political philosophers had mostly either ignored or found justifications for slavery, but in the 1760s the French philosopher Charles de Secondat, Baron de Montesquieu, offered a thorough-going critique of the practice. The influential Scottish economist Adam Smith also registered an unease with slavery, which he saw as incompatible with human advancement. For Smith free will, which slaves so palpably lacked, was the motor that would drive improvement, and free labour was most especially central to his vision of the interplay of morals, economics and governance. If Smith's rationale for opposing slavery was connected to the economic system he thought would improve the world, many anti-slavery activists were motivated by religious sentiment, and a variety of evangelical Christian and other Protestant groups played a significant role in the movement. A religious motivation did not necessarily, or indeed particularly frequently, imply that abolitionists saw slaves as their equals. A common argument wielded by the anti-slavery movement, not dissimilar to Smith's concern about unfreedom, was that slavery degraded and brutalised those who suffered under its yoke. The dramatic speech William Wilberforce delivered in the House of Commons in 1789 claimed that 'all improvement in Africa has been defeated by her intercourse with Britain'. The slave trade, he lamented, had 'enslaved their [Africans'] minds, blackened their character, and sunk them so low in the scale of animal beings that some think the apes are of a higher class'.[4] Many abolitionists saw their role as creating an environment in which Africans could be raised to civilisation, a state they believed fully lacking in their life of enslavement and realisable only through the redemption of Christianity. Note how the chained slave in the medallion in Figure 2.2 is in an attitude of prayer and supplication that would have been instantly recognisable as Christian at the time. The image was widely reproduced and became an enduring symbol of anti-slavery sentiment on both sides of the Atlantic.

Figure 2.2 Anti-slavery medallion created by the Wedgwood factory, 1787
Source: Harris Museum and Art Gallery, Preston, Lancashire, UK/Bridgeman Images

The medallion was the seal of the Society for Effecting the Abolition of the Slave Trade, designed by one of its earliest members, Josiah Wedgwood, the most successful pottery manufacturer of the day. Wedgwood was Charles Darwin's maternal grandfather, and the two families remained staunch opponents of slavery down the generations. When Darwin travelled the world on HMS *Beagle* in the early 1830s, his letters home were full of comments on the iniquities of the slavery he witnessed in the Americas. Darwin's female relatives were prominent in the abolitionist cause. Like many women in Britain, they raised funds and wrote letters of protest. For a substantial group of women, anti-slavery activism opened their eyes to the inequalities under which women in Britain lived, prompting them to fight for women's rights as well.

Britain was not the first country to abolish the slave trade. Denmark passed an abolition law in 1792 which became effective in 1803, and rumours that America planned to do so were circulating widely at the time Britain embraced abolition. (Abolition in the United States came only in the 1860s.) In Britain, the Quakers – an affluent religious sect – had, by the 1770s, broken off all association with slaveholders and slave traders, requiring their members to divest themselves of slave-related business interests. The Mansfield decision, handed down by the courts in 1772, ruled that James Somersett, a former slave now in Britain, could not be forcibly returned to enslavement in the United States because on British soil the former slave was free. The case was important for it destroyed any claims to the legitimacy of slavery within Britain. In 1787, the abolitionist society collected around

60,000 signatures for a petition against slavery, and by 1788 parliament had received more petitions on this than on any other topic. The first bill for abolishing the slave trade reached parliament in 1792, although it failed to pass, not least because of the upheavals in French St Domingue the previous year, which had resulted in a great deal of bloodshed. The eventual abolition of the slave trade early in the nineteenth century was a remarkable moral achievement, a mass mobilisation of public opinion in the face of a trade that, while risky, remained highly profitable. At the same time, however, the push for a free trade system was growing stronger in early nineteenth-century British politics and this, too, helped reinforce the anti-slavery case, for the free trade lobby insisted that labour should be a voluntary contract between worker and employer.[5]

The effect of anti-slavery agitation was, not surprisingly, piecemeal and scattered. Upper Canada ended the importation of slaves in 1793, but Britain did not halt its slave trade until 1807. Indeed a number of MPs agreed to vote in favour only when abolitionists promised not to push for full abolition. Slave emancipation finally passed successfully through parliament in 1833 after a revival of the anti-slavery lobby in the 1820s. Many were horrified by the terms of the emancipation proclamation, which the government justified as necessary to save the planters from economic ruin. Although slavery was abolished as of August 1834, slaves were required for a period of seven years to devote three-quarters of their work hours to their former owners in return for food and clothing. This compensation to the slaveholders was in addition to a generous cash payout totalling about £20 million for the loss of their human property. The seven-year apprenticeship scheme ended earlier than planned, in 1838, but by then it had already led many former slaves to move to uncultivated areas to avoid such onerous service. By the end of the 1830s, some 800,000 slaves had won their freedom in the British colonies of the West Indies and on the sugar-producing island of Mauritius in the Indian Ocean.

The abolition of slavery in the 1830s came very swiftly upon the heels of one of the largest slave rebellions in British territory. In 1831 the 'Baptist War' convulsed large sections of Jamaica. Crops and property were destroyed, and the frustration and anger of slaves was made dramatically visible. Although this uprising alone cannot explain emancipation, it certainly helped sink an even more gradualist plan than that implemented in 1833.

Elsewhere in the British Empire, and especially in East Africa, slavery was not abandoned even after emancipation. At the Congress of Vienna in 1815, at the end of the Napoleonic Wars, Britain was roundly criticised by European leaders for its call for a condemnation of the slave trade; pointing to continued enslavement in North Africa in particular, Britain stood accused of a double standard. The principle of separation between slave trading and slaveholding that had shaped the passage of reforms in Britain continued to influence laws elsewhere. In the last quarter of the nineteenth century slave trading was prohibited in many parts of British Africa, mostly using a strategy known as 'legal-status' abolition. Rather like the Mansfield decision of 1772, this tactic accorded slavery no legal standing, meaning that courts of law could not enforce possession of a slave. The same principle had been applied in British India in 1843, yet in large parts of the Empire, and particularly in regions of Africa, slaveholding was not formally outlawed until the twentieth century.

The number of freed and escaped slaves in the Empire was expanding long before the 1830s. At the time of the American Revolution many former slaves found their way to Canada and Britain, mostly in conditions of poverty. Faced with this unexpected wave of poor migrants, the British established an experimental free black colony in Sierra Leone in 1787 to house freed slaves after the American Revolution. Although the initial scheme failed, the colony nonetheless survived, becoming a Crown Colony in 1808, although never fulfilling the dream of its promoters that it would become a self-sustaining agricultural plantation economy worked by free labour. Keen to demonstrate that alternatives to slavery made economic as well as humanitarian sense, abolitionists promoted similar plans to develop Trinidad as a free labour colony early in the nineteenth century. These experiments were as much a product of slavery as the sugar so avidly consumed by the British in their tea and their cakes.

British trade even after 1807 profited significantly from slave-produced commodities, and British manufacturers remained active in producing goods that were linked intimately to slavery, such as shackles and irons. The abolition of the slave trade did not presuppose any diminution in the export of slave-grown sugar just as the emancipation law of 1833 had no effect on the sale of slave-grown cotton from America to Britain. Long after Britain eschewed slavery legally, its economy and trade continued to profit substantially from slave production. Recent work suggests that even after slavery ended, Britain's elite continued to be concentrated among those who came from slave-owning families. Lower down the social scale, the effects of abolition were felt largely in less stable prices for sugar and, especially in Liverpool, the loss of work related to the slave enterprise.

Since slave-grown sugar was the most valuable British import of the eighteenth century, the West Indies in many ways dominated the late eighteenth-century British Empire; they were the most valuable of British colonies in the eighteenth century. After emancipation the area diminished rapidly in importance. The story was quite different in the era of slavery, when planters not only grew rich from their enterprises but exercised considerable political power. Indeed, the plantation colonies enjoyed significantly more independence than Britain's other colonies in the eighteenth century. The Atlantic colonies were self-governing, with legislative assemblies and a property-based franchise. Barbados led the way, its first assembly convened in 1639. Their value to the health of the British economy also allowed the West Indian planters to extract considerable concessions from the imperial parliament, which increased their wealth and restricted non-British competition. Besides, more than a few members of parliament had significant sugar interests.

One source of irritation that would have significant consequences was the capacity of the West Indian lobby to extract concessions from the imperial government that were opposed by their neighbours in the North American colonies. The Molasses Act of 1733, for example, imposed wickedly high duties on foreign (meaning non-British) sugar imports to the American colonies as well as outlawing the importation of French sugar and molasses into Ireland. Although America went on buying sugar from the French and from other producers when it was cheaper than British sugar, resentment over the preference shown to Caribbean interests at their expense burned deep.

In an era before free trade came to dominate economic philosophy and in which the principles of mercantilism ruled, such protectionist desires were widespread and indeed often secured by naval and military action. Historians of the eighteenth century often describe Britain as a 'fiscal-military' state where close ties between economic policy and diplomacy determined political action.[6] Both economics and diplomacy were intimately connected to the growing profitability of the Empire which helped keep government financially afloat.

A slew of laws governed who could trade with whom and who could transport British goods across the ocean, and in these various laws we see the principles of mercantilism clearly enshrined. The trade in humans followed these same economic principles. The British slave trade had begun as a monopoly venture, the privilege granted first and unsuccessfully in 1663 to the Company of Royal Adventurers, and nine years later to a newcomer, the Royal African Company. In essence, chartered companies – whatever the goods they traded in – paid the Crown in exchange for the granting of a trade monopoly. In 1698 the Royal African Company lost its monopoly and the trade in bodies became one of the very first experiments in free trade undertaken by Britons when the slave trade was opened to private traders.

But though there were, by the middle of the eighteenth century, some 150 British slaving ships actively trading, slaving was not wholly without restraint. In 1713, in the Treaty of Utrecht marking the end of the War of the Spanish Succession, in which Britain also acquired Gibraltar and Acadia (modern Nova Scotia, roughly speaking), Spain granted England for 30 years the sole right (the *asiento*) to supply slaves to the Spanish Empire. The government gave those rights to the South Sea Company, stipulating that they in turn buy their slaves from the Royal African Company (which gave up slaving altogether in 1731, weakened by the competition). British planters, fiercely protective of monopolies that increased their wealth, were deeply opposed, arguing that Spain would get the best slaves and that British planters would have to make do with Spain's rejects.

Mercantilism, then, had very little in the way of a humane face. It was an economic system in which the colonies were expected to supply to the metropolis raw goods in exchange for manufactured ones, and in which each party enjoyed a monopoly position in the market of the other, although the colonies always remained subordinate to British needs. This would be one of the principal sources of tension between Britain and its North American colonies in the second half of the eighteenth century (as Chapter 3 will discuss). This monopolistic exchange of goods was always and ultimately backed by force; in the case of Britain, by the immense power of its Navy. Naval capacity increased enormously in the seventeenth and eighteenth centuries.

From 1651, a series of Navigation Acts regulated colonial trade by ensuring that colonial goods were carried only on English or British colonial ships and by effectively directing almost all export and re-export (with the exception of slaves, Madeira wine and salt for the fisheries) through Britain. Likewise, slaves bound for British colonies were, in the eighteenth century, carried almost exclusively on British slave ships. To sweeten the pill, the colonies in return had a monopoly on the home market. The colonies were thus encouraged, and in some senses coerced, into concentrating on producing goods unobtainable but in demand within Britain and to buying manufactured goods solely from Britain. After 1696 colonial trade was supervised by a new Board of Trade and Plantations, generally referred to simply as the Board of Trade. The Board increased central supervision of private trading, mainly to realise the state's portion of this extraordinary wealth, derived mostly from the collection of customs and excise duties.

Commerce in the eighteenth century was a busy and vigorous enterprise, and social theorists of the period often argued that the elaborate commercial life that so typified the European powers represented the very pinnacle of civilisation. It was not uncommon in the eighteenth century to regard a lack of interest in commerce and business as a defining characteristic of 'primitive' peoples. For an era of colonial expansion premised primarily on trade, it was a perfect justification for colonial conquest and for the appropriation of uncultivated land. Economists, philosophers and politicians generally agreed that less civilised peoples, unappreciative of consumerism, of manufacture and of trade, would benefit from the influences of civilised trading nations. In other eras, differences in religion or skin colour might be the focal point of difference between colonist and colonised, but for the eighteenth century commerce defined civilisation and marked difference. The tendency to encourage a trade in which commodities came *to* Britain and manufactured goods *left* Britain only reinforced this view. The relatively low level of consumption in the colonies was sometimes taken as evidence of the barbarous state of 'native' peoples, a convenient explanation for the distinct lack of interest in British goods traders often encountered in Africa and Asia, and for the poverty among indigenous peoples that so very often accompanied colonial influence. It was also, of course, a convenient justification for Atlantic slavery.

Mercantilism had originated in a desire to acquire ever-greater quantities of silver, then considered the most valuable of all substances. In the mercantilist view the purpose of trade was to increase the store of silver, so wealth-generating trade such as that between Britain and the Caribbean, or the American colonies, was regarded as the right kind of trade. The lack of interest that non-European peoples displayed for European goods was further complicated by the one interest they did show, which was in silver. Silver, the mercantilists complained, was the only item for which Asian traders demonstrated any enthusiasm, but buying with silver obviously diminished rather than increased the stock on hand. In a mercantilist economy, then, a carefully controlled slave trade that disallowed certain kinds of exchanges and that kept trade within a British world was an expression of right, while the Asian lack of interest in British and British colonial goods was evidence of a distance from civilised commerce.

If trade in people as well as goods was one of the most salient characteristics of British imperialism in this period, the other dominant theme was imperial rivalry. The eighteenth century in particular was punctuated by outbursts of naval and military violence between rival European powers, with France, Spain and Britain dominating as the aggressors. The buoyancy of the slave economies of the West Indies allowed politicians to raise revenues for fighting, and it is no accident that the stream of wars that erupted between the main contenders for European expansion was staged not in Europe, but largely in colonial territory. The European colonial competitors fought one another in the Caribbean, in India, in North America, colonial possessions rapidly changing hands with no consideration for the opinions or needs of indigenous peoples.

Throughout the eighteenth century, and in accordance with this primary interest in trade, Britain sought to consolidate its hold in the Mediterranean. The region was of considerable naval and trade importance, and from 1704 when Britain acquired its first Mediterranean foothold at Gibraltar, the plan was to expand British influence there, spreading from the Ionian islands through North Africa and the Middle East.

It was increasingly against the French – themselves interested in control of the Mediterranean – that the British pitted themselves, more especially as the power and significance of the older Spanish Empire – especially in the Caribbean – waned. Between 1680 and 1815, there were seven Anglo-French wars, the most decisive perhaps being the Seven Years' War which ended in 1763. Britain acquired considerable new lands, but at a cost. The war was a huge drain on Britain's finances and on many of its colonies (not least because of trade blockades), and the cost of administering the newly acquired territories was also high. Moreover, the war left Britain vulnerable in one of its most important colonial regions, America. Both British Americans and Britain's European rivals would, not much more than a decade later, exploit that weakness in the American War of Independence.

The British Empire nonetheless grew significantly as a result of the territories acquired in the 1763 Treaty of Paris that ended the Seven Years' War. In the Caribbean, Britain gained Grenada, Dominica, St Vincent and Tobago. In North America, Quebec, Prince Edward Island and both East and West Florida all became British. Britain's interests in South Asia were also expanding considerably at this time. Not surprisingly, many historians see the Peace of Paris as a watershed: where before this, the British Empire was predominantly organised around and acquired for trade, after 1763, the scope, size and heterogeneity of British imperial holdings increased the political, as opposed to the exclusively economic, realm. The rationale for empire shifted at least some degree away from the purely economic.

Yet curiously this growth in the size and diversity of the British Empire coincided with another and very different kind of growth, that of resentment and tension from within. In North America, two major forms of dissatisfaction with British rule were brewing. American colonists in the older territories were chafing at the economic and political restrictions that bound them, and in the previously French territories now controlled by Britain, French-speaking (Francophone) Catholics resented the anti-Catholic elements of the British political system that limited their participation.

Catholic irritation was not, however, confined to colonies such as Quebec. Much closer to the centre of imperial power, Ireland was also in turmoil (as shown in Chapter 1). The 1798 rebellion may have sealed Ireland's fate for more than a century, but it also underscored the vulnerabilities Britain faced within its Empire. Even closer to home than Ireland, the growing anti-slavery lobby threatened the continued use of slave labour at much the same time that a new generation of economic theorists – spearheaded by Adam Smith – attacked the restrictive practices of mercantilism and preached, to considerable effect, the doctrine of free trade. Although hindsight gives us the benefit of knowing that none of these potential and actual crises would bring down the Empire, and that the practice of colonialism would prove flexible enough to incorporate the major ideological changes ushered in by the free trade and anti-slavery lobbyists, those living through these changes must have wondered not if, but when, the Empire would collapse. For many, of course, the events that unfolded in America in the 1770s must have seemed to spell such doom.

Notes

1 Edwin M. Betts (ed.), *Thomas Jefferson's Farm Book: With Commentary and Relevant Extracts from Other Writings* (Charlottesville, VA: University Press of Virginia, 1976), p. 46.
2 Richard Steckel, 'A Dreadful Childhood: The Excess Mortality of American Slaves', in Kenneth Kiple (ed.), *African Exchange: Towards a Biological History of Black People* (Durham, NC: Duke University Press, 1998), p. 220.
3 Vincent T. Harlow, *Christopher Codrington III: 1667–1710* (New York: St Martin's Press, 1990), p. 218.
4 Wilberforce's Parliamentary speech, May 1789, quoted in Barbara Harlow with Mia Carter, *Archives of Empire Vol II: The Scramble for Africa* (Durham, NC: Duke University Press, 2003), p. 97.
5 Seymour Drescher, in particular, has made the case for abolition's success through the mobilisation of moral outrage in *Econocide. British Slavery in the*

Era of Abolition (2nd edn, Chapel Hill, NC: University of North Carolina Press, 2010). The most celebrated and controversial example of the counter-argument, that slavery was no longer profitable and could thus be abandoned, is that of Eric E. Williams in his landmark study, *Capitalism and Slavery* (Chapel Hill, NC: University of North Carolina Press, 1944).

6 Philip Harling and Peter Mandler, 'From "Fiscal-military" State to Laissez-faire State, 1760–1850', *Journal of British Studies* 32 (1993), pp. 44–70.

Further reading

The British Problem, c.1534–1707: State Formation in the Atlantic Archipelago (Brendan Bradshaw and John Morrill (eds), New York: St Martin's Press, 1996) is a helpful introduction to the larger questions posed here. David Brion Davis has been among the most prominent scholars to write about slavery; *The Problem of Slavery in Western Culture* (Ithaca, NY: Cornell University Press, 1966) remains a valuable contribution some 40 years after its first publication. *Discourses of Slavery and Abolition: Britain and its Colonies, 1760–1838* (Brycchan Carey, Markman Ellis and Sara Salih (eds), New York: Palgrave Macmillan, 2004) specifically pairs colonialism with slavery. Colin A. Palmer's *The Worlds of Unfree Labour: From Indentured Servitude to Slavery* (Aldershot: Variorum, 1998) discusses the most characteristic forms of labour that enriched the early Caribbean and Atlantic colonies. Among James Walvin's extensive writings on slavery, see especially *Slaves and Slavery: The British Colonial Experience* (Manchester: Manchester University Press, 1992). For moving reminiscences of slave life, see the stories told in *Africa Remembered: Narratives by West Africans from the Era of the Slave Trade* (Philip D. Curtin (ed.), Madison, WI: University of Wisconsin Press, 1967).

Kenneth Morgan's *Slavery, Atlantic Trade and the British Economy, 1660–1800* (Cambridge: Cambridge University Press, 2000) focuses on the clear economic relationship between slavery and eighteenth-century commerce and trade while *The Many-headed Hydra: The Hidden History of the Revolutionary Atlantic* by Peter Linebaugh and Marcus Rediker (Boston, MA: Beacon Press, 2000) looks at the role of what the authors call 'sailors, slaves, commoners' in the profitable Atlantic trade. A group of scholars working together have highlighted the continued wealth and privilege of slave owning that reverberated in British society long after the demise of Atlantic slavery by logging the compensation payments made to slaveholders at the time of abolition: Catherine Hall, Nicholas Draper, Keith McClelland, Katie Donington and Rachel Lang, *Legacies of British Slave-Ownership: Colonial Slavery and the Formation of Victorian Britain* (Cambridge: Cambridge University Press, 2014).

Soldiers, Sugar, and Seapower: The British Expeditions to the West Indies and the War against Revolutionary France by Michael Duffy (Oxford: Clarendon Press, 1987) puts the slave trade into the perspective of European warmongering, as does Bruce Lenman's *Britain's Colonial Wars, 1688–1783* (Harlow: Longman, 2001). Abigail Swingen's *Competing Visions of Empire: Labor, Slavery and the Origins of the British Atlantic Empire* (New Haven, CT: Yale University Press, 2015) ties slavery, empire and nationalism together.

For the experience of slaves aboard slaving ships, see Stephanie E. Smallwood's *Saltwater Slavery: A Middle Passage from Africa to American Diaspora* (Cambridge,

MA: Harvard University Press, 2007). The experiences of women slaves is explored in *Slave Women in Caribbean Society, 1650–1838* by Barbara Bush (Kingston: Heinemann Caribbean; Bloomington, IN: Indiana University Press, 1990). In *The Caribbean Slave: A Biological History*, Kenneth F. Kiple (Cambridge: Cambridge University Press, 1984) looks at the medical and biological issues slaves faced as a result of their situation. For slavery outside the Atlantic but within the British Empire, see *Gender, Slavery and Law in Colonial India* by Indrani Chatterjee (New Delhi: Oxford University Press, 1999) and Eve M. Troutt Powell's *A Different Shade of Colonialism: Egypt, Great Britain, and the Mastery of the Sudan* (Berkeley, CA: University of California Press, 2003).

The British anti-slavery movement boasts a very large literature. Among the major works in this area are Roger Anstey, *The Atlantic Slave Trade and British Abolition, 1760–1810* (Atlantic Highlands, NJ: Humanities Press, 1975), Clare Midgley, *Women Against Slavery: The British Campaigns, 1780–1870* (London: Routledge, 1992), Charlotte Sussman, *Consuming Anxieties: Consumer Protest, Gender, and British Slavery, 1713–1833* (Stanford, CA: Stanford University Press, 2000) and David Turley, *The Culture of English Antislavery, 1780–1860* (London: Routledge, 1991). In *The Mighty Experiment: Free Labor Versus Slavery in British Emancipation* (Oxford: Oxford University Press, 2002) Seymour Drescher looks at the consequences and impact of the abolition of slavery in the British Empire. It is in his *Econocide: British Slavery in the Era of Abolition* (Pittsburgh, PA: University of Pittsburgh Press, 1977) that Drescher challenges the work of Eric Williams. Christopher Leslie Brown stresses the moral elements of abolitionism in *Moral Capital: Foundations of British Abolitionism* (Chapel Hill, NC: University of North Carolina Press, 2006). The essays collected in *Abolitionism and Imperialism in Britain, Africa, and the Atlantic* (Derek Petersen (ed.), Athens, OH: Ohio University Press, 2010) considerably widen our understanding of who was involved in the abolitionist cause. Paula Dumas looks at pro-slavery activism in *Proslavery Britain: Fighting for Slavery in an Era of Abolition* (New York: Palgrave Macmillan, 2016).

In *Faces of Perfect Ebony: Encountering Atlantic Slavery in Imperial Britain* (Cambridge, MA: Harvard University Press, 2012), Catherine Molineux looks at the ways in which portrayals of black slaves familiarised British people with slavery in the Empire. A dazzling array of images of slavery can be found in *Representing Slavery: Art, Artefacts and Archives in the Collections of the National Maritime Museum* (Douglas Hamilton and Robert J. Blyth (eds), Aldershot and Burlington, VT: Lund Humphries, 2007).

3 Settling the 'New World'

The Atlantic colonies that would, in time, become America were developing at roughly the same time as those of the Caribbean, and indeed the histories of these two sets of colonies are closely linked. Some early settlement attempts in the 1580s, in what is now Virginia and, much further north in Newfoundland (in modern Canada), were succeeded in the seventeenth century by settlements that proved more durable. Founded in 1607, the colony of Virginia was named for Queen Elizabeth (the so-called 'Virgin Queen'). Over the course of the seventeenth century more and more settlers left Britain, some seeking work and some land, and some to gain religious freedom in the new American colonies. This migration led to some characterisations of the colonisation of America as a phenomenon achieved through settlement rather than conquest, and as one in which colonial peoples enjoyed a good deal of political freedom. That view is accurate only if we choose to ignore three important groups: the native American peoples whose subjection and marginalisation by settler society was necessary for the new population to enjoy the freedoms and successes they sought; the convict and indentured labour so important to early American prosperity; and the growing body of slaves carried to the region and forced to work there. All these groups had considerably less freedom than those who came by choice and of their own free will.

Early settlers frequently thought of themselves as British, and of the native indigenes they encountered in the colonies, as well as slaves brought forcibly from Africa, as foreign. The effects of colonisation on America's indigenous peoples were colossal, affecting their health, wealth, social structures, customs and traditions as well as their habitat. Most notorious was the impact of previously unknown diseases unwittingly brought to the continent by Europeans. With no prior exposure to smallpox, measles, influenza, tuberculosis and diphtheria, Native Americans were highly vulnerable, having no immunity. When epidemic disease spread through a Native American settlement, it could easily fell almost every member; in the early days of settlement, epidemics were the most common killer. New forms of land use and the enclosure of land for settlement considerably altered the local ecology over time, often depleting resources such as the wild game that local peoples had traditionally relied upon for food. Changes in land use led also to a gradual shift from subsistence agriculture among Native American tribes to a dependence on trade and commerce. It was a change that made tribes more reliant on settlers, as well as changing radically the seasonal settlement and movement that many tribes had traditionally followed. Fur trading, especially, became a critical source of Native American revenue, but the large-scale trapping of animals took its toll on the environment. The introduction of European-style firearms was also destabilising; the power of guns made them a valuable commodity, and Native American groups competed with one another for possession of them. Such competition led to an increase in inter-tribal conflict, itself made deadlier by the growing use of guns. Still, inter-tribal warfare was less significant in the destruction of an older Native American way of life than were the wars of European settlers. These affected Native Americans even though they were concerned with issues far removed from indigenous life. The rivalry between Britain and its imperial competitors in Europe, and the hunger for large tracts of land, put considerable strain on Native Americans drawn in to these conflicts, weakening their ability to survive in the face of settler America.

Those who did survive, however, not only adapted to the changes around them, but quickly learned the ways of European-style diplomacy. By the eighteenth century, especially as refugees from weakened tribes joined together, their communities became increasingly diverse. Native Americans learned to play the various European rivals off against one another for their own advantage, and there was also a good degree of cross-cultural exchange. The modern American Thanksgiving table owes much to what settlers learned from the locals: turkey, corn on the cob, maple syrup and pumpkins were all foodstuffs that settlers learned how to prepare from Native Americans. Nonetheless, and despite this tough determination to survive in a hostile world, by the time of the American Revolution American Indians along the Atlantic seaboard were largely dependent economically on the European settlers, and this meant they had little political muscle.

The significant support that Native Americans gave to the British during the Revolutionary War was not repaid, and many at the time thought the failure of the peace settlement of 1783 (discussed below) even to make mention of their future was a shabby return for Native American loyalty. Yet the British cultivated Native Americans after white America won its independence from the Empire, although they consistently refused to help them during the wars that would erupt between the new American republic and the native populations in the 1780s and 1790s. Their support for the British during the war did not endear American Indian populations to their new masters, and the treaties America increasingly enacted with numerous tribes were seldom generous to indigenous peoples.

If Amerindian populations were dwindling in the seventeenth and eighteenth centuries in the wake of contact, the settler population was growing fast. Around 20,000 migrants arrived in the New World between 1620 and

1640, in 1730 the population was around 629,000 and by 1783 almost a million and a half Europeans had settled there. By 1800, the population totalled more than 5 million. The earliest migrants were predominantly young, male and single, a typical pattern in settler colonies. In the later period, as the colonies became established, families began to migrate. By the 1630s, some 500 miles of coastline along the northeastern seaboard of North America was British, and by 1759 there were 13 colonies, mostly thriving. The largest populations by the mid-eighteenth century were to be found in the tobacco-growing colonies of Virginia and Maryland, whose combined population totalled some 372,000 by 1750. The New England colonies had the next largest concentration of population.

What made the American colonies so attractive? The story most often told is, of course, that of the 1620 voyage aboard the *Mayflower* that signals freedom of conscience and of religion, and certainly the Puritans do figure significantly in the early history of the American colonies. The bulk of white settlers who came to the Americas were non-Anglican Protestants, and in the eighteenth and nineteenth centuries the colonies became known as places where small religious sects could flourish. One important feature of American life was that, overall, there was no majority religion and this partially explains the strong strand of religious toleration that made America so distinctive. Only 2 of the 13 colonies – Massachusetts and Connecticut – ever had formal state churches, a radically different situation from Britain where the power of the Anglican Church prevented Christian non-Anglicans as well as Catholics and Jews from enjoying full political participation.

Religion, however, was only a part of the complex of reasons why settler colonialism was so successful in America. In the growing commercial environment of the eighteenth century, these colonies offered goods unavailable in Britain as well as becoming an increasingly valuable depot for supplying the nearby slave colonies of the West Indies to their south. North Atlantic markets were of crucial importance for a host of goods: sugar, tobacco, coffee, cotton, cocoa and rum. In the more northerly colonies, timber with which to build and fit ships was equally important and the fur trade, too, was highly profitable. By the middle of the eighteenth century, settler capitalism was well established, and many of the restrictions theoretically imposed by Britain's mercantilist policies were routinely ignored by American merchants and traders with little fear of retaliation.

Land was perhaps the most important factor in colonial advancement, as well as a source of considerable strife between settlers drawn by its availability and cheapness and Native Americans who were increasingly required to abide by property laws alien to their culture. Much of the struggle between the newcomers and indigenous populations reflected a fundamental difference in attitudes and relationship to the land. Both settlers and Native Americans complained constantly about the other's trespass. This persistent tension led to frontier violence and raids, the killing and stealing of livestock, the burning of crops and of compounds; none of this was sanctioned by colonial governments, but it was a fact of life on the frontier. There was no single form of land acquisition in colonial America; different colonies had different methods of parcelling out land. In some colonies, particularly in the north, land was largely allotted to groups and communities, while further south it was more likely to be sold to individuals. In the south, a system known as headright offered free land to those who paid their own passage there. But land was, by British standards, cheap and plentiful and migrants came not just from Britain (the larger number in pre-Revolutionary America) but from Germany and Switzerland, Scandinavia, Holland and Ireland. In the eighteenth century, Scots and Irish migrants became more numerous than the English. Many of the earliest Irish migrants were not Catholic, but Ulstermen who would come to be known in America as Scotch-Irish. They were Scottish Protestants who had left Scotland for Northern Ireland, and came to America in large part because they felt adrift in predominantly Catholic Ireland. Between the end of the Seven Years' War in 1763 and the start of the War of Independence in 1775, some 55,000 Protestant Irish, 40,000 Scots, 30,000 English and 12,000 Germans arrived in the 13 colonies, as did around 84,500 African slaves.

While land was a significant attraction, at least half of all migrants who landed in America in the seventeenth and eighteenth centuries came not to purchase land but as indentured labourers, tied for a fixed term to an employer who paid their passage and guaranteed them food and lodging for the duration of their contract. Although American history is full of grand tales of the poor made good – the 'rags to riches' stories of the popular press – few who started out in America as indentured servants ever saw fabulous wealth. Most stayed poor, remaining waged labourers rather than eventually acquiring land. This suited a society that was increasingly commercially oriented, creating a ready class of labourers. Although such a situation sounds as if it would be favourable to workers since they were in short supply, that was not so: indenture and the mercantilist imposition of maximum wages in many of the colonies served to keep firm the distinction between those who owned property and those who worked for wages. This critical relationship between landowning and labour would re-emerge in colonial Australia (see Chapter 4).

By and large, however, eighteenth-century American society was middle class, with a large population of landholders, a small wage-earning working class and no significant aristocracy. The preponderance among the influential landholding class of non-Anglican Protestants, wedded to a stern work ethic and fervently believing in the importance of the individual, would help shape the new republic in myriad ways. The principle of religious toleration was largely confined to Protestant sects. Life could be very different for settlers in the various regions. The New England colonies were more urban than Virginia, and agriculture in the northern colonies was more diversified than in the plantation colonies to the south. But while settlers may have experienced the colonies differently, for the enslaved and

Amerindian populations violence and conflict dominated their lives in all 13 colonies.

Settler colonies enjoyed a degree of political freedom that was only ever extended to those colonies where a white migrant population came to dominate. The system of 'representative government' in the Atlantic colonies operated via elected assemblies. As in Britain, the franchise was based on property ownership and limited to adult men. Women and landless men were excluded, along with Native Americans. Defence and taxation – which would both prove contentious in the 1770s – remained in the hands of the imperial government in London, but assemblies in the colonies had the power to pass laws of local significance. In the early years of colonisation, and until the mid-eighteenth century, the British government was mostly uninterested in the operation of internal colonial politics unless they interfered with revenue. It was trade that they wished to control, and it was only when trade and politics began to clash that British politicians paid attention to matters of governance in the American colonies.

In part this lack of interest is typical of the eighteenth-century Empire, overwhelmingly concerned with commerce and revenue, and indeed Britain favoured minimal direction from the centre as it passed the costs of governance to the settlers, saving money at home. In the case of the American colonies, it was also because they were regarded as ultimately less profitable than the West Indian colonies. Their main role was to supply the West Indies with foodstuffs, livestock, timber and cloth so that the slave colonies could focus their attention on the products for which they were renowned and on which the returns were so attractive. In return, the West Indies supplied the American colonies with sugar, rum and molasses in a classic example of how the British wanted colonial trade to work: Britain and its colonies linked in a complex network of production and supply, and excluding goods from outside the British world. The steady growth of the settler population in North America boosted this system, making the American colonies increasingly important, but also growingly restive about the limitations imposed from Britain on their trade. By the middle of the eighteenth century, they had moved from relatively lacklustre economic units to become critical markets for both export and re-export alongside their growing role as suppliers both to the West Indies and to Britain.

It was, however, impossible to insulate commerce from the political ferment of an era in which Britain was so often sparring with its European competitors in these very regions. Much of the Anglo-French conflict in the Atlantic and the Caribbean was commercial rivalry, especially with regard to sugar. And it was here that trouble really began to brew between the American colonists and the British government, most especially in and after the Seven Years' War. The lure of wealth often proved greater than the pull of patriotism, and during that war New England colonists resolutely refused to cease their trade with Britain's enemies, sometimes provisioning the very ships that were fighting against Britain. This disregard of wartime loyalties for business reasons may represent an extreme example, but the flouting or ignoring of such sanctions, laws and duties was far from uncommon in the Atlantic economy. For most of the eighteenth century, and despite laws in 1763 and 1764 designed to prevent it, North American traders purchased French as well as English sugar. The impossibility of enforcement in the North American sugar trade became something of a legend in rebel circles; as the economic historian Eric Williams put it, '[L]awlessness was erected into a cardinal virtue of American economic practice.'[1] Trouble was brewing between Britain and its American colonists, and that unrest drew as much on the role of the West Indies in the Empire as it did on local dissatisfactions within the 13 colonies. After the Seven Years' War, right at the moment of swelling restlessness in the American colonies, they became even more important as part of the defence and protection of the neighbouring sugar colonies. Though Britain had gained Caribbean territory as a result of the war, the fighting had been costly and the French still dominated sugar production. Britain's territorial acquisitions and victory had to be carefully balanced against the financial strains they inevitably spawned.

But the war had another cost besides, one that would become increasingly apparent in the 1770s. It fuelled the resentments already being expressed by American colonists regarding the restrictions by which they felt themselves hampered, restrictions that the burden of war had made more apparent. There is no doubt that the Seven Years' War affected the American colonies adversely, even given the deals New England merchants were striking with the enemy French. The war reverberated in America after 1763 in two ways. It spilled over into colonial frustration with taxation by the British. Not wholly unfairly, many colonists argued that they had contributed both soldiers and money to the war effort, and that further taxation was a burden, and though this did not flare into a major issue it burned steadily and rancorously in the background. More pressingly, there was deep resentment not only of the presence of increased troops garrisoned in the colonies, but also of being taxed for their maintenance. The British sought a greater military presence in the region to deter their European rivals and to have troops closer to hand in case of trouble in the West Indies. The Americans did not fully trust British motives, and felt that the troops were a symbol of imperial and authoritarian rule. British insensitivity and obduracy in the following years intensified such suspicions as well as fuelling the dissatisfaction of the Americans, hastening acts of rebellion. The extensive disregard of the many economic restrictions we have already noted is a good index of American discontent with mercantilism.

But alongside the suspicion engendered by the presence of British troops and a resentment of what they regarded as economic inequalities, the colonists also chafed at political restrictions. Their elective assemblies were frequently stonewalled by colonial governors loyal to the English and appointed by the Crown. Rebel colonists felt that their interests – political and economic – were consistently overridden by and subservient to those of far-away Britain. The actions of the imperial parliament in London in the late 1760s and early 1770s did little to appease them. Shortly after the war, in 1764, the Plantation Act (sometimes called the Sugar Act) raised American hackles by calling for the return of sugar duties. Although the rate of duty was lowered, this was the same duty that had angered Americans in 1733 in the Molasses Act (discussed in Chapter 2) and which they had largely ignored. The difference, however, was that this time around there were signs that the duty would actually be enforced. A year later the infamous Stamp Act, levying duties on business and legal transactions, ramped up the level of American anger. Twelve of the 13 colonies protested the Act, and although the British quickly repealed it, their subsequent actions were guaranteed to inflame existing discord. In 1766, a Declaratory Act similar to that relating to Ireland in 1720 (discussed in Chapter 1) asserted parliament's right to impose upon the colonies any taxes it chose. Despite this strong talk, however, by 1768 virtually all duties had been repealed in the face of vigorous resistance. The only one retained was on tea, and it would prove fateful. Ironically, tea was not an important revenue-raising commodity in the Atlantic, and the duty had been retained mostly as a symbol of the principles of the Declaratory Act, of Britain's right as an imperial authority to control taxation. But though tea was of little fiscal importance in this region of the world, it was a major trading commodity elsewhere. Its intrusion into American colonial politics in the 1770s underscores the links between different parts of a growing, and growingly diverse, British Empire in the later years of the eighteenth century.

Across the globe in South Asia, tea was among the most important assets of the fast-growing East India Company which, while Britain was waging war in and near British Caribbean territories, was increasing its territorial and political clout in India. At the heart of the Company's Indian holdings was the province of Bengal in eastern India, and Bengal in the late 1760s was in the grip of a vicious famine that was annihilating both the local population and the East India Company's assets. More concerned with the Company's loss of profits than the hunger of the local population, Britain decided that the Company would benefit from selling its tea exports in America directly rather than through American importers. In reality, the Tea Act of 1773 was not an American revenue measure at all, but rather a scheme to reduce duties by selling directly to the consumer in the hope that an expanded market in the Atlantic would help the East India Company overcome its serious fiscal problems in the east. The Company was much disliked by the American colonists, for whom it was a symbol of the monopolistic trade that so irked them. The result of the Tea Act, which favoured the East India Company over America, was the famous Boston Tea Party of December 1773 in which disgruntled colonists stormed three ships carrying cargoes of tea, and docked in the Boston harbour, throwing the tea overboard in protest. This colourful episode has popularly been seen as the fuse that lit the Revolutionary War, but in fact many Americans were appalled by what they regarded as the extremism of the rebel action.

It was the British response, however, that proved the more troubling. Not only did the British retaliate by closing the ports, putting the livelihood of many unassociated with the action in jeopardy, but parliament withdrew colonial civil and political rights. Early in 1774 they imposed the punitive Coercive Acts and the constitution-changing Massachusetts Government Act which substituted a nominated assembly for the elected one, in essence asserting Britain's political supremacy over the colonies. These actions alone would have been inflammatory given the tense state of the colonies, but another law passed at the same time further fuelled American discontent. In the 1763 treaty ending the Seven Years' War, the British had acquired tracts of French-speaking Canada which they combined into the colony of Quebec. The Quebec Act of 1774 laid down the political system that would govern the new colony, and it was one the Americans did not like at all. Not only did it guarantee religious toleration for Catholics, Quebec's majority population, but it established a nominated rather than an elected assembly in which Catholics outnumbered Protestants. Already dubious about Britain's motives, Protestant Americans worried that such political arrangements would migrate south. The American Mutiny (Quartering) Act of 1765, which enlarged the power of colonial governors with respect to the quartering of troops, did nothing to quell American notions that their political liberties were potentially under threat from the imperial centre. The British clearly had little interest in substantive appeasement, and this slew of aggressive decisions suggests both a certain misplaced confidence in their power and rather poor judgement.

It was in this tense and difficult atmosphere that the two Continental Congresses of 1774 and 1776 convened, the latter producing America's Declaration of Independence. There were plenty of skirmishes between British troops and American rebels in the 1770s before war was formally declared in 1775. Despite their naval power, the British wanted a war waged solely on land, fearing that naval activity would attract the attention of the French, given the proximity of the West Indian colonies over which Britain and France had so recently and so bitterly fought. In the event, land war did nothing to deter the French from seeking an advantage over their imperial rivals. In early 1778, a Franco-American alliance gave the American rebels increased military muscle, and expanded the war from a purely local if serious conflict to one also directly and deeply affecting other colonial sites, principally the coveted West Indies.

To the disappointment of the American rebels, the West Indians did not rally to the cause of independence, instead remaining loyal to the British. This may well have been a strategic choice; as chains of small islands, they were highly vulnerable and had over the years experienced many wars. Since three-quarters or more of the population was under slavery, the question of political freedom was far more restricted than in the American colonies. Planters already enjoyed a good deal of influence in Britain and were generally supportive of mercantilist trade (as we saw in Chapter 2). Dominica,

St Vincent and Grenada fell to the French during the Revolutionary War, but were later restored to Britain. Other colonies experienced considerable disruption both to their trade and in obtaining supplies; it was, of course, most often and most forcefully the slave population who paid the price of this hardship.

By late 1781, it was becoming apparent that the British could not win this war. Spain had joined the forces pitted against Britain in the summer of 1779, laying siege to the British colony of Gibraltar on their southern tip, a long way from America but symbolic of imperial connections. The surrender to the Americans of Charles Cornwallis at Yorktown in October 1781 signalled defeat; the prime minister Lord North, as a result, lost control of the British parliament. The 1779 cartoon in Figure 3.1 shows the British king George III being thrown from his horse while a French soldier, carrying a star-spangled flag, scurries past in the background offering him no help. In February 1782 a motion asserting the impracticability of war passed in the House of Commons, and within the month Prime Minister North had resigned. By November, the basic outline of a peace agreement was in place, and in September 1783 the Treaty of Versailles finally ended all hostilities. Britain won back most of those colonies seized by Spain and France during the conflict, and French colonies captured by Britain reverted to French rule.

THE HORSE AMERICA, *throwing his Master.*

Figure 3.1 The horse America, throwing his master, 1779

Source: LC-DIG-ppmsca-33532, Library of Congress Prints and Photographs Division, Washington D.C. 20540, USA

Britain also agreed to a policy of free trade with the new United States. By 1800 trade between the two countries was running at £40 million a year. Hostility was buried as commerce reasserted its hold; there was a rapid rise in British imports from its former colonies and the loss of the American colonies barely affected British prosperity.

In marked contrast to the abandonment of their Native American allies after the war, the British issued certificates of freedom to runaway slaves who had fought with them for a year or more. Some 3,000 settled in Nova Scotia (Canada), more reached London. Many of the London contingent were among the first to resettle in Africa, in the new colony of Sierra Leone. Those in Canada found life irksome; the land they were given was far harder to cultivate than that given to white loyalists moving north, and they experienced other kinds of discrimination too. Around half left for Sierra Leone in 1792.

The loss of America clearly did not lead to the demise of the British Empire, or to any significant loss of British imperial power. Britain rapidly acquired new territories elsewhere in the world and would, over the course of the nineteenth century, go on to increase its imperial holdings substantially. Why, then, is the American War considered important? In some ways, it was precisely because it shifted the focus of British imperial interest in new directions that would be sustained into the twentieth century. Defeat in the American Revolutionary War was one of only very few defeats Britain sustained during the eighteenth century, and given the considerable fighting in which Britain engaged in at that time, this alone is remarkable. Moreover, while in the earlier wars of the eighteenth century Britain had been fighting against other nations and national interests, this war was between Britons, pitting Britain against a British and Protestant adversary (albeit one enjoying substantial aid from Britain's Catholic rivals). The loss of America and the growing interest in the colonies of Asia made Britain's Empire less Anglophone, less Protestant, less white and less self-governing. And with the French and the Spanish supporting the American colonies against Britain, the war also isolated Britain within Europe.

The outcome of the war affected not just the direction of future growth within the British Empire, but also the fortunes of the West Indies. Over the course of the next 20 years or so, their wealth and power diminished considerably. Competition with the powerful French sugar industry, a declining share of American trade and, in 1807, the abolition of the slave trade spelled the end of West Indian predominance within the British Empire.

Not all of Britain's Atlantic holdings were lost in 1783, of course. American colonists who remained loyal to the English Crown often fled north to the Canadian colonies, and these became an important site for experiments in colonial governance. It would be in British Canada that the new code of 'responsible self-government' would first be instituted. Canada posed some awkward problems for the colonial state, however, since so many of its settler inhabitants were French and Catholic, France having gained a considerable foothold in the North Atlantic by the eighteenth century. Catholicism for the British was still, at the time of American independence, tied symbolically to disloyalty; it was not even a hundred years since the English state had secured a Protestant succession to the throne and passed laws that prevented non-Anglicans of all persuasions from holding public office. The insistence in the new American constitution on separating church and state was a reaction to Britain's restrictive and unequal religious divisions.

In the Canadian context, the loyalty of Catholics living under British rule proved very important, and the constitutional arrangements in late eighteenth- and early nineteenth-century Canada reflect the attempt of imperial politicians to deflect French separatism in the region. Using the experience of America as a guide, Britain granted a limited form of representative government to the Canadian colonies in 1791, with a franchise based on freehold property, and with governors who enjoyed a power of veto. By encouraging British emigration to Canada and awarding land grants to loyalists who left America, the government quietly hoped to increase the British proportion of this mixed population. Lower Canada (Quebec), however, remained predominantly French and by the 1830s rebellion threatened to dissolve the fragile truce between British and French colonists in British Canada. The need to find a system that would quell this tension would result in a solution that would be used in white settler colonies throughout the Empire during the nineteenth century (see Chapter 6). While the system of representative self-government did little to ease the tensions between British Canada and French Canada, it would remain the system that sustained white settler colonialism for the remainder of the nineteenth and into the twentieth century. Canada would prove to be an important resource within the Empire. From a population of some half a million in 1815, Canada grew to almost 19 million people in 1911, and was responsible for 16.5 per cent of British trade. Often neglected in histories of the British Empire, Canada was a significant arena for political experiment as the Empire matured in the nineteenth century.

Note

1 Eric E. Williams, *Capitalism and Slavery* (Chapel Hill, NC: University of North Carolina Press, 1944 (1994 reprint)), p. 119.

Further reading

Bernard Bailyn's *The Ideological Origins of the American Revolution* (Cambridge, MA: Belknap Press of Harvard University Press, 1992) offers a perspective on the political philosophies that informed American discontent in the eighteenth century, while his *Strangers Within the Realm: Cultural Margins of the First British Empire* (Bernard Bailyn and Philip D. Morgan (eds), Chapel Hill, NC: University of North Carolina Press, 1991) looks at the diverse groups who made up this colonial arena. In *British America, 1500–1800: Creating Colonies, Imagining an Empire* (London: Hodder Arnold, 2005), Steven Sarson provides a long view of the expansion of British American colonialism, as do the essays in *The British Atlantic World, 1500–1800* (David Armitage and Michael J. Braddick (eds), New York: Palgrave Macmillan, 2002). In *Replenishing the Earth. The Settler Revolution and the Rise of the Anglo-World, 1783–1939* (Oxford, Oxford University Press, 2009), James Belich looks to explain as well as describe the rapid growth of settler colonies from the eighteenth century to the outbreak of war in 1939.

Crucible of War: The Seven Years' War and the Fate of Empire in British North America, 1754–1766 (New York: Knopf, 2000) by Fred Anderson presents a detailed account of the impact on the American colonies of what was perhaps the key colonial war of the eighteenth century for this region. P. J. Marshall's *The Making and Unmaking of Empires: Britain, India, and America c.1750–1783* (Oxford: Oxford University Press, 2005) is a valuable perspective on the relations between the different colonial possessions of the period. Philip Lawson's *The Imperial Challenge: Quebec and Britain in the Age of the American Revolution* (Montreal: McGill-Queen's University Press, 1990) underscores the significance of Canada in the eighteenth-century Empire. In *Subjects and Sovereign: Bonds of Belonging in the Eighteenth-century British Empire* (New York: Oxford University Press, 2017), Hannah Weiss Muller explores questions of allegiance to the Empire and what it meant to be a subject of it.

Two books which do a lot to flesh out a picture of life in colonial America are *Down and Out in Early America* (Billy G. Smith (ed.), University Park, PA: Pennsylvania State University Press, 2004) and *The Creation of the British Atlantic World* (Elizabeth Mancke and Carole Shammas (eds), Baltimore: The Johns Hopkins University Press, 2005). *Born to Die: Disease and New World Conquest, 1492–1650* by Noble David Cook (Cambridge: Cambridge University Press, 1998) vividly describes the toll disease took on indigenous peoples as they encountered microbes new to the region. Tracing the migration of some 5,000 people to the Atlantic in the 1630s, Alison Games shows how varied the settlements in the New World were in their early years in *Migration and the Origins of the English Atlantic World* (Cambridge, MA: Harvard University Press, 2001).

In *Epic Journeys of Freedom: Runaway Slaves of the American Revolution and Their Global Quest for Liberty* (Boston, MA: Beacon Press, 2006), Cassandra Pybus tells of what happened to slaves who took the opportunity offered by the revolutionary war to escape enslavement. *Indians in the Fur Trade: Their Role as Hunters, Trappers and Middlemen in the Lands Southwest of Hudson Bay, 1670–1870* (Toronto: University of Toronto Press, 2nd edn, 1998) by Arthur Ray discusses the centrality of indigenous peoples to the colonial economy.

4 After America

At the end of the eighteenth century, although it had lost a good deal of its North American possessions, Britain was a major colonial power, with territorial possessions spread far and wide, in which there were a multitude of languages, customs and religions. After a century of recurrent warfare – mostly with the French and the Spanish – the British had established their supremacy among European expansionist powers. In part, this was due to Britain's considerable maritime power, developed because, as a small island, Britain needed to protect its shores.

With the loss of the American colonies and the decline in the importance of the West Indian colonies, British imperial interests began to shift from the Atlantic world towards the Pacific and Asia, which had been steadily developing as colonial sites of interest since at least the 1750s. The new forms of white settlement that would emerge in the Pacific at the end of the eighteenth and into the nineteenth century were politically very different from those of the 13 American colonies. By the 1860s these new colonies of settlement, Australia and New Zealand, had followed the Canadian colonies in being granted 'responsible self-government', and they would remain central to the growing idea of a British Commonwealth.

Exploration in the Pacific preceded actual settlement, and the 1760s and 1770s were particularly active decades of maritime exploration. The motives for the many voyages to the Pacific region in these years were varied. There was, of course, the constant search for resources and wealth that had long prompted entrepreneurs and explorers to set sail for distant lands. There was also a keen interest in finding good ports and harbours where ships could dock, rest and resupply on long sea voyages. Beyond this, eighteenth-century science was closely associated with imperial exploration, revealing new flora and fauna as well as different cultures.

The work of explorer-scientists in this era influenced poetry and art as much as it shaped the course of empire; the romantic view of the South Seas and the Pacific became part and parcel of English culture. Late eighteenth-century expeditions rarely sailed without a retinue that included artists as well as scientists. The most famous of the British sailor-explorers of this era, Captain James Cook, who had fought in the Seven Years' War and played

Figure 4.1 John Webber, *Poedua, daughter of Oreo, chief of Ulaietea, one of the Society Isles*, 1785. Te Papa Tongarewa, New Zealand
Source: Pictures from History/Bridgeman Images

a crucial role in the siege of Quebec, hosted a large group of scientists on his Pacific adventures, many of whom would be active in subsequently promoting the commercial development of the Pacific and other regions of colonisation. Artist John Webber sailed on Cook's third expedition (1776–80), sketching and painting the landscapes and peoples of the Pacific. This portrait (see Figure 4.1) of the high-born Poedua, one of the earliest images of a Polynesian woman seen by western audiences, may seem tranquil but was made while she was a hostage – along with her father and brother – aboard HMS *Discovery*, as Cook angled for the return of two sailors who had deserted.

Cook's first Pacific voyage left English shores in August 1768, landing at Tahiti some nine months later. Samuel Wallis had already staked a British claim to Tahiti in 1767, but Cook sailed more extensively in the area, landing at several spots on the east Australian coast during the first of his three voyages, and claiming the Australian continent in the name of Britain. Other European colonisers were close behind, spurred by the increased British interest in the region. The Spanish and the French mounted Pacific expeditions in the 1770s, and what would become Australia was commonly known as New Holland at this time, reflecting the active Dutch presence in the region. There was also a growing American interest in the Pacific, dominated by the trading ships of New England.

The British made no attempts to settle these Pacific islands, although the impact of contact with Europeans would still have a devastating impact on the local population; Tahiti's population diminished from around 40,000 in 1770 to a tiny 9,000 in the 1830s. It would be 1788, and the creation of the first penal colony in the Pacific, before permanent colonialism would emerge in this region. But why did Britain choose to send convicts on such a long, expensive and perilous voyage? Throughout the seventeenth and early eighteenth centuries, *Terra Australis* (or New Holland) had generally been regarded as a fabulous and mythic spot rather than a land that would realise profit for European commerce. The Pacific voyaging and exploration that gained ground in the eighteenth century significantly altered that opinion, even though it was only the eastern Australian coastline that was known. Britain had lost its main penal colony after the American War of Independence, but not its desire to transport convicts. The waters around Britain were littered with convict ships, known as hulks, where convicts were locked up at night, spending their days working in the ports and harbours where these unsanitary ships were moored. Though few of the convict hulks were seaworthy, this style of imprisonment reveals the depth and centrality of Britain's maritime personality. Sailing convicts to a distant land seemed a routine activity, and if that land might offer naval and commercial advantages as well, then the state would win on numerous counts, offloading unwanted peoples and, through their labour, gaining potential profits, goods and bases for future commerce and military security.

After the American Revolution, government quickly turned its attention to establishing an alternative penal colony, for the Americas had absorbed around 1,000 transportees annually. Africa was considered and rejected, and in 1786 Botany Bay on the east coast of New Holland was adopted. This was to be a penal colony principally for white convicts; those in the Indian Ocean (at various points Bencoolen; Penang; Mauritius; Malacca; Singapore; the Andaman Islands; and the Burmese provinces of Arakan and Tenasserim) housed colonial, and especially Indian, convicts. Nonetheless African, Indian and Chinese convicts did sometimes end up in Australia, though never in large numbers.

New South Wales was a site from which escape would be unattractive and difficult, and whose distance from home might be seen as a disincentive to would-be criminals. There was a hope, too, that the harbour would provide a naval base for further expansion in the region, and that whaling, also lost after American independence, might be profitably resumed in these waters. Norfolk Island, an isolated island some 1,400 kilometres east of Botany Bay, also offered the prospect of both a timber and a flax industry, commodities vital to the navy. Since European imperial rivals were also scouting the area, establishing a working, occupied colony would strengthen Britain's own claims in the region.

This was, of course, a hugely ambitious project, not only because of the distance and uncertainty regarding the land but because it was to be a colony built in effect by convicts, by Britain's discards. This posed interesting questions regarding how the colony would be administered. Clearly, it could not operate as the American colonies had done, since prisoners by definition were not free, and aside from them the only other settlers were the marines who accompanied them and who acted as their guards after the voyage was over. The new colony, as a result, was a curious hybrid, a military colony run by naval officers, but with a civil legal system since this was the system under which the convicts had been sentenced. The hope was to transform criminals into productive colonists who would ready the land for profitable settlement.

The First Fleet, consisting of 11 ships carrying around 1,050 people (of whom some 750 were convicts) as well as animals, farm implements and food supplies intended to last two years, left Portsmouth in May 1787. The fleet reached Botany Bay in mid-January of the following year but quickly realised that it was by no means an ideal landing spot. Sailing north, they docked instead 12 kilometres away at Port Jackson on 26 January 1788, a date still celebrated annually as Australia Day.

The new migrants had arrived at the hottest time of year and soon found that raising crops was a difficult business and that the unfamiliar timbers of the region did not yield easily to their axes. Life was hard and sparse for these first settlers; only 12 acres of land had been successfully cultivated after six months in the new colony, the livestock, unused to the harsh conditions of an Australian summer, were dying and food and medical supplies had to be strictly rationed. A party sent east to Norfolk Island was similarly impoverished as neither the pine trees nor the flax there proved usable. In 1803, Van Diemen's Land (renamed Tasmania in 1856), an island off the south-east corner of Australia, was also settled. Sealing was already an established industry there before formal colonisation began but it, too, provided a far from easy living.

Despite these unpromising beginnings, the settlements slowly but surely gained a foothold, even if in the first decade or two shortages and crises recurred regularly. The Napoleonic Wars of the early nineteenth century brought hardship but, at the same time, increased British attention to the region. Fighting against the French, whose interest in the Pacific had not waned, Britain's presence on the east coast of New Holland was an important strategic and military one. Yet the war also brought about a decline in transportee numbers since ships were diverted to wartime use, and passage across the waters became less safe. Still, the colony's future was assured by 1815, when the Napoleonic Wars ended. By 1800, there were some 5,000 white colonists on the eastern mainland and another 1,000 on Norfolk Island, and although it was already becoming popular in England to regard the convict's lot as a happy one resulting in substantial land ownership, convicts were daily reminded that theirs was a punitive condition. In the earliest years, convicts were assigned either to public works or to an individual master, and were allowed time to work for themselves and earn an income alongside the work they performed as part of their sentence. Women convicts, far fewer in number, worked mostly in domestic service or on production lines in the female factories while the work for men covered all areas, since the colony was quite literally being built by them. Floggings were plentiful for those who challenged the system and convicts were expected to return to work the day after a lashing, whatever their physical condition. By 1800, many of the private employers reliant on convict labour were themselves former convicts who had served out their sentences or who had received an early pardon. Two-thirds of the colonists were free by that date, though few had the means to return to England and many chose in any case to stay on in what was now called New South Wales.

In the mid-nineteenth century, convict conditions, if anything, became harsher. Convicts could no longer work for themselves: the free time in which to do so had been taken away. Many fewer were pardoned early, and the fractious were far likelier to be sent to one of the isolated settlements now developing up and down the coast and on Van Diemen's Land to the south. The land grants that had made the English public so sceptical of transportation as a punishment disappeared, creating a landless workforce of former convicts to people the industries of the new colonies.

When the Napoleonic Wars ended, transportation once more quickened. By 1820, there were 32,000 colonists in New South Wales and Van Diemen's Land, and by 1850 the white population had grown to 400,000. In addition to a constant flow of migrants, both voluntary and convict, the dramatic growth in population was also a result of natural increase. The settler population was mostly a youthful one, and the growth in the number of children in the colony was striking. Children constituted some 3 per cent of the initial settlers (some born on the voyage, a few accompanying their parents). By the end of 1799, they accounted for almost 17 per cent of the population.

The youth of the settlers was only one reason for this rapid increase in population. Though women colonists were small in number, colonial policies all aimed to domesticate them and to foster the principles of Christian family life at the centre of colonial culture. The early land grants given to convict men (but not to women) on the expiration of their sentences were augmented if the man was married, and boosted even further if he had children. Women's reproductive potential was, in a sense, part and parcel of the social landscape envisaged by the architects of the new settlement. Women represented approximately one-sixth of all transportees, and were invariably of child-bearing age; they were a conscious instrument of colonial policy and, by the early 1800s, the larger number of them were either formally married or cohabiting with men.

Their lives were certainly no easier than those of the men. Women were severely economically disadvantaged, since they were not entitled to land grants in their own right and were restricted in the employments open to them, despite the fact that many of them had labour skills from their prior life in Britain. Unlike men who could, should they choose, work their passage home as shipboard labourers, women seldom had the means or opportunity to return to Britain. In the first days of settlement, women's rations were two-thirds those awarded to men. It would be the early twentieth century before there were roughly equal numbers of men and women in the population. Interestingly, however, the Australian colonies would be among the first places to grant women the right to vote. South Australia led the way, women there acquiring voting rights in local government elections in 1861 and in parliamentary elections in 1894.

Women were not the only group of convicts singled out for differential treatment. Political prisoners, many of them Irish, were routinely separated from one another, for fear they would organise rebellions, as some indeed did. Another interesting group is the thousand or so Africans, former slaves, who had been taken to Britain and were subsequently convicted of crimes and sentenced to transportation.

Transportation came to an end in 1867. New South Wales had abandoned transportation in 1840, resuming the practice briefly in 1847. Van Diemen's Land discarded the practice in 1853. The Swan River Colony (now Western Australia) began transporting convicts only in 1850, and it was here that the last transport deposited its human cargo in 1867. In the years between 1788 and 1867, somewhere between 150,000 and 160,000 convicts arrived in Australia; about 60 per cent were English, 34 per cent Irish and 5 per cent Scots.

All of this activity was unfolding against the backdrop of a substantial indigenous population whose principal experience of colonialism was the loss of their hunting grounds, their livelihood and their place in the world. Regarded as primitive by the settlers because they wore scant clothing, did not engage in settled agriculture or build in western ways, the Aboriginal population suffered considerably at the hands of the continent's new residents, despite spirited attempts both to resist and to live amicably alongside them. The extension of western-style agriculture severely limited Aboriginal movement and access to foodstuffs, as that most distinctive of western ideas, private property, was fenced off or actively policed. As in colonial America, diseases brought from the west wreaked havoc on populations exposed to them for the first time. The size of the Aboriginal population plummeted from roughly 300,000 at the moment of initial white settlement to some 80,000 in the 1880s, leading many white Australians as well as anthropologists and scientists, to classify them – wrongly – as a dying race.

In the very earliest days of settlement, officials exercised some caution in their relations with Aboriginal Australians, although Aboriginal men were kidnapped and held in the white settlements in the hope that they would act as translators of indigenous custom and culture. Needless to say, such tactics were much resented, and men thus confined almost always escaped as soon as they could. By the 1790s, punitive raids against resistant Aboriginal groups were sanctioned, and the killings began to mount. Yet far more Aboriginals died because of disease or malnutrition than from the guns of settlers. It was exposure to unfamiliar diseases and the loss of traditional forms of food-gathering that ultimately had the most devastating effect on Australia's earlier inhabitants.

Outside the cities, on farms and sheep and cattle stations, Aboriginal labour was key to success, for settlers relied upon indigenous knowledge of a harsh land where water was sparse and dangerous storms could blow up in minutes. Aboriginal trackers assisted surveyors, settlers and others to navigate and pass through the hinterlands, yet despite their importance in helping settlers, Aboriginal workers were often poorly treated. Unlike white workers, they were frequently paid in rations rather than in money, a practice long since abandoned in western labour markets where waged work was a central symbol of the modern workplace. Local peoples, as in many other colonies, were regarded as pre- or un-modern, unlikely and often unable to adapt to the modern western conditions that colonialism brought with it as it swept the globe. As in the case of Australian labour practices, this led to massive inequalities between settlers and indigenous peoples all over the Empire. Though the Australian colonies were, by the late nineteenth century, a shining example of new and progressive labour conditions and practices, these benefits were restricted to white Australians.

The most notorious relations between white settlers and Aboriginal Australians were to be found in Van Diemen's Land. By 1830, the Aboriginal population had already been severely diminished by settler violence. The colony's governor, George Arthur, acknowledged in correspondence with the colonial secretary in London that the local Aboriginals were complaining that 'the white people have taken possession of their country, encroached upon their hunting grounds, and destroyed their natural food, the kangaroo'.[1] The killing of some settlers prompted Arthur to declare a state of martial law, and his 1830 'Black Line' plan – literally a human chain stretched across the island comprising some 2,000 armed soldiers as well as civilians – was designed to force what was left of the Aboriginal population southward, and then to round them up and contain them on allotted lands. The plan was an abject failure. In its wake, Arthur commissioned a tradesman, George Robinson, to bring in the island's Aboriginals. Using less confrontational methods, Robinson's success probably sealed the fate of the black population for this apparent exercise in protection isolated the entire population on inhospitable Flinders Island, where their numbers declined precipitously. By the 1880s there were no full-blood Aboriginals left on Van Diemen's Land. The last was Truganini, a Nuenone woman who died in 1876. She had been one of Robinson's guides, teaching him the language and customs of her people. Although by all accounts, Truganini had made it known that she did not wish to be an object of scientific study after her death, the Royal Society of Tasmania were given leave to exhume her body in 1878 on condition that it be accessible only to scientists. By 1904, however, her skeleton was on public display at the Hobart Museum and Art Gallery where it remained on view until 1947.

From the start of white settlement, indigenous Australians both fascinated and, at times, disturbed the newcomers. Long before Truganini was displayed in Hobart, artists sketched and painted the locals. Convicts were among the first artists to paint scenes of Aboriginal life. They depicted family life, hunting scenes, disputes, landscapes, documenting everyday life for both settlers and Aboriginal Australians in the early days of white settlement. Thomas Watling (see Figure 4.2) was one of the best known of the early convict artists, a Scotsman convicted of forging bank notes and transported in

Figure 4.2 Thomas Watling, *A group on the North Shore of Port Jackson, New South Wales*

Source: Natural History Museum, London, UK/Bridgeman Images

1791. In Australia, his talents became quickly known to the authorities and he was given work illustrating local plants and animals as well as scenery.

The idea of Aboriginal protection became popular around the 1830s at about the same time slavery was abolished. It found a more sympathetic audience in Britain than in the colonies themselves. The imperial parliament in London established a formal investigation in the mid-1830s of the effect of colonialism on native peoples in British colonies, while concerned humanitarians, mostly evangelicals, founded the British and Foreign Aborigines' Protection Society. In time, the Australian colonies would introduce Aboriginal Protection Acts, the first of which was in the colony of Victoria (in south-east Australia) in 1869. Despite their name, the Acts were more concerned with control than protection, routinely prescribing where Aboriginals might live, who they could marry, what work they could do and addressing many other aspects of their daily life. This was paternalist legislation founded on a belief that Aborigines were incapable of making responsible decisions; such laws also effectively drew distinct boundaries between white and Aboriginal spaces, invariably to the disadvantage of the latter.

Land, and the use of land, was at the heart of much of the conflict between the Aboriginal and the settler inhabitants of the new colony from its inception. The Cambridge University Le Bas Prize for 1873 went to J. Langfield Ward for his essay 'Colonization and Its Bearing on the Extinction of the Aboriginal Races' in which he argued 'we cannot allow what will give such an increase to the sum of human happiness, to be hindered by the claim of a tribe to acres over which it occasionally roams'.[2] In other words, where land was not cultivated, those who lived on it could be forced to forfeit it for the larger good. Since, in British eyes, Aboriginal populations did nothing productive with the land on which they lived – no settled agriculture, no market in agricultural produce, no farming of the land – it was just and proper to turn it over to western use. That view failed, of course, to understand the rich alternative ways in which Aboriginal peoples sustained themselves through the land. After all, when white settlers first arrived the Aboriginal peoples were healthy and numerous, living well for the most part off land which looked to British eyes uncultivated. It was this colonial perspective that led to the development of the legal doctrine of *terra nullius*, in which the British reasoned that land not put to productive use was available for settlement, denying the principle of Aboriginal land title that would not be restored until the landmark legal case of *Mabo v. Queensland* in 1992. This concept justified the seizing of huge areas of the continent, pushing indigenous peoples increasingly to the margins of newly farmed, cultivated and built-upon soil.

Land was a key component in the shaping of the new colony's culture and politics. The ability of settler colonialism to survive was staked on the promise of what the land might productively yield and, as the various Australian colonies grew economically, older British ideas about property ownership re-emerged. As we have seen, the very earliest years of settlement relied not just on convict labour but on a hope and a belief that giving men, even former convicts, land would be an incentive for them to work hard and produce wealth. The slow but steady success of that gamble in a sense also effected its undoing; as in Britain, a line was increasingly drawn in settler Australia between the propertied and the unpropertied as well as between white and Aboriginal. By the mid-nineteenth century, land was made available for purchase rather than being given away free, although there were those known as squatters who had illegally but successfully assumed control of vast tracts of land, principally for the grazing of animals. Their position would be much debated in government, although it remained largely unresolved, at least at the legal level. Still, by mid-century, and most especially in the cities, white Australian society was clearly divided among those who owned property and those who sold their labour to property owners. Wholly different from Britain, however, a universal male franchise was typical for the lower chamber of government, the Assembly, after responsible self-government was conferred on the colonies of New South Wales, Victoria and South Australia in 1855, in Tasmania in 1856 and in Queensland in 1859.

What did this term 'responsible self-government' mean? Imported from the British Canadian colonies (see Chapter 3), it was a device that distinguished settler colonies from the larger portion of the Empire where far fewer Britons lived, and where they did so generally on a temporary basis only. It drew on the forms of governance that had been in place in the Atlantic in earlier years. Unlike colonies where there were few white settlers and which were increasingly considered incapable of managing their own affairs, the Australian and other white settler colonies were regarded as outposts of British society and civilisation. Responsible self-government created colonial mini-versions of parliament, a two-house government in which the assembly approximated the House of Commons as an elected house, while the council consisted of those appointed by the colonial governor. Since there was no formal aristocracy to inherit seats in the new colonies as there would have been in the British House of Lords, this upper house had appointed members. Prior to responsible self-government, the governor wielded considerable power. He made legal decisions, ruled on economic and fiscal matters, on the granting of land, on marriage contracts and on many other facets of colonial life.

Throughout the first hundred years of settler colony history, however, many key powers remained with the imperial parliament at Westminster. Governors were appointed by the Colonial Office in London, rather than in Australia, just as they had been in the Atlantic colonies. Laws passed in the colonies could be overturned by the imperial parliament which also retained control of fiscal, monetary and tax issues, and of defence. Furthermore, when responsible self-government was granted not only was the decision to do so taken in London but it followed that the governing structures of the colonies would closely resemble those at the centre of the Empire.

Responsible self-government depended upon the colony's acceptance of political structures created in an English idiom.

The creation of a series of 'miniature Britains' in the 1850s rested on the transformation of the Australian colonies from penal settlements to free settlements. Free settlers had been coming to the Australian colonies in significant numbers since 1793. From the 1830s, sponsored colonisation began to alter the social structure of Australia as free settlers rapidly outpaced the prisoner population. By the late 1840s, free migrants – many of them poor – outnumbered those whose passage to the colonies had been via the criminal courts.

Before the 1840s especially, there were also a good few British indentured servants in the Australian colonies, but indenture proved unpopular and unsuccessful. Employers complained that the indentured were lazier than the convicts, while those under contract chafed at the disparity between their low wages and what free labourers could command in a still sparsely populated country. They energetically sought early release from their contracts and seldom renewed them on expiry. Indenture among whites in Australia simply faded away over time, although this did not mark the end of indenture in the Australian colonies.

State-assisted migration from Britain began in 1831, with free passages and cheap land on offer to those willing to start new lives across the globe. Agents for the scheme were paid per head for those they signed up, and the numbers of voluntary migrants rose dramatically. In the 1820s, before these schemes were introduced, some 8,000 free settlers arrived in the Australian colonies. Those numbers, not surprisingly, jumped dramatically with the introduction of state-assisted schemes. In the 1830s, around 30,000 made the journey, rising to about 80,000 in the 1840s. The free and assisted passages that made emigration an option for poorer Britons were financed by a shift within Australia from land grants to land sales; the Colonial Land and Emigration Commission, established in 1840, used some of the proceeds from colonial land sales to fund emigration to the Empire. The new settlers to Australia were largely people of modest means, many of them from the rural regions of southern England where wages were low and social relations between employers and workers still very rigid. Over time, and especially once famine hit Ireland, a significant proportion of migrants would come from poverty-stricken Ireland. There was also a concerted, though not always successful, push to encourage single women to migrate as a means of solving the distinctive imbalance between male and female populations. Maria Rye and Jane Lewin founded the Female Middle-Class Emigration Society in the 1860s to promote the emigration of single women to the colonies. Rye herself accompanied parties of women to Australia and New Zealand in the 1860s.

With so many migrants arriving, settlements spread further and further and new colonies beyond New South Wales were created. By the late 1850s, there were six colonies, by no means identical in population, politics or governance, but a sure sign that what, from 1814 or so, was called Australia, would endure. The Swan River Colony was first established in 1829, and that of South Australia in 1836. The founding of new colonies was prompted not only by the tide of emigration from Britain but by a variety of local political interests as well. As had been the case with Van Diemen's Land at the start of the century, the Swan River Colony was initiated in large part to deter the French from attempts at settlement on Australia's western coast. It was planned initially as a settlement solely of voluntary migrants, although including those under indenture, but the struggles of the early residents led to the late introduction of transportation in 1850. Despite the Swan River Colony's desire to be convict-free, it would be, as we have seen, the last of the colonies to abolish transportation.

South Australia, by contrast, proved successful in limiting its population to free settlers. Here the principles of 'systematic colonisation' laid out by Edward Gibbon Wakefield were implemented, as they would be, too, in parts of New Zealand. Wakefield proposed to create communities that were aligned to the laws of economics as they were popularly understood in the nineteenth century. Arguing that selling land too cheaply upset the critical balance between land, labour and capital, Wakefield looked to create both a landowning class and a landless labouring class, replicating the traditional contours of British society. He saw this social structure as guaranteeing a labour supply, in this case composed of free settlers rather than convicts forced to work. If everyone could afford land, he argued, then labour costs would rise prohibitively since there would be no inducement to seek waged work. It was a classically nineteenth-century statement of the relationship between the social order and the economy. After some initial struggles – typical of settler history in these lands – South Australia thrived. It remained a free settler colony and, unusually, one in which the ratio of men to women was more balanced than in the other Australian colonies.

Vital to the expansion of Australian settlement was exploration. Matthew Flinders, a naval officer, had sailed around Australia at the start of the nineteenth century, proving that it was indeed a continent. Inland, explorers heading west from Port Jackson crossed the Blue Mountains in 1813, enabling settlement towards the interior of the country. In the 1820s many new penal stations were established up and down the east coast. Major expeditions to northern and central Australia in the 1840s also opened up the interior, although the settler population clung mostly to the coastal areas, as the population still does today. As a result, and despite the emphasis on land acquisition and the development of large-scale pastoral agriculture, Australia developed as a highly urbanised culture, the vast majority of its population (although not always its wealth) clustered in cities by the middle of the nineteenth century. In 1850, 40 per cent of the population already lived in urban environments, a proportion that would grow substantially over time.

The characteristically urban profile of the Australian colonies should not blind us, nonetheless, to the central importance of pastoral agriculture to the economy. Wool and, later, dairy and beef cattle dominated the economy, although in the very earliest years whaling and sealing had been key industries. The penetration inland and the creation of large sheep and cattle stations so destructive to Aboriginal lifestyles made wool a staple of the Australian economy by 1850. Coal mining was on the rise by the early 1800s and gold became significant in the 1850s. Copper and silver also proved economically important.

As convict labour diminished, a dual labour system grew up, quite distinctive when compared with many of Britain's other colonies. As we have seen, changes in land policy led to the creation of a large white working class, many engaged in much the same kind of work as might have been on offer in Britain. But in the tropical northerly reaches of the continent, as settlement expanded, fears of climatic unsuitability had a striking effect on the labour market. There was some use of Aboriginal workers but many white Australians regarded them with suspicion and hostility, and many Aboriginals in any case had little interest in the kind of work offered by white employers. Instead, there was a growing use in the north, and at a time when its use was waning elsewhere in Australia, of indentured labourers, some of whom were from India and China, but who mostly came from nearby Melanesia. Pacific Islanders worked in plantation-style agriculture, especially in the growing sugar industry of Queensland. The use of non-white indentured labour in Australian colonies lasted into the early twentieth century, long after white indenture had disappeared. It was more commonly in use in places where there was no white labour force to be employed, and it was crucial to the cultivation of the northerly tropical regions of Australia. The networks that allowed workers from different parts of the Empire and beyond to take work in other lands is a fascinating, and often quite brutal, example of transnational colonial connections at work (as we shall see in Chapter 8).

Some 1,600 kilometres south-east of Australia, and across the Tasman Sea, lay what would become in the 1840s the new British colony of New Zealand, also a white settler land although in many respects markedly different from Australia. First claimed for Britain by Cook in 1769, and initially a dependency of New South Wales, New Zealand had a less harsh climate and a more tractable soil than Australia's east coast, and it had timber suitable for ship-building. There was considerable commercial activity there even before formal colonisation. Both the Americans and the French operated whaling stations, and wealthy Australian speculators were busy buying up tracts of land. In 1839, Edward Gibbon Wakefield's New Zealand Company undertook the organising of a permanent settlement on the North Island. All of this activity was the work of private entrepreneurs and would have been unthinkable without the acquiescence of New Zealand's indigenous Māori peoples. The government's lack of interest in pursuing more formal colonisation had more than a little to do with the perception of Māori society as well organised and militarily proficient, and thus not all that easy to subdue.

Life would change for both the Māori and the early settlers when, in 1840, New Zealand became a Protectorate (as a dependency of New South Wales) after the signing of the Treaty of Waitangi. Prompted in part by concerns about increased French activity in the region, the treaty was engineered largely by missionaries and reformers who argued that the intense economic speculation in New Zealand was producing anarchic conditions harmful most especially to the Māori. Protestant missionaries were also anxious to curb their French Catholic rivals, already quite active on New Zealand's South Island.

The treaty was a curious one for, in principle, it recognised Māori ownership of land, a very different context for colonisation from that experienced by the Aboriginal Australians. The treaty offered protection and British subjecthood to the Māori in exchange for an exclusive British right to purchase lands the Māori might wish to sell. In practice, Māori reluctance to sell was often overlooked, and the effect of the treaty was the acquisition of a very substantial quantity of land by colonisers at extremely low prices. The shift of land ownership not surprisingly precipitated increasing friction between Māori and Pākehā (as the white settlers were known by them) over governance. By the mid-1840s, the New Zealand Wars had begun, initially in the north. The ultimate, though not easily achieved, defeat of the Māori had the inevitable consequence of dispossessing and marginalising New Zealand's indigenous peoples as white settler colonialism spread. By 1861, two-thirds of New Zealand land had been sold, with the inevitable result that there was a rise in the white settler population and a corresponding decline in the Māori population. In the 1840s alone, Pākehā numbers in New Zealand rose from 2,000 to about 10,000 while the Māori population, over the course of the nineteenth century, halved from around 200,000 to 100,000. Still, when white women were awarded the vote in 1893 (the earliest granting of a national franchise to women in any British territory), the Māori were also enfranchised, just one month later. This, and the four Māori seats in parliament that had been guaranteed since the 1860s, did little to restore the previous prosperity or dominance of New Zealand's indigenous peoples. It nonetheless offers a very different version of settler colonialism than that of neighbouring Australia. As was always the case, however, settler colonialism relied on the subjugation of claims by prior residents. New Zealand's economic situation remained precarious throughout these years of war, although the Australian gold rush of the 1850s eased things by providing a local market for New Zealand produce. New Zealand acquired a federal constitution and a general assembly in 1852, and the two islands (north and south) were united as one state in 1876, a quarter of a century before Australia's federation. The ecological effects were dramatic as large-scale agriculture and bush clearance transformed the landscape dramatically.

The white settler model was not the only form of colonialism operating in the region as British attention turned east from the late eighteenth century. In South-East Asia and the Malay archipelago, the British were by no means the dominant imperial power. The Dutch had a long history in the region, as did the Spanish and the French. In the sixteenth century, the East Indies – the chain of islands comprising Java, Sumatra, the Bandas and the Moluccas – were assumed to be the most profitable, and India (see Chapter 5) was often regarded as a stop en route to reach these sources of wealth. But the Spice Islands proved tough for the British, both because of the actions of local elites and rulers and because of the success there of their European rivals. In 1700 the British had only one settlement in the area, administered by the East India Company, at Bencoolen on Sumatra's west coast where slaves did a large amount of the necessary work.

Typically, the British took advantage of wartime conditions to wrest control of some of these places from their European competitors. During the Napoleonic Wars, Britain captured many of the Dutch possessions in this region. But the balance of power and of economic profitability had shifted considerably, and the British no longer coveted the Spice Islands for their commodities, but rather for protecting India from territorial encircle-ment by the French, since the Dutch, at this time, were under the influence of Napoleon. By 1811, Britain had captured all the major Dutch colonies, among them Java, Mauritius and the Trincomalee harbour at Ceylon. Though most were restored to the Dutch after Napoleon's defeat when a new kingdom of the Netherlands was established, Britain was careful to maintain a strategic and commercial foothold in the region. The Dutch were welcome to return as long as a place for British trade and passage was guar-anteed. In 1819, adding to the British possessions on the Malay peninsula around the Straits of Malacca, Sir Thomas Stamford Raffles acquired for the East India Company an island that in 1826 would become part of the new colony of the Straits Settlements: Singapore. In its early years Penang was the principal settlement at the Straits, but over time Singapore would come to dominate the colony, economically and politically. In these early years, since the colony was an East India Company possession, it was administered via India. The Straits became a Crown Colony in 1867, and it was only then that more complete British intervention in the area developed. Even before then the colony was both a highly profitable acquisition and a valuable loca-tion from which to conduct diplomatic relations with both Siam (modern Thailand) and the Malay states.

The period between the loss of the Americas and the end of the Napoleonic Wars was, thus, a busy period of colonisation for the British, and the Napoleonic Wars in particular saw an active period of acquisition on the part of the British. The motives were partly strategic and partly eco-nomic, limiting the power of rivals and simultaneously maximising profit-ability. The introduction in 1815 of the Crown Colony reflects this period of activity and also a change in thinking about the process of colonisation and the future of the British Empire. This new device, which placed a colonial territory under the direct authority of the British Crown, allowed the use of British laws and institutions (such as courts and police forces) without the need for any local ratification. The imperial parliament in London had full control in such colonies and local legislative bodies could be required to assent to London's decisions. Not all colonies were Crown Colonies, of course. India, for example, never had that status and nor did many colonies designated as Protectorates. Technically, the Protectorate remained under the sovereignty of a local ruler under British protection and gave the inhabitants no right to British citizenship. In practice, Britain acquired a good deal of control, and most of its Protectorates moved to Crown Colony status at some stage. Most white settler colonies were granted responsible self-government by mid-century, radically altering their political relationship with the centre. Essential to this expansion was the principle that colonies should be self-financing entities.

The one settler colony without responsible self-government by the 1850s was the Cape Colony in coastal southern Africa, and since the settlers there were largely in this period not British and struggles between them, the Africans and the British were common, this is not surprising. The British had first occupied the Cape in 1795, mostly to prevent the French from doing so. It was only after occupation that its value as a port en route to India really became clear. The area catapulted back and forth between Dutch and British claims in the early 1800s, until at the end of the Napoleonic Wars it was formally ceded to the British as Cape Colony. The Dutch settler farmers – the Boers – who had been there for a hundred years or so, thus became British subjects, a change that in the 1830s would cause considerable disruption in the area. Enraged by the British abolition of slavery in 1833, and the abolition of indenture among the indigenous Khoisan people in 1828, some 15,000 Boers (known also as Afrikaners) attempted to found their own land to the north across the Orange River. This exodus in 1835, known as the 'Great Trek', forced Britain's hand: were the Boers to be permitted secession or should Britain bear the expense of administering another colony? Southern Africa was not yet a really valuable economic location, for the discovery of gold and diamonds was still decades away. Nor was plantation-style agriculture yet fully established. The British, thus, took their time in deciding how to react to this Boer challenge, and it was almost a decade before, in 1843, they chose to move, annexing what the Afrikaners called Natalia. The Dutch settlers scattered throughout the region, winning a pocket of independent land – the Transvaal – from the British in 1852.

Tensions would mount between the Boers and the British throughout the century, though they often had a more deleterious effect on local African populations than on the Europeans. British numbers swelled at the launch of the Cape Emigration Scheme, which hoped to introduce English settlers to the region, offering free passage and land to men who agreed to bring with them ten more English labourers. The scheme was inundated with applicants and around 4,000 emigrants arrived from Britain in 1820, only to find themselves in conflict with local peoples who fought vigorously to prevent their lands from being given away to the newcomers.

Beyond its southern tip, Africa was of limited interest to the British before the late nineteenth century. There was little colonisation of the continent prior to the 1890s, other than in West Africa at Sierra Leone and The Gambia. Both of these were colonies directly related to Britain's new policies on slaving: Sierra Leone was created as a site for the return of freed Africans while The Gambia housed Britain's naval anti-slaving squadron.

There was expansion in this period, however, in other regions. The tiny and isolated Falkland Islands in the South Atlantic (called by the Spaniards, the Malvinas) aroused European interest in the late eighteenth century because of their proximity to the route between the Atlantic and the Pacific Oceans. Not surprisingly, therefore, they also became the subject of European rivalry between the French, the Spanish and the British. The first white settlers there were French: two years later, in 1766, a small British contingent settled to the west. Together the French and the Spanish tried to drive out the British in 1770, but though the British remained unsubdued, it was not a territory for which they were willing to fight. They withdrew their settlement in the late 1770s, though continuing to claim ownership. The Spanish, who had taken control of the French settlements in 1767, withdrew in 1811 and little attention was paid to these remote islands until, in the early 1830s, newly independent Argentina claimed possession on the curious grounds that the Falklands had once been, like Argentina, part of the Spanish Empire. Britain promptly despatched a naval expedition to the South Atlantic and declared the Falkland Islands a Crown Colony in 1832.

Although friction with France dominated much of Britain's colonial doings in the early nineteenth as well as the eighteenth century, the British and the Spanish also clashed, as in the Falklands and in many of the complicated wars discussed in Chapters 2 and 3. One other long-term bone of colonial contention between the two countries was Gibraltar, on the southernmost tip of Spain. This promontory on the Iberian peninsula, just a few kilometres from the North African coast, was first claimed by the British in 1704. By the 1713 Treaty of Utrecht, resident Gibraltans continued to enjoy rights that, had the territory been wholly British, would have been denied them as Catholics. Gibraltar proved useful for British naval forays in the Mediterranean where, as a result of the Napoleonic Wars, they added Malta (1814) and the Ionian Islands (1815), off the coast of Greece, to their colonial spoils, extending the Empire quite significantly into European territory.

Such captures as these demonstrate just how much of Britain's imperial strength derived from its naval prowess. The colonial acquisitions and consolidations we have tracked gave Britain an immense advantage, in effect a global chain of harbours, a powerful and dominant navy and an empire that, by 1815, was the largest in the modern world. From a concentration for most of the eighteenth century on the Atlantic, and centred on the West Indies and America, the Empire had not only expanded considerably in the Pacific but had secured an impressive network of ports and harbours that gave Britain the imperial pre-eminence that would so colour its modern history.

By the start of Queen Victoria's reign, Britain's Empire was a global political force of considerable significance. The champions of a humanitarian imperialism, who had promoted the abolition of slavery and the idea of protecting indigenous rights (in South Africa, in Australia, in New Zealand and elsewhere), had been marginalised. The claims of land-hungry settlers were increasingly successful and the introduction of white self-government did not bode well for indigenous peoples. Indicative of this changing mood was the ejection from active politics of leading reform figures such as Thomas Fowell Buxton and Charles Grant. Buxton lost his seat in parliament in 1837 after almost 20 years representing the constituency of Weymouth. A prominent figure in the abolition of slavery, he was also one of the guiding lights behind the appointment in the mid-1830s of the House of Commons Select Committee on Aborigines that considered the plight of indigenous peoples in Africa, the Americas, the Pacific and had recommended 'fair dealing and Christian instruction' as the way forward.[3] Meanwhile, Charles Grant (Lord Glenelg) resigned as colonial secretary in 1839 under pressure from his detractors. Like Buxton, he had spoken out for the rights of indigenous peoples in many of Britain's colonies, and had clashed with influential opponents over imperial policy, in particular in Canada and in South Africa. With the disappearance from politics of men such as these, there were far fewer voices calling for ethical versions of imperialism which, while invariably paternalist, nonetheless defended the rights of the colonised.

Notes

1 George Arthur to Viscount Goderich, 10 January 1828. Parliamentary Papers, House of Commons 1831 (259), *Van Diemen's Land. Copies of all Correspondence between Lieutenant-Governor Arthur and His Majesty's Secretary of State for the Colonies, on the Subject of the Military Operations lately carried on against the Aboriginal Inhabitants of Van Diemen's Land 1831*, p. 4.

2 J. Langfield Ward, 'Colonization and Its Bearing on the Extinction of the Aboriginal Races' (Leek, Staffordshire: William Clemesha, 1874), p. 12. The Le Bas Prize was established in 1848 by former pupils of Charles Webb Le Bas, principal of the East India Company's Haileybury College from 1837–43. Before becoming principal, Le Bas had taught mathematics at Haileybury for many years.

3 House of Commons Parliamentary Papers, 1837 (425), *Report from the Select Committee on Aborigines (British Settlements)*, p. 44.

Further reading

For an overview of the expansion of this era, Philip Lawson's *A Taste for Empire and Glory: Studies in British Overseas Expansion, 1660–1800* (Brookfield, VT: Variorum, 1997) is helpful and comprehensive. '*A free though conquering people': Eighteenth-century Britain and its Empire* by P. J. Marshall (Aldershot and Burlington, VT: Ashgate, 2003) covers some of the same territory. In *The Global Reach of Empire: Britain's Maritime Expansion in the Indian and Pacific Oceans, 1764–1815* (Carlton: Miegunyah Press, 2003), Alan Frost reminds us of the critical importance of Britain's naval power for colonial expansion in this period. C. A. Bayly's *Imperial Meridian: The British Empire and the World, 1780–1830* (London: Longman, 1989) offers a broad and important perspective on the global reach of Britain's imperial interests. For a wide and lively survey of the Empire before 1800, see Miles Ogborn, *Global Lives: Britain and the World, 1550–1800* (Cambridge: Cambridge University Press, 2008). The essays in *A New Imperial History: Culture, Identity, and Modernity in Britain and the Empire, 1660–1840* (Kathleen Wilson (ed.), Cambridge: Cambridge University Press, 2004) are a rich resource for understanding the importance of empire in Britain in this era.

Stuart Macintyre's *Concise History of Australia* (2nd edn, Cambridge: Cambridge University Press, 2004) and Philippa Mein Smith's *Concise History of New Zealand* (Cambridge: Cambridge University Press, 2005) are excellent introductions to the histories of these respective colonies.

In *Invisible Invaders: Smallpox and Other Diseases in Aboriginal Australia, 1780–1880* (Carlton South: Melbourne University Press, 2002), Judy Campbell explores the impact of European diseases on Aboriginal populations, while James Belich reads New Zealand through the lens of racial inequality in *The New Zealand Wars and the Victorian Interpretation of Racial Conflict* (Auckland: Auckland University Press, 1986). *Encounters in Place: Outsiders and Aboriginal Australians, 1606–1985* by D. J. Mulvaney (St Lucia: University of Queensland Press, 1989) discusses some of these same questions in the Australian context.

Aboriginal history, and the effect of settler colonialism on the earlier inhabitants of Australia, are discussed in Richard Broome, *Aboriginal Australians: Black Responses to White Dominance, 1788–2001* (3rd edn, Crows Nest: Allen & Unwin, 2002); Henry Reynolds, *Frontier: Aborigines, Settlers, and Land* (St Leonards: Allen & Unwin, 1987); and *Contested Ground: Australian Aborigines under the British Crown* (Ann McGrath (ed.), St Leonards: Allen & Unwin, 1995). In *Dancing with Strangers: Europeans and Australians at First Contact* (Cambridge: Cambridge University Press, 2005), Inga Clendinnen looks at the earliest relations between settlers and indigenes. Anne Salmond does similar work for New Zealand in *Two Worlds: First Meetings between Māori and Europeans 1642–1772* (Honolulu, HI: University of Hawaii Press, 1991). Zoe Laidlaw and Alan Lester's collection of essays, *Indigenous Communities and Settler Colonialism: Land Holding, Loss and Survival in an Interconnected World* (Basingstoke: Palgrave Macmillan, 2015) offers a wealth of information on relations between indigenous peoples and settlers across the Empire.

Depraved and Disorderly: Female Convicts, Sexuality and Gender in Colonial Australia by Joy Damousi (Cambridge: Cambridge University Press, 1997) offers an excellent account of the life and status of women convicts in early Australian history. Marie Ruiz's *British Female Emigration Societies and the New World, 1860–1914* (Basingstoke: Palgrave Macmillan, 2017) is a thorough analysis of free female migration to Australia and New Zealand.

P. J. Marshall and Glyndwr Williams in *The Great Map of Mankind: Perceptions of New Worlds in the Age of Enlightenment* (London: Dent, 1982) do a wonderful job of mapping changing British perceptions of the world as news of the imperial explorations of the era came home. In *The Trial of the Cannibal Dog: The Remarkable Story of Captain Cook's Encounters in the South Seas* (New Haven, CT: Yale University Press, 2003), Anne Salmond details Cook's voyages in the Pacific.

5 Britain in India

In the colonial scheme of things, Britain's imperial interests in India had been among its most important from as early as the seventeenth century. Though it would be the middle of the nineteenth century before the British government laid formal claim to ruling large parts of India, British India was central to Britain's Empire at a far earlier date.

India was not a single country or entity, but rather a collection of states ruled in different ways, and frequently with markedly different languages and customs. There was no single Indian language or religion. Small and large areas were governed by local dynasties, and by the eighteenth century much of northern and central India was ruled by the powerful Mughals. British imperial influence in the subcontinent came on the heels of the Mughal Empire. The last wave of Muslim Mughals had arrived in India from central Asia in the sixteenth century, forging alliances with powerful Hindu elites and rapidly establishing significant control. Mughal power and wealth was considerable and early British traders were obliged to pay homage to the Mughal rulers. In the seventeenth century European merchants typically traded in Asia by permission of local rulers whose power and military might were at least the equal of the Europeans.

The dominating British enterprise in India was the East India Company (EIC), launched in London in 1600 by a powerful financial elite. The EIC was a chartered company, enjoying a monopoly over British trade with the east. Its charter afforded it control of trade between the Cape of Good Hope in Africa and the Strait of Magellan, a natural passage between the Pacific and the Atlantic Oceans to the south of South America. The chartered company was an economic and political device of mutual benefit to a company and its backers and to the government of the country in which it was established. By the eighteenth century, in return for a share of the profits (and sometimes also favourable loans), the government granted these companies tremendous political and military as well as economic freedom in a given area. The EIC enjoyed not only a trade monopoly but the government's agreement that it might directly negotiate with local rulers. Though it was entitled to engage in warfare to defend its privileges, it was forbidden to initiate hostilities. The Company also had the right to mint currency, build forts and control British citizens within its territories. It created courts and imposed laws, actively prosecuting traders who sought to encroach on its territories. As a joint-stock enterprise, the EIC was well suited to expensive long-distance trade for its size meant it could raise more money and spread the risk involved over a larger group of investors, a strategy unavailable to small traders. These monopolistic policies, part of the mercantilist system, were typical of the way in which global business was conducted before the free trade era of the nineteenth century. Clearly, such policies married economics and governance in important ways, since much more than merely control over commerce was granted to those doing business across the globe.

India was of growing importance among Britain's colonies even beyond its commercial capacity. The EIC's hold on India was tightening at much the same time that the American colonies broke away from Britain. The failure of British trade in the East Indies (Indonesia and the Spice Islands), and the barriers to trade in China before the 1840s, made India a particularly important site of British interest, and their principal foothold in Asia. Success in India acted as a counter-balance to Britain's inability to rein in the American revolt. India became more and more important not only for its products but increasingly as a symbol of Britain's overseas power after the loss of America. India would occupy British attention until the middle of the twentieth century, strongly influencing other colonial decisions and acting as a training ground for scores of colonial officials.

The need to protect India from the encroachment of rival powers often shaped colonial policy in the nineteenth century, just as in the eighteenth century protection of the sugar colonies had been paramount. Fear of neighbouring Burma led to the first of the Anglo-Burmese wars in the mid-1820s, prompted by Burmese expansion into Indian territories. Friction with the Burmese kingdom of Ava led in 1886 to Britain's annexation of parts of Burma, taken under the wing of Indian administration. Rivalry with European powers also prompted land-grabbing. Britain had seized Mauritius from the French, and Java from the Dutch in 1810. In Ceylon, the British poached on territories formerly under the control of Portuguese and Dutch interests, annexing the island in 1796. To the east, the British commandeered interests (including Singapore on the Malay peninsula) that, in their earliest colonial days, were administered, like Ceylon, through the EIC. The Malay colonies were used early on by the Company, in an echo of Australian transportation, as a dumping ground for Indian convicts used as forced labour, as were the first convict settlements on the Andaman Islands in the Indian Ocean (1789) and on the island of Mauritius (1815). There were also a whole series of strategically placed sites en route to India and seized by the British during the French War, including the Seychelles (1794), the Cape of Good Hope (1795) and Malta (1800; annexed 1814).

To the east, China was closely connected to British interests in India, for a significant fraction of EIC profits derived from the sale in China of opium grown in India. The efforts of the Chinese leadership to stem the flow of

Indian opium would lead in 1839 and again in 1856 to war and to Britain's acquisition in 1842 of the island of Hong Kong, just off the southern coast of mainland China. In 1839, Britain also took possession of Aden, its proximity to the Red Sea and the Arabian Sea making it a vital coaling station for ships bound for India. Aden, significantly, was governed from Bombay for almost a hundred years.

With these new, and sometimes temporarily held, colonial possessions, Britain formed a protective circle around India, near and far, and in essence the EIC became a transnational corporation with tentacles all over the world, holding together both its fiscal and its political interests. These close ties – political, military, geographical, economic – exemplify the interconnectedness of imperial interest and expansion, each colony influencing and shaping other British possessions. A mass of factors was always involved in the acquisition and the maintaining of colonies; it was never a single factor that decided which areas of the world would come under British rule. And as the Empire grew in size, these global considerations became increasingly important. India – and before 1857, the EIC – was frequently central to these considerations.

Yet in the late 1680s, the Company's future in India had been uncertain. The sum of £15,000 in compensation for defensive military actions paid to the Mughal Emperor Aurangzeb helped ensure that the EIC did not lose its trading rights, but what this failed military aggression clearly demonstrates is that the Company, even before the dawn of the eighteenth century, no longer felt constrained to engage only in peaceful trade. That important shift in policy would have far-reaching consequences. By 1700 the Company had established the three presidencies of Bombay (to the west), Madras (in the south), and Bengal (to the east). Attempts to fashion them as settler colonies in the seventeenth century had failed, despite the Company's shrewd assessment that attracting women as well as men would help shape a settler culture.

Though they were small in area, the Company had also, by this time, leased more than 20 trading posts from the Mughals. In return for these, the rulers of India expected aid in stemming piracy and, perhaps most importantly, in organising the collecting of land revenues. The EIC's role in collecting taxes from property (especially in Bengal) brought huge wealth both to the corporation and to individual officials. Over time, and despite its origins as a trading entity, the EIC's focus shifted from trade to taxation.

Company trade was regulated by a *firman* from the emperor, which granted the Company trading rights in designated areas in return for either rent or an annual fee. In its early years, the Company enjoyed jurisdiction over very small areas of India, but the Mughal Empire was changing direction, moving from a heavily centralised power to a more regional entity and Europeans interpreted this change as indicating its decline. These changes rendered the Mughals vulnerable to attack and invasion, as well as to the intrigues of other Indian rulers (of whom there were many), anxious to enjoy a share of India's lucrative trade. The Company, too, had been transformed early in the eighteenth century. After far-reaching criticism of its methods and practices, it had reformed in 1709 as the United Company of Merchants Trading to the East Indies. Its new system made it highly profitable, and between 1709 and 1748, there were only two occasions on which the Company was unable to pay dividends to its shareholders. At the start of the eighteenth century, some 90 per cent of its major cargoes originated in India. Textiles and opium were the most profitable of its goods. In Sumatra, the Company also traded in pepper and in China in tea, silk and chinaware.

It was when the EIC defeated Mughal forces in 1757 that the expansion of British India really began in earnest. The Company had explicitly violated its agreement with the Mughals by fortifying Calcutta (the centre of British Bengali operations) against the French. They also engaged in a host of illegal and dubious commercial practices in the region. Angered, the nawab of Bengal, Siraj-ud-daula reacted by capturing Calcutta from the Company in June 1756. His imprisonment of Europeans in what became notorious as the 'Black Hole' of Calcutta – and the death of some of the prisoners held there – ignited widespread British anger. The quick and decisive defeat of the nawab's forces by Company troops, led by Colonel Robert Clive at the Battle of Plassey, resulted in the establishment of a new nawab. Mir Jafar was very much under the British thumb, at least early in his rule. Bengal, and especially Calcutta, quickly became the central power base of the Company. The growing importance of Bengal in trading also helped enhance its supremacy.

From the 1760s, as more territory and power accrued, the presidencies increasingly fulfilled responsibilities traditionally the province of governments rather than commercial companies. With their courts of law and their armies, the three presidencies effectively ruled larger and larger tracts of the subcontinent, deploying their armies against intractable rulers as much as against the French whose interest in the region had not waned, and who hoped to weaken the British through supporting local rebellions. The decisive defeat of the French interest came in the early 1760s when victory in a series of skirmishes in south-east India consolidated Britain's position. The Company took advantage of the ousting of the French from India and the failing power of the increasingly fragmented Mughal Empire. British patronage of regional rulers speeded the disintegration of the older Mughal power structure while stabilising and entrenching a British foothold. Coupled with Britain's willingness to colonise, if sometimes only temporarily, in regions helpful to Indian expansion, such as Mauritius and Java, these tactics secured the Company's extraordinary transformation. And the fact that it still continued to pay fat dividends to its British shareholders gave the Company considerable weight at home.

Yet there was serious internal dissension and concern in government circles about the conduct of individual officials and about the Company's arrogation of power. EIC officials came to be seen as greedy, unscrupulous and self-seeking, and those who ostensibly controlled direction and policy from London felt increasingly in the late eighteenth century as if they could not control their own employees. Novelists, playwrights and cartoonists poked fun at the 'nabobs' who were often resented and despised in Britain, seen as a corrupt and spoiled *nouveau riche*. The most famous of the nabobs was Robert Clive who won battles, commercial concessions and territory for the Company. Always a provocative figure, Clive did much in the 1760s to steer the Company towards its new role in India, though at times he was more popular with the public than with his employers. His most celebrated accomplishment besides the victory at Plassey in 1757 was engineering the *diwani* of Bengal (revenue collection) in 1765. By this agreement (also known as the Treaty of Allahabad), the Company won sole right to collect revenues on behalf of the emperor, now Shah Alam, in Bengal and in neighbouring Bihar and Orissa. In return the emperor was to be paid the enormous sum of 2.6 million rupees a year. Clive enriched his own coffers considerably, returning to Britain immeasurably wealthier than when he had left.

Figure 5.1 Brighton Pavilion: built in 1784 and purchased in the early nineteenth century for the Prince Regent. John Nash oversaw the rebuilding of the palace between 1815 and 1821 in a mixture of classical and Indian styles, often labelled 'Hindoo-Gothic'. The construction of this marvellously eclectic building on England's south-east coast suggests the significant influence exerted by India in the imperial era

Source: Paul Thompson Images/Alamy Stock Photo

This intensification of the Company's financial role not only altered its own profile but had a lasting impact on patterns of land ownership in eastern India. The 'Permanent Settlement' engineered by Lord Cornwallis in 1793 created a new landowning class of local wealthy Indians who had functioned previously as tax collectors. Tax assessments on land remained unchanged over time, offering an incentive for a new and profitable form of property-holding by purchase. The effect was to alter the basis of property ownership substantially, investing individuals with rights of ownership previously shared among all those with an interest in the cultivation of land. While the system significantly enriched the affluent tax-collecting *zamindari* or *talukadar* and, of course, the Company, ordinary farmers and agricultural labourers were forced to pay substantial land taxes. Since these remained unchanged whatever the yield of the harvest, they paid heavily under the new system for their traditional livelihood. It was – for the wealthy, at least – a profitable system that put India at the centre of British imperial interest.

For all the wealth this created, and despite Clive's considerable political skills, the Company ran aground in the late 1760s. Political intrigue, charges of corruption, expensive military campaigns and a market crash that seriously threatened EIC stock pushed the British government into action. It was abundantly clear by the 1770s that the government needed to regulate the affairs of the Company if Britain's national interests in India were to remain viable. India was too profitable and prestigious a possession by then to risk losing, and in 1773 the prime minister, Lord North, changed the course of British colonialism in India. His Regulating Act, though cautious and exploratory, established government authority over the Company's activities in India. The Act created the position of governor-general to oversee all three presidencies. The Court of Directors made the nomination, but could appoint to the position only with government approval. Judges appointed from London presided over a new supreme court at Calcutta in Bengal, which now replaced Delhi as the centre of power in India. The system created considerable resentment in the presidencies, angered by their loss of autonomy, as well as among the Company's directors in London who resented government interference.

This tension between officials on the ground and government in London would become an enduring hallmark of British imperialism. It had, in some senses, already been apparent in the American context, for it was opposition to what American colonists regarded as undue control from London that had catalysed rebellion and ultimately independence. The principle of government intervention was the chief cause of friction. Warren Hastings, the first governor-general in India from 1774 to 1785, endured almost constant disharmony in relations between London and the colonial government. Despite long experience in the Company's service in India, he faced opposition on a number of fronts; his uncompromising views on imperial Indian governance made him invariably controversial. India in these years received a tremendous amount of attention in the London press, with vigorous debates about the moral status both of British and Company involvement.

It was in part because of some of the stalemates Hastings faced in his years in office that Pitt's government reconsidered the 1773 Act under which Hastings had been appointed. That Act was replaced by a more comprehensive law after 11 years, and after the fall of the British government at the end of 1783 over its policy on India. By then, the American rebels had changed the face of British imperialism, making India an even more important and attractive possession, and tilting the axis of British imperial expansion eastward. And unlike the 13 colonies, there was next to no settler tradition or elective government in India to challenge the new structures. In many respects, the India Act of 1784 extended and expanded upon the earlier Act, strengthening both the power of the governor-general and of the profitable Bengal presidency over those of Madras and Bombay. The governor-general acquired the power of veto over his council and over the decisions of the two other presidencies. His appointment remained officially in Company hands, but since government had the power of recall, the procedure became one of careful negotiation between government and the Company; after Hastings, those appointed to the position were routinely outsiders to the Company. The governorship, in short, became a political appointment. The Act also created a Board of Control based in Britain. The Company did not lose its trade monopoly, its role in revenue collection or its right to appoint and dismiss its own officials but the Board now had jurisdiction over the Company's civil, military and revenue affairs in India. The law gave Britain's politicians new power to control the political and diplomatic roles of the Company. The shift from control by a chartered corporation to direct government rule was not complete until 1858, but a heightened degree of government supervision and interest was already changing how large parts of India were ruled and by whom.

For all the expansion of power, however, the EIC found its prominent new role in British India a costly one, and its growing control of India was accompanied by an anxiety over balancing the books and realising the necessary profits. The heavy cost of the machinery of government as well as of maintaining standing armies, as the Company did in all three presidencies, cut into profits considerably prompting government, always concerned with the profitability of trade, to intervene in Company affairs. Governor-general Cornwallis had begun the task of professionalising the Company's growing administrative staff, creating competitive pay scales and a merit-centred ethos long before the British civil service adopted such practices in the 1850s. It was a policy prompted in large measure by the perpetual outcry in Britain over the corrupt practices of Company servants. After 1805, Company civil servants were sent to the EIC's own college in Britain, Haileybury, where they underwent a two-year preparatory training before being posted to India. Along with Calcutta's College of Fort William (founded in 1802) where new recruits received language training, Haileybury gave the Indian civil service a unique level of preparation among government servants.

Each presidency also supported its own army, composed largely of Indian soldiers (sepoys) commanded by a white officer class. In the second half of the eighteenth century their numbers swelled strikingly. There were some 18,000 troops in the three presidencies in 1763; 40 years later there were more than 150,000. In Bengal alone, the 1756 contingent of 3,000 soldiers rose in a mere decade to 26,000. The soldiers were needed to keep order at a time of increasing restiveness among local rulers and to ward off threats, especially in the late 1790s from the French, who continued to show interest in the region. Yet the expansion of territory effected by this soldiery was also the source of their financing; without the revenue brought in by what the military achieved, there could be no expansion in their number. The military component of the Company was a self-propelling entity necessary for rule but also itself creating the need for the relentless expansion of territory and therefore revenue so characteristic of the later eighteenth century. The high expense of the military continued into the new century, directly influencing the course of economic policy.

In the years after 1858 the composition of the army in India would change radically, but in the years of Company rule the presidency armies were overwhelmingly Indian. Poor men were recruited into the armies by the promise of regular pay and food and a pension. At a time when the British army was regarded contemptuously as a haven for those who needed to hide, the armies of the Company were well trained and well disciplined. Indians employed in the civil administration, equally, were well educated, though in the 1830s there was considerable debate over the wisdom of encouraging an English-style education among Indian elites. Much of urban India (in cities such as Lucknow and Calcutta) possessed an active elite culture with a lively literary and theatrical scene and well-established music and dance traditions. The issue for the British was whether or not an English education would secure the long-term loyalty of this essential class of administrators. They were necessary not only because, like all colonial ventures, success relied in part on a degree of local collaboration and collusion, but also because there were insufficient numbers of Britons to keep the enterprise afloat. Without the work of Indians – in clerical and administrative positions, in farm labour or building construction, or in the armed forces – British India simply could not have functioned.

The number of Britons residing in India remained small until after direct rule was imposed in 1858; in the 1830s, the British component of the population was 45,000 out of a total population of 150 million. Even after 1858, British numbers were not vast, though there were significant changes in who came to India. In the earliest years of British influence, aside from the occasional adventurer, the majority of Britons in India were Company officials working either in trade or in the military. As the Company became a political body, traders gave way to emissaries and administrators. The numbers still remained small, and this population was almost exclusively male, for there were no job opportunities for British women. The Company rarely permitted officials to bring their wives with them to India, and the military allowed marriage for only a small percentage of the rank-and-file. The trickle of British women coming to India grew in the nineteenth century, as first missionaries and then other women began to settle. However, the majority of women in India throughout the colonial period were the relatives – wives, daughters and sisters – of officials, civil and military. As a result, the British areas of Indian towns and cities were slowly transformed into family-oriented areas resembling more and more the environment left behind in Britain.

The indigenous population, meanwhile, became increasingly mobile. Changes in land use and in patterns of land ownership under both Mughal and British rule disrupted traditional occupations. Shortages and famines – never unknown in the region – became more frequent and more severe. The Bengal famine of 1770, caused by a mix of high taxation and a drought, killed a third of the local population. Many sought new job opportunities catering to British needs as traditional employments diminished. From the 1830s many Indians signed on as indentured labourers, either on the tea plantations in Assam in eastern India and nearby Ceylon, on the rice plantations in British Burma or in more distant lands. Almost a million Indians worked under colonial indenture before the system was abolished in 1917. The abolition of slavery in 1833 created a new workforce to replace slave labour, especially in agriculture. The early abandonment of apprenticeship schemes for former slaves in 1838 quickened the pace of recruitment. India's large rural population seemed an obvious source for plantation labour and recruiters targeted areas where work was scarce. A system of debt bondage, where debts were paid off through the labour, often of a younger family member, pre-dated the British colonial presence in India, and perhaps made the prospect of indenture less alarming; certainly the severe depression of the late 1820s to 1850s spurred the supply of such workers.

A very different set of political influences, meanwhile, was at work in Britain. The influence of the free trade movement, hostile to the protectionism and monopoly that had so characterised the eighteenth-century mercantile system, was mounting in Britain, and when the EIC's charter came up for renewal by parliament in 1813, the free trade lobby was ready to do battle. Its success was such that the Company lost most of its monopoly in India, retaining it only on opium and salt. Since together these items represented 25 per cent of the Company's income, and since trade played less and less prominent a part in the Company's operations, the loss was in some ways symbolic, more a reflection of political than economic concerns. Though the Company experienced some diminution in its commercial ventures, its power in the three presidencies was more and more comprehensive, and its military was untouched by the changes to the charter. The charter renewal did introduce, however, a small contingent of around 40,000 royal forces to

India, supplementing the growing size of the EIC armies. Twenty years later, in the 1833 charter renewal, the free traders fully prevailed: the Company lost its last remaining monopoly in China, and India was opened fully to private traders.

The activities of the EIC over the course of the first half of the nineteenth century make it hard to remember that this was a trading and commercial organisation. Philip Lawson describes the Company after 1813 as 'a department of state'.[1] From the 1820s on, and acting exactly like a government, Indian administrations tackled a host of social improvement issues in India, moving away from the earlier principles of 'orientalism' that had eschewed overt influence on local cultures. This new direction in policy was typified by Thomas Babington Macaulay, a member of the Bengal Supreme Council, and by William Bentinck, governor-general from 1828 to 1835. Macaulay, in a famous tract known as his 'minute on education' (1835), argued that English should be the language of state in India, and that westernisation would improve the condition of India and guarantee the loyalties of India's educated classes. Bentinck, meanwhile, presided over a series of social reforms in the 1830s that attacked what were regarded as barbarous local customs.

In the same year that Bentinck was appointed governor-general, Ram Mohan Roy, a Calcutta-based activist and prolific author, founded a reform organisation, the Brahmo Samaj, that would be of tremendous influence in eastern India. A Hindu-based organisation dedicated to extirpating idol worship and the caste system, the Brahmo Samaj was also active in social reform. Many of the same issues on the organisation's agenda attracted Bentinck's attention, prominent among them the ancient practice of widow sacrifice (*sati*), in which a widow threw herself upon her husband's burning funeral pyre, dying in recognition of his centrality to her existence. An EIC regulation of 1813 had declared *sati* legal as long as it was a voluntary act. Roy, arguing that the practice was not necessary to religious observance, published in 1818, in both Bengali and English, a tract condemning the practice. For Roy and his followers the practice was a brutal corruption of Hindu tenets, while journalistic and literary accounts of women's hideous screams of agony captured the British imagination. In 1829 Bentinck outlawed *sati*, though this did little to stem its incidence. In remote areas few would have known of the change in the law, and in any case the incidence of *sati* seems to have been regionally specific and confined to the higher castes. Some historians have argued that the law was counter-productive, advertising the practice more widely, and also making it seem an act subversive of British rule.

The ban on *sati* was only one of a number of reforms undertaken in the years of EIC governance and aimed at Indian women. In 1856, a widow remarriage act permitted Hindu widows to marry again, but forced them to forfeit rights in their deceased husband's estate. This was also an issue that Indian reformers, led by Ishwar Chandra Vidyasagar, had campaigned around for decades. But the form the law took robbed low-caste women of economic opportunities, since the prohibition on remarriage had, like *sati*, generally been practised only among the higher castes. In other castes, women had routinely remarried, but under the new law could no longer inherit from their deceased husbands when they did so.

Widow remarriage and *sati* reform alike failed to take into account the differences between practice in elite and in poor families. In taking high-caste Brahmin orthodoxy as the norm, reforms of this sort often made the lives of lower caste and poorer women more difficult, and neither British nor Indian reformers saw any need to consult Indian women in formulating their actions. All these laws presumed the lesser status of women in Indian culture and society and emphasised a highly elitist interpretation of Hinduism based solely on Brahmin texts. This thinking became the basis for much of the colonial accommodation to local custom in the nineteenth century, a policy that reinvested the Hindu caste system with power and gave the men of the priestly Brahmin caste a disproportionate influence in discussions of what constituted proper Hinduism and proper Indian behaviour. It was a colonial tendency that would recur in other parts of the Empire with equally detrimental and divisive results. It reflected, too, a conscious power shift on the part of the British, favouring Hindu over Muslim.

Measures of reform almost always involved a critique of what were seen as typically Indian behaviours or ideas, and implemented conduct and values favoured by British elite culture. With each successive diminution effected in Company power by charter renewals, the metropolitan voices of reform – spearheaded by free traders and evangelicals – became more influential. Bolstered by Indian activism in many of the same areas of concern, early nineteenth-century governments intervened ever more closely in Indian religion, culture and social life. The effect was often to emphasise the more conservative strands of local society. The Hindu caste system, now enforced through the courts, became, if anything, more pervasive and more stultifying, while Britain's interest in maintaining Indian princes as local rulers helped to keep tradition securely in place. British economic policy discouraged competition with the metropole, making large parts of India more rural and agrarian just as Europe was industrialising.

These reforms point to the declining role of the EIC and the rising government interest in India; many of them would likely not have been initiated by the EIC alone. The Company's long-standing policy on religion had been one of toleration and non-intervention, a principle that had led them to keep missionaries out of the country. Christian missionaries thus arrived in India only after 1813 when the evangelical lobby finally overcame the EIC's mistrust. Even then their victory was only partial. Missionaries required licences to work in areas under Company control and were watched carefully. It would be another 20 years before missionaries gained complete freedom of mobility and organisation in India.

For all the interest in the alleged social ills of the country, there was one critical arena that remained untouched, and that was the opium trade between India (the source of production) and China (the principal point of sale). The dulling and addictive effects of opiates were already known in Britain, and in the popular imagination opium was associated with the 'Chinaman'. Throughout the nineteenth century, colonial Chinatowns (whether in Britain, Australia, Hong Kong or Canada) were invariably depicted as teeming with haze-filled opium dens where insensate addicts dozed and dreamed. Yet the trade – unwelcome to the Chinese authorities – was hugely lucrative for the EIC and for the Chinese middlemen to whom they sold the drug. The Chinese government's hostility to the importation of opium to China did not deter Indian production, although it did force the Company to find ways around Chinese anti-opium laws. In effect, the Company endorsed a huge and sophisticated smuggling ring. In terms of income, it was worth the risk. Without opium the Chinese trading route would show a trade deficit. China had little interest in the other goods available from British traders; its own pottery and textiles were far superior, and it had tea in abundance. If the Chinese did not buy the Company's opium, there was little else to sell them, and tea bought from China had to be paid for in cash since the Chinese were uninterested in the other goods on offer. The only way to address the deficits that this large outlay of cash entailed was from the sale of opium.

Although illegal in China, the opium trade was enormously profitable and constantly growing, with the result that opium became one of the most important products managed and traded by the EIC. Large numbers of workers in India relied on the income from growing poppies, and the Company offered hefty incentives to farmers involved in its production. The Company thus invested considerable time and effort in developing this trade. Before the large-scale cultivation of opium poppies in India, Turkey had been the world's principal source of opium. The disintegration of the Ottoman Empire during the nineteenth century made the development of Indian cultivation a viable business proposition, so much so that in 1830 the British government gave permission for more extensive opium cultivation in India. The effect, not surprisingly, was to reduce cultivation of other agricultural products in the race for the easy profits associated with the opium poppy.

The Company's monopoly on opium had been the work of Warren Hastings, first governor-general of India. Over time, the monopoly tightened; by 1793, poppy growers in India could sell only to the EIC. Despite its central role in the movement of opium from India to China, the Company worked hard to disguise its position in the trade. It sold the opium at auction in Calcutta, from where it was shipped by private firms rather than in Company vessels to China and then distributed by smugglers. The proceeds from the sales, however, were always paid to the EIC's own China office.

A clash between China's Manchu leaders and British traders over the illegal importation of opium into China of huge quantities of the drug was inevitable. China was concerned both about high levels of opium addiction among its populace and about the drain on the country's stock of silver, which was being diverted to pay for opium. The first of the two Opium Wars broke out when Chinese customs officials impounded opium shipments arriving at Canton (now Guangzhou). Britain, already irritated by a Chinese offensive to curb the trade, deployed a naval detachment to shell important Chinese ports and trading sites in protest. The attack not only forced trade concessions from the Chinese, but led to Britain's acquisition of the important new colony of Hong Kong, a small rocky island off the south coast of mainland China.

This three-year war, from 1839 to 1842, occurred at much the same time as social reformers were declaring the moral bankruptcy of Indian society. Yet other than the evangelical lobby, surprisingly few British voices were raised in protest over the selling of opium until the appointment of a Royal Commission to investigate the opium trade half a century later in 1893. The first Anglo-Chinese (or Opium) War was depicted in the British press and in parliament as a principled dispute over free trade rather than about drug peddling. Both the British government and the EIC focused attention on China's refusal to allow foreign merchants commercial access to the country. The continued monopoly the Company enjoyed in trading opium was conveniently forgotten, as was the fact that its sale violated Chinese law. In practice, the war – conducted not by the Company but by the British government – was a convenient way to force open a China trade that had for so long eluded the British. In his 1845 novel, *Sybil*, future Conservative prime minister, Benjamin Disraeli, caricatured the most famous of the opium merchants, William Jardine, as the fictional 'McDruggy fresh from Canton, with a million in opium in each pocket, denouncing corruption and bellowing free trade'.[2]

The 1842 Treaty of Nanking made no mention of opium despite the fact that it had been the catalyst for the war. By 1849, the trade through Hong Kong was worth about £6 million a year, and opium exports to China rose substantially after the signing of the treaty. India's second largest source of revenue after land taxes, the opium trade remained the province of highly respectable business ventures; some of the most prominent of Hong Kong's commercial entities owed their success to the drug. After the Second Opium War (1856–60), the trade was effectively legalised by the establishment of formal tariffs for the importing of opium.

Opium's huge profitability has always been more important to those who trade in it than have been the consequences of addiction to it. What makes the colonial opium trade so interesting is that it was controlled not by underground and illegal organisations but by some of the largest and most successful businesses of the period, and with the direct knowledge of successive British governments. Moreover, in the case of the EIC, it was a business enterprise involved simultaneously, via its political wing, in the implementation of law and order in British India. In effect, then, the nineteenth-century opium trade was more than connived at by government;

it was actively encouraged. And that encouragement did not deter officials from claiming moral, religious and civilisational superiority over both those who grew the product and those to whom they trafficked it. Few outside the highly moralistic circles of evangelism saw the contradictions at work in an arena where politics, economics, religion and culture so fully coalesced. Ironically, the Treaty of Tientsin in 1858, which put opium trading on a legal footing, also saw the opening of China to Christian missionaries for the first time. The age of reform and of high morals was also quite palpably an age of rapacity.

The EIC had imposed direct rule over Assam in north-east India in 1838, a move not unrelated to the growing tensions with China. In the 1830s, China dominated the trade in tea, an increasingly important commodity in Britain and the largest import from the east. Uneasy with this economic dependence on China, the Company sought alternative arenas for growing and processing this popular product, especially in India. Governor-general Lord Bentinck formed a Tea Committee in 1834 to investigate the possibilities of commercial production in India. Annexation followed quickly when it was realised that Assam had an indigenous cultivable tea plant. The Assam Company, founded to establish the local tea industry, was created in 1839, the same year Britain waged its trade war against China.

The first half of the nineteenth century was a time of considerable expansion in British India. Annexation and a series of military skirmishes all required considerable military force, and the military in India was the largest in Asia, with 16 European regiments and 170 sepoy regiments. In the first quarter of the nineteenth century, the Indian army was involved in a series of colonial wars which augmented Britain's territory in the region substantially. Britain annexed the Carnatic in 1801, Sind in 1843, the Punjab in 1849 and Oudh in 1856. These were often brutal affairs in which colonial troops burned villages and crops and killed livestock to subdue local resistance.

The EIC was increasingly acting like a government, imposing British values and British definitions, while incorporating more and more territory. From the mid-1840s, under the ambitious leadership of Lord Dalhousie, the tentacles of westernisation spread further and further. Dalhousie eased the way for the construction of railways, steam-shipping and irrigation schemes. He laid plans for Indian universities and introduced changes in the military, and in 1854 set up a postal service. He altered the systems of land tenure that hampered cultivation. He also ushered in the deeply unpopular 'doctrine of lapse', which broadened British opportunities for expansion by requiring that independent Indian states without a male heir be forfeited to the British. In the process of these many reforms, Dalhousie angered many entrenched interests.

Local dissatisfaction with this system of dual government found many outlets. The Company had won the right in 1813 to introduce a non-fixed tax system (*ryotwari*) in newly acquired territories. Peasant cultivators in these areas were heavily taxed to compensate for the situation in Bengal where, under the Permanent Settlement, taxes could not be raised. Intervention in a few social issues by no means signalled an intent to overhaul and certainly not to modernise India. Local rebellions and resistance to Company rule were not uncommon, and there was a general feeling that the British imposed alien values on local peoples. In the Company armies, there was resentment at British insensitivity: for example, a new army regulation in 1856 required soldiers to serve wherever they were posted, potentially jeopardising the standing of high-caste Hindu sepoys, since crossing the 'black waters' (meaning shipping overseas) forced them to share food and utensils with other castes aboard ship. Yet during the latter half of the nineteenth century, the army required such service of Indian soldiers in large numbers. They were deployed in many colonial hotspots: in Ethiopia in 1867, in Egypt in 1882, in Burma in 1885 and in many parts of Africa in the 1890s and beyond, including in the South African (Boer) War. The defence of imperial interests globally was a major reason for the maintenance of the Indian army.

The army was often a restive institution, and it was a military rebellion that prompted the end of dual government in India. The fuse that lit the 1857 rebellion among Indian soldiers was religious taboo. Though it was mostly a catalyst for a broad range of differences between the sepoys and their command, the rumour that the cartridges of the new-issue Enfield rifles were greased with animal fat found fertile ground. The very breadth of the rumour – that the fat was both beef and pork, and thus anathema to Hindu and Muslim alike – itself suggests a profound degree of unhappiness, as does the long history of prior if less widespread mutinies among Indian soldiers. Earlier mutinies – at Barrackpur in 1824, in the Northwest Provinces in 1844 and in the Punjab in 1849, to name just a few – had been stopped before they could spread. In 1857, however, tensions between the British and their Indian subjects (and not just in the army) had mounted considerably and resentment at the EIC's often high-handed methods of governance was common. Moreover, soldiers understood only too well that Dalhousie's army reforms imperilled their long-standing privileges. What began as a military mutiny in the Bengal Army spread to include agrarian protest and much more, though it remained focused in the north of the country. The 1857 revolt (see Map 5.1) was far more than merely a soldiers' protest. It expressed in many ways the burgeoning gulf between British authority and its Indian subjects. This revolt cohered a whole range of frustrations – over extortionate tax demands, extensive overt racism, insensitivity to local culture and religion and incessant territorial expansion.

The rebellion, which began at the military cantonment of Meerut in May 1857, spread rapidly and caught the British by surprise. It was more than a year before the uprising could be fully contained, and in the meantime there was much destruction of life and property. Violence was met with violence.

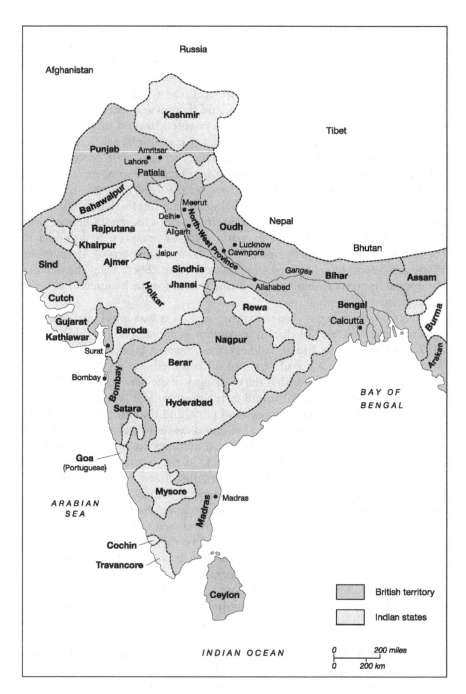

Map 5.1 India in 1857

Source: *British Imperialism, 1750–1970*, Cambridge University Press (Smith, Simon c. 1988), p. 52, © Cambridge University Press, reproduced with permission of the author and publisher

The British exacted brutal punishment for the revolt, reacting to some of the more violent episodes of the rebellion. Many Britons were murdered, and it was the slaying of British women and children that most angered the British, both in India and in Britain. Accounts of the rebellion often focused on this, an emphasis that made the Indians seem cowardly, cruel and unchivalrous. Such a focus also allowed British opinion to minimise other elements of the rebellion. Civilian and in some areas even landlord support for the mutiny was, in many regions, quite strong and often explicit in demanding the reinstatement of pre-British ruling dynasties, most particularly the Mughals and the western Indian Marathas, only recently subdued by the British. These political elements of the rebellion were played down while violence against unarmed British citizens was accentuated.

In any event, not only were the British less than gracious in victory but the result of the mutiny was to oust the EIC and to impose direct British rule in its place, through the Act for the Better Government of India, passed in August 1858. The EIC was dissolved and a new Indian civil service established, with appointment by competitive examination. Officials reported directly to the British government via the newly created India Office in London. Unique among British colonies, India now had its own separate government department. The governor-general, also called the viceroy to indicate that he was the formal representative of the Crown, reported directly to the secretary of state for India; the three presidency governments were subordinate to him.

The dissolution of the EIC did not, of course, bring all of India under British control. Several hundred independent territories dotted the subcontinent, and in these the principle of paramountcy governed relations after 1858. Queen Victoria's proclamation of 1858 guaranteed the princes in these independent states their territory in exchange for a pledge of loyalty to the British Crown. The British retained the right, however, to intervene where a ruler colluded with an enemy of the Crown or in cases of 'gross misrule'. In reality, as had been the case under EIC governance, many of these princely states were independent in name only, and were subjugated to British interests and needs. As the nationalist movement took hold in parts of India from the 1880s onwards, many regarded these hereditary princely states as anachronistic holdovers of an earlier era deliberately kept alive by the British for their own political ends. It would be 1971 before India would fully abolish the principle of rule by inheritance in these states. By then, the full complement of the problems associated with it were apparent. The continued impasse over Kashmir, still simmering today, can be traced in part to this policy; it was one of a handful of princely states unwilling in 1947 to accede to one or other of the newly created nations of India and Pakistan. Today both countries lay claim to Kashmir.

In practice, much stayed the same after 1858. Officials often continued in the same positions. Lord Canning remained in office as governor-general. Instead of being employed by the Company, officials and soldiers now became Crown employees. The new Council of India, advisory to the secretary of state and replacing the old Board of Control, was at least partially in the hands of Company men for some time. Their experience and knowledge was invaluable, but their loyalties were sometimes to an older tradition of rule. A good example of this continuity can be seen in the central Asian states that sit between Russia and India. Fears, likely unwarranted, that Russia had plans to wrest Indian territories away from the British engendered a long period of diplomatic tensions between Britain and Russia played out principally in Afghanistan. Russia was anxious to prevent the British from incursions into central Asia while British officials argued that Russia might use Afghanistan as a route into India. This Anglo-Russian rivalry lasted most of the nineteenth century, spilled over into a series of military skirmishes and despite a series of treaties and agreements demarcating territories, was still a source of anxiety on the eve of the First World War.

For the Indian population, the most obvious difference between EIC and government rule may well have been the increase in the presence of British soldiers on Indian soil. Shaken by what was read as the disloyalty of Indian soldiers to the military establishment, the new system, still reliant on military muscle, doubled the number of British soldiers in India. After the 1857 rebellion, there were never less than 60,000 British soldiers stationed in India, constituting more than a third of the entire British army. Cantonments grew to accommodate their numbers and the military lobby demanded ever-fatter budgets. Sepoy numbers, though reduced, continued to outstrip those of white soldiers, but the palpably larger presence of British soldiers was seen as a deterrent to further trouble. Changes to local recruiting practice were made, with preference being given to illiterate and ill-educated men who were thought likelier to accept an unquestioning oath of loyalty as well as to the so-called martial races, often conveniently defined as those who had remained loyal in 1857. It was the much-hated land taxes imposed on locals that paid for this immense military undertaking.

The first few years of direct rule saw a great deal of activity codifying and establishing new policy and rule. In 1860 an Indian Penal Code, and in 1861 a Code of Criminal Procedure, laid down the legal principles which would henceforth govern Britain's Indian subjects. In 1861 the Indian High Courts Act created courts at Madras, Calcutta and Bombay which exercised civil and criminal appellate jurisdiction similar to that in Britain. In 1871 the British inaugurated a decennial census in India, and seven years later a survey, instruments similar to those operating in Britain and designed to make control of the population easier.

In the late nineteenth century India witnessed the flourishing of a nationalist movement as middle-class urban populations most especially grew frustrated with their lack of a political voice. India remained a major market for British trade, its chief export market in the early twentieth century. India, meanwhile, remained predominantly agricultural, aided by the rapid growth of railway lines to and from the major ports. Land revenues prevailed, and Britain made little effort to stimulate or modernise the Indian economy,

And there was a huge prestige factor, for now Britain could boast the largest single territory under European rule in the world. 1858 represented for Britain a commitment, not only to long-term rule in India, but also to a broader, deeper vision of the British Empire than had hitherto been possible, and while that year might not be a watershed in Indian history, it was a major one for the history of the British Empire.

Notes

1 Philip Lawson, *The East India Company: A History* (London: Longman, 1993), p. 144.
2 Benjamin Disraeli, *Sybil, or: The Two Nations* (Harmondsworth, Middlesex: Penguin Books, 1954), p. 55.

Further reading

C. A. Bayly's *Indian Society and the Making of the British Empire* (Cambridge: Cambridge University Press, 1988) is a comprehensive view of relations between Britain and India. P. J. Marshall has written extensively on the early British Empire in India. Among his many works, see in particular *East Indian Fortunes: The British in Bengal in the Eighteenth Century* (Oxford: Clarendon Press, 1976) and *Problems of Empire: Britain and India 1757–1813* (London: Allen and Unwin, 1968). Useful general texts include *Modern South Asia: History, Culture, Political Economy* by Sugata Bose and Ayesha Jalal (2nd edn, New York: Routledge, 2004) and *Ideologies of the Raj* by Thomas R. Metcalf (Cambridge: Cambridge University Press, 1994). In *Inglorious Empire: What The British Did To India* (London: Hurst, 2017), Shashi Tharoor takes aim at the effects of colonial rule on India.

In *The Company State: Corporate Sovereignty and the Early Modern Foundations of the British Empire in India* (New York: Oxford University Press, 2011) Philip Stern makes the case for the EIC as a sophisticated governing corporate body at an early stage. A good general history of the Company can be found in Philip Lawson's *The East India Company: A History* (London: Longman, 1993). In *Reading the East India Company, 1720–1840: Colonial Currencies of Gender* (Chicago, IL: University of Chicago Press, 2004) Betty Joseph provides a cultural perspective on the Company era.

Lata Mani's *Contentious Traditions: The Debate on Sati in Colonial India* (Berkeley, CA: University of California Press, 1998) offers a broad reading of gender relations under colonialism in early nineteenth-century India. Andrea Major also focuses on campaigns against *sati* in *Sovereignty and Social Reform in India: British Colonialism and the Campaign against Sati, 1830–60* (London: Routledge, 2011). Durba Ghosh's *Sex and the Family in Colonial India: The Making of Empire* (Cambridge: Cambridge University Press, 2005) explores the relationships between English men and Indian women in the early years of British influence and rule.

In a series of imaginative essays, Bernard S. Cohn discusses language, clothing, textiles and much more in his innovative *Colonialism and Its Forms of Knowledge: The British in India* (Princeton, NJ: Princeton University Press, 1996).

In *The Indian Princes and Their States* (Cambridge: Cambridge University Press, 2004), Barbara N. Ramusack gives a helpful history of those princely states formally beyond British control but often a critical component of colonial rule. The economics of colonial India are the topic of Neil Charlesworth's *British Rule and the Indian Economy, 1800–1914* (London: Macmillan, 1982). In *Nabobs: Empire and Identity in Eighteenth-century Britain*, Tillman Nechtman paints a vivid portrait of the 'nabobs', both in India and on their return to Britain. Thomas R. Metcalf's *Imperial Connections: India in the Indian Ocean Arena, 1860–1920* (Berkeley, CA: University of California Press, 2007) helpfully puts colonial India in a broad regional context.

6 Global growth

Over the course of the nineteenth century, Britain added 10 million square miles and 400 million people to its colonial holdings. It would, by the end of the century, be the largest of the European empires, scattered across the globe in a bewildering variety of political and administrative forms. The diversity of this Empire was not only geographical and cultural, but also administrative. There was no one formula for rule or appropriation and, much like the Empire of the eighteenth century, there was perpetual debate about both the moral standing of colonialism and about the value of particular colonies.

But while there was no singular and characteristic policy dominating the seemingly unstoppable growth of the Empire, that does not necessarily mean that British colonialism was somehow an accidental or even a reluctant series of random acquisitions. Such a view, most famously voiced by the nineteenth-century historian John Seeley, has enjoyed considerable popularity among historians. Seeley's elegant quip – that Britain's eighteenth-century Empire was acquired in a 'fit of absence of mind'[1] – has influenced many interpreters of British imperialism.[2] Others, not pushing the point quite so far, see the British political establishment as dominated, especially after the 1850s, by reluctant imperialists, unwillingly annexing territory or unenthusiastically nudging local rulers into accepting British influence.[3] Yet given the vast areas brought under British sway during the course of the century and under leadership from a variety of political standpoints, the image of a reluctant or accidental imperialism is not awfully persuasive. Huge areas of Africa became British; only in North Africa, dominated by the French, was British influence negligible. Dozens of small islands in the Pacific were appropriated as well as large portions of the Malay archipelago in South-East Asia. India came under direct rule. Much of Burma, to India's east, was brought under the Indian administration. Australia and New Zealand developed rapidly, and huge tracts of westerly land were added to Britain's Canadian possessions. Hong Kong, first acquired in 1842, expanded its boundaries over the course of the century. In many of these places, the British fought wars to hold on to the territories they had acquired, as well as negotiating treaties that favoured British influence in areas where outright control was not considered feasible. Though parliament after parliament worried over the potential costs, this vast, constantly growing proliferation of territory and over so long a period can hardly have been an accident.

The influential work of Ronald Robinson and John Gallagher, who coined the much-used phrase 'the imperialism of free trade' in the 1950s, sees Britain's acts of nineteenth-century colonisation as formal only when

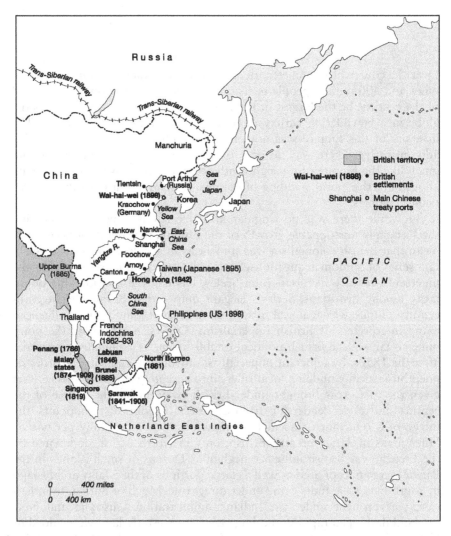

Map 6.1 Britain's holdings in East and South-East Asia

Source: *Cambridge Illustrated History of the* British *Empire*, Cambridge University Press (Marshall, Peter 1996) p. 55, © Cambridge University Press, reproduced with permission of The Licensor through PLSclear

absolutely necessary.[4] They regard British imperialism as shaped by informal imperialism (in China, in the Middle East and in South America, for example) as much as by formal annexation, a reading that stresses economics above all else, and in which Britain undertook formal colonisation only as a last resort.

Robinson and Gallagher's assessment reminds us usefully that the British Empire was a complex entity with tentacles that reached beyond legal and political borders. Still, the implication that the British were reluctant colonists minimises the huge territorial gains of the nineteenth century. Certainly the British Empire was neither a simple, nor a simply defined, beast, but its heterogeneous structure should not lead us to minimise its effects and power throughout its history.

As the territory under British stewardship accrued, events in distant places forced the British into unanticipated action to protect acquisitions and to stem unrest. Unforeseen problems certainly meant that both politicians in Britain and colonists in the field sometimes had to extemporise, and this on-the-spot decision-making could be described as accidental in that it was not specifically planned. The stratagems of expediency were often weighed against the consequences for related possessions and for the Empire as a whole. Britain may not have wanted to expend money on its colonies, but it was hardly a wallflower among the European imperial powers. Colonial acquisition during the course of the nineteenth century was neither accidental nor reluctant, but a fundamental part of an aggressive expansionist policy designed to bolster Britain's leading world role in politics and trade. Empire was about making money, it was about visible forms of power and it was about the moral high ground. The civilising mission was also a money-making mission and both were trumpeted as elements of Britain's heritage and history.

The intense period of colonial rivalry in Africa in the last 15 years or so of the nineteenth century has encouraged historians to see these years as Britain's most expansionist, yet the entire century is marked by expansion. The shift to direct rule in India in 1858, the occupation of Egypt in 1882 and the chartering of a trio of commercial companies in Africa in the 1880s characterise the later era, but in the first half of the century British India spread in a number of directions, Hong Kong and Singapore came under British control, and British influence and territory grew considerably in southern Africa.

There was also considerable administrative reorganisation. In 1768 parliament had created the new post of secretary of state for the American or Colonial Department, a position abandoned after American independence. In 1801, the position was revived as secretary of state for the War and Colonial Departments, the title acknowledging the often aggressive means by which colonial territory became British. The Colonial Office and the War Office became separate entities in 1854. These bureaucratic changes suggest that government was by no means uninterested in the supervision of the growing Empire even early in the century. We might fruitfully, then, see the nineteenth century as one of imperial gain and aggrandisement, perhaps with different motivations at different moments, but with a forward momentum throughout the entire century. In Christopher Bayly's words, the partition of Africa at the end of century was 'a mere footnote' compared with acquisitions earlier in the century.[5] The nineteenth century generally was, for the British Empire, a time of sweeping conquest, land reorganisation and vast growth, helped along by the waning power of older empires.

The nineteenth-century Empire was a diverse and scattered assortment of territories, some hugely valuable in commercial or strategic terms, others of little more than psychological value. No single policy connected them, no studied philosophy of governance reigned over them all; no one motive had driven this diverse agglomeration of possessions. The forms of rule were as different as the languages spoken, the food eaten and the customs observed in the motley collection of lands that in the nineteenth century succumbed to British power or influence. There were settler colonies where, in the mid-nineteenth century, significant strides towards self-government were made. There were territories conquered by troops or handed over to British rule by local rulers. There were places where British agents and residents offered advice but could not, at least formally, make local rulers knuckle under the British thumb. There were treaty ports in Asia (at places such as Nagasaki and Okinawa) where the British had significant economic power and no mean amount of political sway as well. And there were those places where no formal trappings of British rule existed, but that came within Britain's 'sphere of influence', a favourite phrase of the day. Most curious of all, perhaps, were colonies run not by government appointees but by individuals such as James Brooke, a British soldier who, through his aid to local rulers, was given his own kingdom, Sarawak, on the island of Borneo in 1841. Despite allegations of misrule, Brooke's rule was legitimised when the British appointed a consul to the colony in 1863.

One of the most important principles of colonialism to emerge during the nineteenth century was 'responsible self-government'. The Upper Canada Assembly had promoted the principle of a united legislature in Canada from 1822, and the theme was taken up in Lord Durham's 1839 report on how best to manage the Canadian colonies. Durham envisaged a united Canada exercising control over its internal affairs, with the imperial parliament in London maintaining control over constitutional questions, foreign policy and trade. Canada was a vital element in the Atlantic Empire, and self-government was a way to secure its continued loyalty, especially given the tensions between French and British Canadians. Within a decade, self-government began to take shape not just in Canada, but across all the white settler colonies. Those colonies deemed sufficiently politically mature were granted authority to pass laws on their own behalf in a two-thirds elective (one-third appointed) political system modelled on the British parliament. The imperial government in Britain maintained authority in key areas such as defence and foreign policy, although as a cost-cutting measure Britain abandoned its military presence in all these colonies in 1870. This experiment in government occurred mostly in the 1850s in colonies of white settlement (outlined in Chapter 4), revealing the racial distinctions in colonial governance. The only areas considered fit for this experiment in self-determination were those where white European settlers had stayed to build new lives; non-white populations were invariably classed as too backward to be entrusted with such powers.

The creation of elected assemblies occurred mostly in the 1840s and 1850s with the various colonies of what would, in 1867, become the Dominion of Canada the first to benefit. By 1854 Nova Scotia, the Province of Canada, Prince Edward Island and New Brunswick all enjoyed responsible self-government. The bulk of the Australian colonies followed suit in the 1850s. Only Western Australia, the last of the penal settlements, would have to wait until the 1890s. New Zealand acquired responsible self-government in 1856. Until 1872, the Cape Colony in southern Africa had the lesser status of representative self-government, in which a British-appointed governor-general retained a much higher degree of control. In both responsible and representative self-government, the governor retained the right to veto laws passed by the elected representatives, but his control over a representative government was far greater. The hurried passage through parliament of the Colonial Laws Validity Act in 1865 gave Westminster the right to invalidate laws passed by colonial assemblies that ran counter to British statute law. This brake on white settler rights would remain a bone of contention among the white settler colonies until the law was dissolved in 1931.

Responsible self-government was attractive to British politicians because it was a cheap form of rule. Colonies paid for their own administration and their own troops, and it was no coincidence that in Australia, self-government followed the discovery of gold, and in Cape Colony diamonds. Although no such distinctive riches prompted the changes in the Canadian provinces, the prospect of losing the remaining British North American lands to the United States would have been both politically humiliating and commercially costly. Economic considerations were central to these decisions, for beyond the cost of maintaining a colony, there were also crucial trade relationships. White settler colonies, particularly early on, needed British markets and Britain needed imports from these areas. Responsible self-government allowed Britain to maintain favourable trading relationships on the cheap, while bolstering the fledgling economies of the settler lands.

The new elective system was at first sometimes unstable, with governments often failing before their term of office formally expired. Yet there was no question of these colonies being returned to dependent status. The only incidence of that came some 30 years after the end of slavery when the white elites of the West Indian sugar colonies (with the exception of Barbados) opted out of responsible self-government to avoid facing a majority black electorate. The workings of race in determining how a colony would be administered were always and everywhere crucial. Writing in 1906, Colonial Office civil servant W. H. Mercer unapologetically distinguished between colonies 'occupied for the purposes of taking the products of the country with the aid of coloured labour', and colonies 'which are meant to be settlements of men of white race', underlining the crucial distinction between colonies of extraction and of settlement.[6]

While settler colonies moved in the direction of independence, many other areas were, over the course of the century, brought under direct British rule. Some were captured during war, such as Hong Kong, Mauritius and the Seychelles. Some, as was Fiji, were ceded to the British by local rulers. The Fijian Islands are an uncharacteristic example of reluctant British imperialism. Plagued by local rivalry the Christian ruler, Thakombau, had been trying for some time to relinquish the islands to a western power. The British accepted his offer in 1874, largely to prevent Fiji's acquisition by another European power. In other instances, simple annexation sufficed, as in Ashanti and North Borneo. Singapore was acquired by purchase. These new territories were largely tropical or semi-tropical with little or no European population prior to colonisation. Some became Crown Colonies, although in Africa Protectorates were more common. In these there was no governor; instead the top-ranking colonial official was a commissioner. The thinking behind these forms of rule was closely linked to British attitudes to peoples they regarded as backward and savage.

These were the principal forms of colonial rule in the nineteenth century, but they do not exhaust its diversity. India, after all, though its form of governance resembled that of a Crown Colony, had its own London administration: the India Office. And India itself administered a number of colonial territories: Burma from 1824, Aden from 1838, Purim from 1857, Socorro from 1886 and the Andaman Islands (on and off from 1789) as well as parts of the Malay archipelago into the 1830s.

Closer to home, there was Ireland. The 1800 Act of Union had resulted in a small number of Irish MPs being elected to Westminster (see Chapter 1). The complicated divisions between rich and poor, Protestant and Catholic, landowning and peasant classes in Ireland were in no manner solved by union. Indeed, Ireland would be, throughout the nineteenth century, a problem that would bring down British governments. Long before the severe famine of the mid-1840s forced mass emigration from Ireland and caused incalculable misery and suffering, Irish nationalists and those championing the cause of its dispossessed peasantry reminded British politicians that not all imperial questions were located at a distance. Throughout the century, Irish activists destabilised politics within Britain in their quest for self-determination. That threat did not go unnoticed in the corridors of power; Britain routinely maintained around 18,000 troops in Ireland.

⚓ This lack of colonial uniformity reflects some interesting characteristics of the British imperial order. In every case, finding the least expensive method of colonisation was a priority though seldom one which prompted Britain to get out of the business of expansion. Relatedly, since sending a military detachment to subdue people was a costly business and not a guaranteed success, there was also always a question about what rule was appropriate and in which contexts. A consideration of these factors helped to determine what kind of colonial presence would be imposed.

There were also significant areas with no formal British presence but where Britain still exercised substantial influence. For the most part, this occurred in areas not considered suitable for direct rule but where there were strategic or commercial considerations important to British interests. In Central and South America, for example, Britain had very few formal possessions – only British Honduras and British Guiana – but wielded considerable economic influence, especially in the former Spanish colonies of Argentina and Brazil. Every country in South America had a British-owned railway by the end of the nineteenth century, and British investors were also heavily involved across Latin and South America in nitrate production, ranching and the wool and meat trades alongside banking, insurance, transport and more. In his 1875 novel *The Way We Live Now*, Anthony Trollope paints a vivid picture of the speculation involved in such ventures. British trade dominated these countries and their debt burden made them heavily dependent on British investors, allowing a significant British foothold in the region without any need for formal colonial governance. In part, the reluctance to colonise formally was a fiscal one, since conquest was invariably an expensive business. The Latin American case, however, was more complicated. Britain mostly worked to acquire free trade treaties which gave preference to Britain. The policy was successful insofar as Britain was, throughout the century, the main European nation trading in the region. The British seldom chose to colonise in places where there was already a European presence or a European style of rule. Alongside the long history of Spanish and Portuguese colonial rule, the increasing presence and interest of the United States in the region further complicated the picture.

A trade treaty with Siam (now Thailand) signed in 1855, and which effectively ushered in a free trade policy in the South-East Asian kingdom, became the model for Britain's informal imperialism. Though it was strategic reasons that made the states along the Persian Gulf important to the British in this period (rather than oil, which would only become essential later), here too treaties in the nineteenth century made many small countries effective satellites in the British colonial system. The sheikdoms of Bahrain (1861 and 1892), Kuwait (1899) and the sultanate of Muscat and Oman (1891) all came within the sphere of British influence during the course of the century.

One of the most politically complicated of the possessions acquired in the nineteenth century was Egypt, on the tip of north-east Africa and across from the Arabian states of the Persian Gulf. Britain's involvement pre-dated the military occupation it undertook in 1882 and was closely tied to the fate of the Ottoman Empire and to shipping routes to India. Egypt was nominally a part of the Ottoman Empire, though the sultan was too weak by the mid-nineteenth century to wield any genuine control there. For most of the century, British colonial interests dictated a pro-Ottoman policy despite public and political misgivings about many aspects of culture and rule in the Ottoman lands. The vast Ottoman holdings stretched from North Africa to the Black Sea, encompassing a diverse multi-ethnic array of peoples within a Muslim state, and straddling eastern and western cultures. In the nineteenth century, the Ottoman Empire was struggling to maintain its integrity. A strong internal military resisted the changes demanded by its western allies. Minorities were increasingly vociferous, and in 1829 Greece won its independence. Syria almost followed suit in 1831. Growing Austrian and Russian interest in the Ottoman's Balkan possessions weakened another flank of the Empire, while in 1853 Russia's invasion of Ottoman territory set off the Crimean War.

Britain stood by the Ottoman Empire for most of the century, seeing it as a critical barrier to French and Russian interests in the all-important routes to India. It was this concern that prompted Britain to send aid when Syria threatened to break away, and again during the Crimean War. One of the major overland trade routes to India was through the Syrian desert, a route the British were anxious to protect. But British support came at a price. In 1838, the British forced a free trade treaty (Balta Liman) on the Ottoman sultan that had detrimental effects on the local economy while benefitting the British, a situation further undermining the sultan's hold. The reluctance to seize Ottoman lands dwindled in the face of British need. In 1878, needing a supply line to the eastern Mediterranean, Britain seized and colonised the Ottoman island of Cyprus, and at the end of the century, when the British entered into a power-sharing condominium in the Sudan with Egypt, Ottoman claims were simply ignored.

It was on Egypt, however, that British interests in the region came to focus. Over the years, a large European trading population had moved there, controlling the considerable export and import trade. The Europeans prospered under the Ottoman legal system of 'Capitulations', which allowed them freedom from local jurisdiction. Cotton had become an especially important export when, during the American Civil War, Britain's supplies of raw cotton had been compromised, seriously affecting the prosperity of the British textile industry. With the building of the Suez Canal, begun in 1855 and opened in 1869, Egypt became even more important to the British. The canal, located in Egypt, gradually eliminated the longer overland routes to India. When the British intervened in Egyptian affairs, the bulk of the shipping passing through the canal was British, and in 1875, the prime minister Benjamin Disraeli engineered Britain's purchase of a 44 per cent stake in canal ownership.

In the face of economic chaos in Egypt, the British and the French assumed dual control of the Egyptian economy to manage the country's considerable debt and to protect the financial interests of their own investors.

Their intervention was disrupted in 1882 by a nationalist uprising spurred by resentment of this foreign interference. The French were less and less interested in managing Egyptian affairs, so Britain unilaterally embarked in July 1882 on a naval bombardment of the port of Alexandria. Instead of quelling the unrest, this show of force sparked riots. A manoeuvre intended to display British force and persuade the Egyptians to accept informal British influence backfired, and the nationalist refusal to surrender forced Britain into military action. By September 1882, Egypt was under military occupation and became a part of the British Empire. Lord Cromer, who had served in the 1870s as Egypt's British controller-general handling the country's finances, was named consul-general, and Egypt remained under British influence until the 1950s despite nominal independence from 1922.

The colonisation of Egypt came at the start of a very busy period of British expansion in Africa. Often known as the 'scramble for Africa', the period from about 1885 until the end of the century was one in which colonial growth was predominantly, though never exclusively, centred on Africa. Africa had been an important site of colonial trading in the eighteenth century. A smattering of British trading stations had grown up along the West African coast from the sixteenth century, and in the nineteenth century some of these were placed under Crown rule: Sierra Leone (whose port of Freetown was an important fresh-water stop on many international shipping and trade routes) in 1808, The Gambia in 1816 and the Gold Coast in 1821.

Africa's colonial importance before the nineteenth century lay not in territorial possession but in its provision of a critical export: human slaves. In this respect Africa was at the heart of the Atlantic slave trade (see Chapter 2) and crucial to many of Britain's other colonies as well as to the slave states of America. After the ban on slaving imposed by the British in 1807, The Gambia became Britain's base for the anti-slaving squadron that began operating in the 1820s. Often ineffective, the squadron faced an arduous task for many involved in the trade saw no reason to abide by British injunctions to cease business. Upwards of 3 million slaves made the grim journey to the Americas before the naval patrols ended in 1870, while the squadron freed some 150,000. In the 1830s, when the institution of slavery was fully abolished in the British Empire, West African slave traders – who were not British subjects – received no compensation for their losses, unlike the West Indian planters. The loss of income must have been severe and not easily replaced. Slavery was also part of the rationale for the occupation of Lagos, on the West African coast, in 1861. It was an aggressive move designed to open up trade, to display British force to local rulers, to break up continued slaving and to prevent further French incursion in the area. As the institution of slavery slowly ebbed, trading interests in the region began to shift to palm oil which, before the mass export of petroleum oil, was of crucial importance in the lubrication of machinery as well as a major component in soap-making.

These changes reoriented the geography of colonial interest in Africa to other parts of the continent and away from the Atlantic routes. The mid-century years saw a tremendous amount of African exploration by British adventurers; David Livingstone traversed the continent in 1853, John Hanning Speke reached Uganda in 1857. Southern Africa, meanwhile, attracted British interest from early in the century. The Cape was a perfect stopping point for ships sailing between India and Britain, which made securing the region for British interests a priority. Annexation of land in the region began in earnest in the early 1840s. British Kaffraria was established in 1847 as a home for the Xhosa people, and incorporated into Cape Colony in 1866. The incentives in southern Africa were considerably intensified by the discovery of gold and diamonds. Diamonds were first found in the region in 1867; the discovery of gold in the Transvaal followed a few years later. Griqualand West was annexed in 1871 to ensure that its recently discovered diamond deposits remained British property. The prospect of the wealth that these precious finds would bring made southern Africa a newly important focus of British interest.

Yet even here, the typical method of colonisation the British favoured was commercial, a strategy that in some ways returned them to an earlier era of colonisation. For it was the chartered company that, in Africa especially, was responsible for much late nineteenth-century colonisation. The state moved in with formal or semi-formal administrative arrangements only late in the proceedings, if at all. From the late 1880s, three new chartered companies – the Royal Niger Company (West Africa, 1886), the British East Africa Company (1888) and the British South Africa Company (1889) – paved the way for imperial expansion in Africa, a method much cheaper for government than formal direct rule. The smaller British North Borneo Company, established in 1881, heralded the revival of imperial expansion through the mechanism of the commercial charter which accounted for the majority of African acquisitions after 1880.

It was in some respects a curious practice for, other than a few major products, Africa offered a relatively scant array of exportable items. Ivory was as important as gold or diamonds in this period, and 85 per cent of the world's ivory came from Africa. In West Africa, the growth of the palm oil industry was certainly important. But overall, Africa was a less economically profitable environment than many of the other areas coveted by the British. It attracted less British investment, except in the gold and diamond industries of the south, than other areas of the Empire and throughout the colonial era remained considerably less developed.

In part, this was also because colonisers had to deal with indigenous African powers, themselves interested in expansion and by no means always deferential to the British. They had also to contend with the spread of Islam in the region, a phenomenon that tended to produce resistance to European colonisation. In the Sudan and Somaliland, in particular, Islamic rebellions reminded the British that their rivals were not solely

European. The Mahdist jihad in the Sudan in the 1880s produced one of the great mythic tales of British expansion, the death of General Gordon at Khartoum. The Ethiopians were an expansionist force to be reckoned with in this region but the British found resistance and competition throughout Africa, from the Baganda in East Africa to the Ndebele in South Africa. Attempts to avoid clashes with these powers was one reason why the policy of indirect rule, so eloquently enunciated by Frederick Lugard, was the chosen method for late nineteenth- and early twentieth-century African colonialism.[7] Accommodation with local rulers and an insistence on retaining customary practice meant less likelihood of unrest, a built-in tendency to conservatism and less need for a large locally based British bureaucracy.

In this way, during the last 15 years of the nineteenth century, the British feverishly acquired territory all over Africa. The Niger Districts Protectorate was established in 1885, the chartering of the Royal Niger Company following in 1886. In 1890, Britain concluded agreements with Germany and France to resolve disputes about ownership of African lands in Zanzibar, Tanganyika and the Niger region. The year 1891 was a busy one for colonisation and diplomacy; treaties with the Italians, the Dutch and the Portuguese delineated territory in and near Africa. In that same year Britain created the Central African Protectorate and allocated Northern Zambesia to the British South Africa Company. The rest of the decade was one of intense growth and diplomacy in the region, and by the end of the 1890s, tropical Africa had been divided fully between the major European powers, with scant regard for indigenous claims.

Resistance to British annexation and rule was by no means confined to Africa. The 1857 Indian rebellion may be the best known of the uprisings of the period, but it was by no means the only moment of dissatisfaction with colonial authority. Some ten years earlier, a rebellion in Ceylon had been quelled by British troops. In the same year as the Indian rebellion, there was a Chinese uprising in Sarawak with another close on its heels in 1859. In Hong Kong, a Chinese plan to poison the local white residents by lacing their bread with arsenic caused a great deal of sickness. Riots destabilised much of the Malay archipelago in the 1850s and 1860s; the Straits Settlements became a Crown Colony in 1867 in part to control such unrest and violence. The threat to British trade was likewise a factor in the 1874 Treaty of Pangkor whereby protected Malay states agreed to allow British residencies. The Perak War of 1875 was prompted by the assassination of the local British resident; and in a reaction to the assassination and subsequent riots, Britain's quelling of the rebels led to growing colonial influence in the region. The residency plan focused on restoring order to the region by reducing dynastic conflict between local rulers, and between different ethnic Chinese groups. British suspicion that other European powers might have designs on the region also played a significant role.

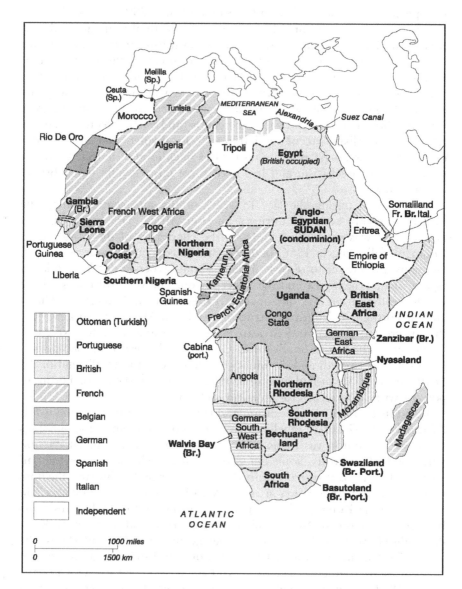

Map 6.2 Africa after the Boer War

Source: *British Imperialism, 1750–1970*, Cambridge University Press (Smith, Simon c. 1988) p. 76, © Cambridge University Press, reproduced with permission of the author and publisher

Colonial wars abounded. 1879 was a bad year for the British who suffered defeat in Afghanistan and at the hands of the Zulus at Isandhlwana, as well as major disputes with the Irish Land League. Across the Pacific, the Māori wars engulfed the new colony of New Zealand in the 1860s.

A major rebellion at Morant Bay in Jamaica in 1865 made headlines in Britain. Governor Eyre was vilified by some and acclaimed by others for his swift and brutal response to this uprising among former slaves; his prosecution became something of a metropolitan *cause célèbre*. The press in Britain reported insurrections of this sort avidly. The response of colonised peoples will be considered more closely (see Chapter 8), but here I want to suggest that the eagerness of the press in reporting colonial agitation hardly suggests a nation indifferent to colonialism, or shying away from expanding the boundaries of its formal rule. Many historians have favoured this idea that the British were reluctant colonialists. However, the speed and scope of growth, the public interest in colonial conquest evinced by story books and exhibitions, the formation of pro-imperial bodies such as the British Empire League (1894) and the Imperial Federation League (1884), and the constant attentiveness of the press to colonial affairs, hint rather at a nation whose very identity was bound up with possessing, ruling and keeping hold of an empire of epic proportion. There were always critics of imperialism as well, of course, but overwhelmingly the populace approved Britain's possession of an ever-expanding empire, regarding it as proof of and often the reason for English pre-eminence.

✳ Many factors played into the palpable growth of the British colonial world in the nineteenth century. In some cases there were economic or strategic reasons for Britain's interest. Technology significantly altered the possibilities for rule and this, too, played a part. The re-emergence of serious rivalry with other European powers (a major theme in eighteenth-century diplomacy) as the latter caught up to Britain's industrial pre-eminence increasingly influenced the colonial power structure. In addition, as an island Britain had attended carefully and for a long time to its naval defences, a strategy that had given it unparalleled command of the world's oceans. As the Empire grew, the need to defend existing territory often resulted in expansion to increase buffer zones or to provide ships with convenient safe harbours on long voyages. Britain's commitment to remaining in India, cemented in 1858 with direct rule, resulted in colonial growth elsewhere in the world. There were the coaling stations and ports for ships bound for India, there was the Suez Canal and there was expansion on the ground in South Asia, in response to a perceived Russian threat in what is now Pakistan. The borders of British India pushed further north in the nineteenth century, along with incursions into Afghanistan in the name of defending India. The fear of Russia as a rival expansionist power had been growing since the defeat of Napoleon in 1815. Britain's support of the Ottoman Empire, as we have seen, was maintained in part because Russian interest in Ottoman territories threatened shipping routes to India. Britain's role in the Crimean War and in the Russo-Turkish War some 20 years later was premised on protecting India and routes to it. The build-up of the Russian military presence in central Asia in the 1860s and 1870s intensified fears in India, though the Russians never in fact got even as close to India as Afghanistan.

Towards the end of the century, rivalry between Britain and other European powers began once more to intensify. Many of the gains on the African continent and in the Pacific were motivated by a perceived need to counter or to keep up with what other European colonists were doing. Belgium, Germany and France, in particular, vied for African lands, often quietly fomenting local discontent to weaken the territories of rival powers. Elsewhere, the substantial Dutch and French interests in South-East Asia influenced British decisions in the region, as did the growing imperial aspirations of Germany under Chancellor Bismarck. Germany in the years after its unification in 1871 began actively colonising not only in Africa but in South-East Asia and the Pacific. It was fear of German predominance that led the British to support American colonisation of the Philippines in 1898 and to annex – via Queensland – a large segment of New Guinea in 1884. The Berlin Conference of 1884–5 underlined the colonial prominence of newly unified Germany. This meeting of the European colonial powers, the USA and Turkey to establish the principles of European colonial conquest in Africa was initiated by Bismarck and held on his territory. Fourteen nations met for 15 weeks, and ended by endorsing, without reference to indigenous desires or needs, free access for European powers to the African interior. The claim to territory had to be proven by what the conference chillingly called 'effective occupation'. Though the conference agreed in broad terms on the need to respect the welfare of local peoples, their claims to sovereignty were passed over and they were treated exclusively as peoples in need of European protection. Under the terms of the Heligoland-Zanzibar Treaty of 1890, Germany ceded to Britain, among other lands, the small sultanate of Wituland on the East African coast in exchange for the Heligoland Islands and other territories which would form the core of German East Africa. The local population in Wituland, however, wished to remain under Germany's protection. They protested this change to no avail; the Sultan, Fumo Bakari ibn Ahmad, was deposed when he and his supporters resisted, and Indian police were soon brought in to impose British authority.

Following this extraordinary dismissal of the rights of colonised peoples, the conference also staked Germany's claim as a major European colonial power. The emergence of new rivals as well as the reassertion of old competition marked a new economic phase in both Europe and the colonies. Britain was no longer the dominant economy on the world stage, and indeed by the 1860s it was apparent that such predominance would not easily be regained. But what Britain already had was a substantial and credible empire, and this, in the second half of the nineteenth century, was the basis of the country's continued claims to global political authority.

Although many of the new territories claimed by Britain in the later nineteenth century offered little practical benefit by way of valuable goods for export, the size and intensity of British imperialism gradually came to overtake economic supremacy in Britain's quest for continued political predominance. Certainly many of the colonies could and did provide Britain with valuable trade (and it was not always a mutually beneficial relationship, by any means). Australia, New Zealand, India, southern Africa, Singapore, Hong Kong and the sugar colonies of Fiji and Mauritius created tremendous wealth, but many of the territories acquired later were never particularly profitable. Tropical colonies provided three major export groups: agricultural raw materials including rubber, palm oil and cotton; foodstuffs such as cocoa, coffee, tea and sugar; and minerals (petroleum oil, tin, copper, diamonds and gold). But in many of the newer colonies, production was slow or limited, distribution was difficult and yields were unimpressive. Nonetheless, taken as whole, their presence on the British map added to the influence of the Empire, and to its prestige as the largest of the European empires of the era.

Britain was, by the mid-1870s, experiencing a serious if unevenly distributed economic depression. Prohibitive tariffs imposed by other European nations (Germany from 1879, France from 1881, Italy from 1887, and the USA after 1890) undermined the principle of free trade, and it was becoming increasingly clear that Britain would never again dominate world trade and industry as it earlier had. Investment and interest shifted slowly towards the colonies, which provided less restrictive export and import markets. In theory, the colonies operated in a free trade environment, but in practice most were dominated by Britain as supplier and as buyer, and when free settler colonies began to seek trade agreements with other nations, as Canada did in the late nineteenth century, British authorities were alarmed. The effect of British predominance in colonial economies was not always beneficial, however, for the system tended to focus production on a narrow range of commodities needed by the British and developed in response to British markets. This lack of diversity inevitably made colonial economies vulnerable to market shifts, a susceptibility exacerbated by the distinct lack of industry in most colonies, making them dependent on the UK for industrial products and machinery. It was not until Joseph Chamberlain headed the Colonial Office in 1895 that colonial development became an important item on the political agenda. Most of Chamberlain's schemes for development proved unfeasible, but his term of office made the issue more prominent with later administrations.

Britain's share of world trade may have been dropping, but there was one economic arena in which the country remained supreme, and that powerfully helped sustain the Empire and drive home its importance for Britain's global authority. London, by the start of the twentieth century, was the centre of international commerce and finance, which in turn made sterling the most important currency. London was where investment, insurance, brokerage, valuation and more happened, and this gave Britain a vast influence in the world of economics and trade.

The new technologies of the period contributed considerably to the expansion of empire. It became quicker and easier to traverse the world as ship-building techniques improved along with innovations such as the Suez Canal. The advent of the telegraph in the 1860s made communications immediate in hitherto impossible ways. The railway cut through the interior of continents, allowing quick transport of goods to shipping ports, and goods could now be refrigerated during lengthy voyages, a process that brought meat and dairy products literally across the world from Argentina, Australia and New Zealand to the United Kingdom. New Zealand's first shipment of frozen lamb and mutton, celebrated in the issue of a new postage stamp, left Port Chalmers in February 1882. Troops, too, could be moved more easily as transport options multiplied, and new long-range rifles and machine guns increased their firepower. Yet as late as 1931, the Indian census showed less than 10 per cent of the country's population working in industrial occupations.

In the long term, technological innovations cut prices. In the short term, they were often costly and while Britain wanted a large empire, it wanted it as cheaply as possible. The revival of the chartered companies and the use of new forms of governance such as Protectorates requiring less administration were strategies designed to minimise the Empire's cost to Britain. Year after year, budgetary discussions in parliament focused on the expense of colonialism, and this is another of the reasons that historians have seen the British as only reluctant conquerors. Even given the many penny-pinching tactics employed, the Empire was never cheap to run, for it necessitated a large body of troops and a smaller but still size-able body of administrators in the colonies and in Britain. But the burden nonetheless lay disproportionately with those colonised rather than with the colonisers, for the principle, as we have seen, was always that the colonies, other than militarily, should be self-financing. In most colonies outside the white settler arenas, little substantive economic development occurred under nineteenth-century colonial rule, and in many places the encouragement to produce goods for the British market helped the British more than it did the producers. The export back to Asian and African colonies of cheap finished cotton goods hurt indigenous textile trades, for example, and in Africa and Malaya, products valuable for the growth of British industry were exported in huge quantities, but there were few attempts to locate those industries more locally.

A good example of this inequality at work can be seen in the develop-ment of the railway in India. Private investors in Britain, who were offered a return of 4.5 per cent to 5 per cent on their investment, grew wealthy as the railways expanded in India, but little of the wealth produced stayed in India. Even the equipment and the stock used were more likely to have been exported from Britain and Europe than produced locally. For all this, the railways were nonetheless a huge success, not only in facilitating more effective colonial rule but in their widespread use by local peoples as well.

White settler countries, by contrast, actively promoted industrialisation, especially those outside Africa. Though these colonies were encouraged to cater to British markets and needed that trade for their own economic well-being, they experienced industrial and economic development on a scale utterly unknown in the dependent non-migrant colonies. Here in lands more and more peopled by an influx of British and European whites, we see all the trappings of nineteenth-century industrial capitalism, opening ever wider the gulf between colonies of settlement and dependent colonies, as well as between settlers and increasingly marginalised indigenous peoples in the settler lands.

The effects of colonisation were, then, as varied and diverse as the forms of colonialism that took root in this period. More often than not in the nineteenth century, the experience of colonisation was deeply affected by race. White migrants intent on making a new life in places such as New Zealand and Canada might feel they had a stake in this new land, but indigenous peoples mostly experienced colonisation as upheaval. Land use and ownership, occupational prospects, laws and customs, language and culture were all changed by the white colonial presence. This was as much the lot of Aboriginal Canadians and Australians, New Zealand Māori and many southern African peoples as it was of those in non-settler environments. In both instances, for example, the zeal for social reform already so fashionable in Britain was imported to address the alleged savageries of local culture. Alongside reforming politicians, scores of lobbyists demanded reform in a wide range of activities from customs around dress to the treatment of new-born children, from sexual mores to religious rituals. Missionaries, feminists, humanitarians, doctors, teachers and a host of others called on colonial governments to end what they saw as barbaric practices and to encourage Christian and western behaviours. This was the 'civilisational' model of imperialism, the common and popular argument that allegedly backward peoples were well served by good colonial administration that would educate and Christianise them, help them curb disease and poverty (neither of which the British were showing much sign of controlling at home), and fit them for a place in the after-life. These were powerful and deeply felt arguments and many people genuinely believed in the good they felt colonial rule could do in improving 'backward' and difficult lives.

The nineteenth century, then, was a time of tremendous change, expansion and experimentation in colonial terms. The land mass of the Empire was massively augmented, the range of export and import goods considerably broadened, and the types of rule employed hugely expanded. British imperial interests were not confined to a particular region. The entire century was a period of major global expansion in which the British Empire guaranteed Britain a prominent role in world politics and trade out of all proportion to island Britain's size, commodities and production. In the nineteenth century, and despite fears over cost and complex negotiations, a British future without the Empire was an impossible notion.

Notes

1 J. R. Seeley, *The Expansion of England* (London: Macmillan, 1883), p. 8.
2 See, for example, Bernard Porter, *The Lion's Share: A Short History of British Imperialism, 1850–1995* (Harlow: Longman, 1996), pp. 11–12, 28–9.
3 Peter J. Durrans, 'The House of Commons and the British Empire 1868–1880', *Canadian Journal of History* 9, no. 1 (1974), pp. 19–44; Ronald Hyam, *Britain's Imperial Century, 1815–1914: A Study of Empire and Expansion* (2nd edn, Basingstoke: Macmillan, 1993), p. 116; Timothy Parsons, *The British Imperial Century, 1815–1914: A World History Perspective* (Lanham, MD: Rowman & Littlefield, 1999), p. 15. In *Colonialism and Development: Britain and its Tropical Colonies, 1850–1960* (London: Routledge, 1993) Michael Havinden and David Meredith see such reluctance as a 'passing phase' (p. 24).
4 Ronald Robinson and John Gallagher, 'The Imperialism of Free Trade', *Economic History Review* 2nd series, 6, no. 1 (1953), pp. 1–15.
5 Christopher Bayly, 'The British and Indigenous Peoples, 1760–1860', in Martin Daunton and Rick Halpern, (eds), *Empire and Others: British Encounters with Indigenous Peoples, 1660–1850* (Philadelphia, PA: University of Pennsylvania Press, 1999), p. 37.
6 W. H. Mercer, *A Handbook of the British Colonial Empire* (London: Waterlow and Sons Ltd, 1906), p. 2.
7 Lugard (1858–1945) was a soldier turned politician whose lengthy career in Africa was divided mostly between Uganda and Nigeria. His many years in India (where he was born and lived as a child, returning in the late 1870s as an army officer) clearly influenced his philosophy of indirect rule.

Further reading

A good number of general histories of empire in this period have been published in the last few years. Among them are Dane Kennedy, *Britain and Empire, 1880–1945* (Harlow: Longman, 2002), Timothy Parsons, *The British Imperial Century, 1815–1914: A World History Perspective* (Lanham, MD: Rowman & Littlefield, 1999), Andrew S. Thompson, *Imperial Britain: The Empire in British Politics, c.1880–1932* (Harlow: Longman, 2000), and Willie Thompson, *Global Expansion: Britain and Its Empire, 1870–1914* (London: Pluto Press, 1999). Steven Press investigates the colonies that emerged not from formal governance but from private individuals seeking power, wealth and glory, in his highly readable *Rogue Empires: Contracts and Conmen in Europe's Scramble for Africa* (Cambridge, MA: Harvard University Press, 2017).

There is also, of course, a huge literature on the individual history of particular colonies. *India and the World Economy 1850–1950*, (G. Balachandran (ed.), New Delhi: Oxford University Press, 2003) is a helpful overview of India's place in the increasingly global economy crafted by colonialism in the nineteenth and twentieth centuries. The growing colonial interest in Africa is discussed in Roland Oliver and Anthony Atmore, *Africa Since 1800* (5th edn, Cambridge: Cambridge University Press, 2005), in *The Scramble for Africa, 1876–1912* by Thomas Pakenham (New York: Random House, 1991) and in *Africa and the Victorians: The Official Mind of Imperialism* by Ronald Robinson, John Gallagher and Alice Denny, first published in 1961 and much reprinted and revised thereafter (London: Macmillan). For East and South-East Asia, John M. Carroll's *Edge of Empires: Chinese Elites and British Colonials in Hong Kong* (Cambridge, MA: Harvard University Press, 2005) does an excellent job in revealing the collaboration necessary to successful colonisation. Carroll's *A Concise History of Hong Kong* (Lanham, MD: Rowman & Littlefield, 2007) is a very good introduction to the history of the colony. Nicholas Tarling's *The Cambridge History of Southeast Asia. Volume II. The Nineteenth and Twentieth Centuries* (Cambridge: Cambridge University Press, 1992) offers an extensive overview of British interests in the region.

7   Ruling an empire

Ruling a colony was serious business and though, as we have seen, it has some-times been fashionable to represent the British Empire as something inad-vertently acquired, neither accident nor serendipity could get the job done once a territory became British. Consider the scope of the enterprise: by the start of the twentieth century, Britain administered 47 territories, of which a mere 12 were self-governing. As already noted, the population in this vast swathe of land numbered some 400 million, and the range of languages, religions and cultures was huge. Maintaining order in such a diverse array of regions and among such different peoples required something more than merely muddling along.

There were key moments, mainly crises of rebellion, when British administrations needed to stop and take stock, to consider with all pos-sible seriousness what empire was and what it was not. And, of course, the answer to such questions did not remain the same over time, for imperial rule and attitudes changed with the times, moving in tandem with other cultural and political developments. In the 1780s, the loss of America, a major turning point for the Empire's future even if mainly in psychological terms, led Britain to explore more fully other regions of the world, while in the mid-nineteenth century the uprisings in India and Jamaica took Britain's leaders in a different direction, imposing more direct and autocratic forms of rule in some regions. Many factors – economic, racial, cultural, stra-tegic – help explain these varied tactics and responses: here we will explore those factors in the context of the lives, experiences and attitudes of those charged, whether at home in Britain or stationed in the Empire, with ruling a colony.

Many Britons firmly believed that imperial supremacy was the national destiny, a sentiment that certainly in both the nineteenth and the twen-tieth centuries peppered the public utterances of politicians, the writings of historians and journalists and the teaching of British schoolchildren. This patriotic reading of expansion and colonisation saw British law and govern-ance as the finest and noblest expression of humanity. Britons were kinder and more just as colonists, according to this view, and their colonial power was used to benefit the colonised. The English, claimed a school textbook from the start of the twentieth century, 'are especially fitted by nature' to be colonists because they are 'persevering, unflinching ... patriotic ... [and] love order and justice'. According to Sir Lepel Griffin, an experienced and long-term Indian civil servant, the 'secrets of government ... in the modern world' belonged 'to the Anglo-Saxon race alone'.[1]

Figure 7.1 Golden Jubilee wallpaper, 1887. Pro-imperial and patriotic décor, crockery and fashions were heavily promoted in the late nineteenth century, especially during celebrations such as a Jubilee

Source: © Victoria and Albert Museum, London

By the late nineteenth century, fiction for both children and adults was saturated with this point of view. Much of the impetus behind the new scouting movement established by Robert Baden-Powell in 1908 derived from an imperially suffused patriotism. It was a powerful rallying call that often worked well for politicians. Yet it was by no means the only or always the dominant attitude within Britain and among the British. As Britain's economic and political dominance came to be challenged in the mid-nineteenth century by new industrial and imperial competitors, many saw the Empire as a means of political and economic survival rather than a blessing for the less fortunate. In 1906, Viscount Milner, one of the leading pro-imperialists in Britain, told the Manchester Conservative Club that if Britain did not remain 'a great Power ... she will become a poor country'. Britain was too small to compete alone but 'Greater Britain may remain such a Power ... for ever', a guarantee of future prosperity.[2] His colleague, Cecil Rhodes, thought civil war likely without settler colonialism to absorb population and buy British goods.

This was clearly more a pragmatic than a moral stance, less concerned with Britain's duties than with its political and economic success. It shared, nonetheless, with the promoters of progress a strong belief that those colonised by the British were weaker and inferior peoples. While the moralists saw it as a duty of imperialism to take civilisation to lesser peoples, those more concerned with British survival in a competitive arena regarded the failure of the colonised to use their resources productively as the principal justification for empire. Both camps of colonial boosterism, then, saw the colonised as lacking intelligence, social organisation and, of course, civilisation. The idea of the 'civilising mission' was a surprisingly broad umbrella.

The distinction between those who ruled and those who were ruled took many different forms within the Empire, as we have already seen in the contrasts between varied forms of governance. These differences, however, became much more visible as the Empire expanded and as the non-settler colony became more typical of British imperialism. In much of the world in the eighteenth century, colonists lived in close contact with indigenous populations, and in many instances were dependent upon them. Mughal rule dominated those areas of India where Britain's growing commercial interest lay, and the British needed permission to trade, to live and to build there. In the American colonies, relations with Native Americans were far more central than they would become when indigenous peoples were pushed to the margins. The early settlers traded, bargained with and learned from local peoples, and often had no choice but to accommodate their needs. Gradually, as British power and wealth spread across the globe, compromise and negotiation became less common than conquest and autocratic rule, and increasingly the alleged savagery and lack of civilisation of other cultures became a major justification for this slow but palpable change of overall policy. Even in those areas where Britain's imperial influence was informal, in Latin America, for example, a strong

Figure 7.2 Thomas Joshua Alldridge (1874–1916), a district commissioner in Sierra Leone in the 1890s. Alldridge's sense of authority and superiority comes through vividly in this picture. Even the armed officer with him is depicted as subordinate, standing back slightly, and bare-footed in contrast to Alldridge's meticulous uniformed presence

Source: Cambridge University Library: Royal Commonwealth Society Library, T. J. Alldridge Sierra Leone collection, 1890s, Y30446F

sense of British superiority was increasingly discernible. This hierarchical self-confidence, typical of the western and Christian world, was buttressed by Britain's constant and mostly successful colonial expansion. Figures 7.3 and 7.4, with their boast of the size and success of Britain's imperial ventures, exemplify this self-congratulatory pride. Figure 7.3, dating from the early twentieth-century reign of King Edward VII, offers miniatures of the British royal family, the viceroy of India and the Indian princes, with the latter grouped in one vignette while each of the British occupy their own cameo, establishing a pecking order of importance. Figure 7.4, an advertisement from some 20 years later, puts the boastful and popular claim that the sun never set on the British Empire, so great was its global reach, to commercial use. In the late nineteenth and well into the twentieth century, the Empire was a frequent backdrop for commercial advertising. Advertisements for soap, chocolate and many other commodities invoked the Empire.

Figure 7.3 The Empire on Whom the Sun Never Sets postcard
Source: Courtesy of the Kenneth Robbins Collection, University of Michigan

Alfred Milner and Cecil Rhodes (founder of the diamond company, De Beers), working in South Africa in the late 1890s and early 1900s, personify this hardening set of attitudes. Milner as high commissioner of South Africa and governor, first of Cape Colony and then of the Orange River and Transvaal territories, and Rhodes as prime minister of Cape Colony, actively promoted British business interests in the region at the expense of local peoples. Rhodes engineered legislation to limit the black African franchise and to ensure an African workforce for western concerns. Milner precipitated a scandal over labour conditions when he persuaded the Home Office in 1904 to permit the importation of Chinese indentured workers to the South African goldfields. Both men worked actively to extend British

Figure 7.4 Craven tobacco advertisement, 'The Sun never sets'
Source: *Punch*, 22 July 1931

landholdings in the region. Northern and Southern Rhodesia (now Zambia and Zimbabwe) were named after Rhodes who died in 1902. In a paper he wrote in 1877, Rhodes proclaimed that 'more territory simply means more of the Anglo-Saxon race more of the best and most human, most honourable race the world possesses'.[3]

This pride in British worth was invariably undercut by anxiety. Would the Briton abroad 'go native' and be tempted to behave in un-British ways that would undermine British rule? Would the effects of 'lesser' cultures corrupt Britain at its centre? These were fears that beset Britain's ruling class throughout the years of imperial rule. In the eighteenth century, West Indian planters and returning East India Company (EIC) employees (the so-called 'nabobs') were often regarded with mistrust and satirised for their distance from 'proper' English behaviours and their fondness for 'native' customs. In the nineteenth and twentieth centuries, marriages between local women and colonising men were discouraged in an effort to keep coloniser and colonised separate. Assimilation at the height of Britain's imperial power was very much a one-way street, with colonised peoples expected to conform to British behaviours and values. Movement in the other direction was considered contamination, not assimilation.

Imperial anxiety was not limited, however, to the fear of contagion or pollution. The immense sense of difference and alienness experienced by Britons living abroad in other cultures is something many memoirs of imperial service mention. Sir John Strachey, who spent his career in India, wrote in 1911 that the colonial official 'has to wage constant warfare against strange barbarisms, horrid customs and cruel superstitions, ancient survivals, ready, at any moment to start into activity'.[4] This sense of strangeness and incomprehension kept alive an undercurrent of uncertainty about whether and, sometimes, when those being ruled might refuse to submit. The fear of rebellion and resistance was no fantasy; violence underpinned imperial might but worked in both directions. Slave rebellions, wars, mutinies and riots litter the history of the Empire, as we have seen. Even in settler colonies, imperialism could be fraught with uncertainties. Frontier societies, such as those in Canada, South Africa and Australia, proved hard to domesticate into a British image of respectability. Men striking out to tap gold deposits or to work in mining and logging had little interest in, or opportunity for a settled, demure lifestyle that emphasised religious duty, marriage and family. The existence of disorderly white communities in outback territories undermined claims of empire as a civilising mission.

Migration, an important feature of British colonialism, fed many of these fears, as more and more Britons moved to imperial locations, permanently as settlers or temporarily in colonial employment. Where the eighteenth century saw a vast number of people moved by force as slaves, the nineteenth century was characterised mostly by voluntary migration, although the many indentured labourers who criss-crossed the Empire after the end of slavery often made constrained choices and, in some instances, were the victims of kidnapping (see Chapter 8). Likewise, a large percentage of free migrants were prompted by poverty at home, though they journeyed freely enough to new lands. Almost 23 million people left Britain between 1815 and 1914, and although the United States absorbed the greater proportion (62 per cent), until around 1870 the Canadian colonies were the most popular destination. Those headed for the Empire went mostly to white settler lands, attracted in large part by the prospect of owning land often for the first time in their lives. In the twentieth century, settler options expanded as large tracts of southern and eastern Africa, notably in Rhodesia and Kenya, were given over to white migrants. In Kenya, there were two principal classes of migrant: poorer whites from South Africa, and an upper class, about 3,000 strong by 1905, from Britain. The less affluent were given parcels of cheap land, around 1,000 acres each, while the wealthy settled on vast estates in the highlands of central Kenya where their lifestyle became legendary for its decadence. By the mid-twentieth century changes were afoot, and many of the white migrants moving to Africa and other colonies were skilled workers and professionals rather than poorer unpropertied folk looking to start anew.

Outside the settler lands, British populations in the colonies tended to be small and often quite scattered. Colonial Office staff posted abroad never numbered much more than 6,000. The Colonial Office had one of the smallest staffs among major government departments. With numbers on the ground so thin, there was a good deal of room for improvisation, especially in minor matters that might not attract attention in London. In Africa imperial rule was for the most part a loose and highly decentralised business, depending very heavily on a localised prefectural administration. The two largest groups of Britons in the non-settler colonies were almost always civil servants and troops. There was also a smattering of medical workers, teachers, missionaries and business people. In most places, and as far as possible, British officials from an early date relied on manipulating local knowledge and systems of communication to their advantage, developing networks of informers as well as collaborators.

In the early years of colonialism, men had been prohibited or severely discouraged from bringing their families to live in the Empire; in India, for example, for most of the eighteenth century, the male to female ratio would easily have approached 50:1. By the mid-nineteenth century, changing attitudes meant that wives more frequently accompanied husbands appointed to colonial positions. Although children often spent the first few years of their lives in the family home, those who could afford the expense sent their children back to Britain at quite a young age.

Children were sent home for a host of reasons: to ensure they were schooled in the British way and to root out any local culture they might have picked up, but also because in many colonial environments they were vulnerable to diseases unknown or uncommon in the British Isles. Neither the cities nor the countryside of Britain were free of disease in the eighteenth and nineteenth centuries, and epidemics of many dangerous illnesses coursed through the country well into the twentieth century. There was, however, a deep fear that tropical colonies were especially unhealthy environments for whites, where they would be susceptible to fevers and melancholy, to lassitude and sickness. In places such as northern Australia and the West Indies, fears that manual labour for whites would prove physically impossible prompted the use first of slaves and later of indentured labourers. In the eighteenth century, parts of Africa were known as the 'white man's grave' since mortality rates among Europeans were so high, as was the death toll among troops sent to the Caribbean in the eighteenth century. This vulnerability was not, of course, limited to colonists, but the devastation wreaked on local populations was often deemed a regrettable part of bringing civilisation to savage lands, whereas white mortality was a danger to be guarded against. Colonial medical practice, not surprisingly, was more concerned with protecting white colonial populations than with the health needs of the colonised. It would be inaccurate to suggest, however, that indigenous peoples were clamouring for western health care. On the contrary, they were often suspicious and even resentful of it. Still, the discrepancy between access to medical care for colonist and colonised was always substantial, and is certainly suggestive of the relative value in which their lives were held. The exception is the active work of overseas missionaries. Medical care, especially in isolated rural communities, was among the most common of the activities which missionary groups abroad embraced.

The inequalities so typical of colonial health care are just one example of the gap that divided the colonist and the colonised in imperial settings. A civil servant or plantation overseer posted to a remote location might be the sole Briton for miles, but most colonists lived in or close by towns and cities where racially exclusive neighbourhoods sprang up to service them. The distance between colonists and locals was both spatial and social in most cases. Whites lived in enclaves where their social life revolved around a racially exclusive club, a Christian church and neighbours of mostly similar background, experience and attitude. Such neighbourhoods were less crowded than those where indigenous populations lived, and the architecture was intended to evoke Britain, adjusted for the local climate but often distinct from the usual building styles of the region. To this day one can visit typically Victorian churches in the cities of India, and grandly appointed hotels and official buildings in European style in many former colonies.

Frontier conditions for white settlers were considerably less comfortable. In British Columbia in the Canadian north-west, labourers lived in basic conditions in logging and mining camps. Less well-to-do settlers in Rhodesia and Kenya often lived isolated and harsh existences on rural farmsteads, though they would have employed black servants and farmhands from among the local population. Class played an important role in the colonies as it did in Britain itself, and working-class colonists (loggers in Canada, soldiers and sailors in Asia, farmhands in New Zealand, to name just a few) were separated from the wealthy whites of the colonies as firmly as were the locals. There was some slippage in the middle ranks, and those of humble background could sometimes rise further in a colonial than in a British setting. Yet colonial white society was governed by rigid social hierarchies even after some of these social barriers had begun to be relaxed in Britain. The humbler commercially employed whites in India, sneeringly known as 'box-wallahs' by those above them in rank and station, were as fully removed from the higher rungs of the colonial social world as were the vast majority of Indians. Poor whites, and especially vagrants and other considered unrespectable, were a source of concern for colonial authorities, seen as disrupting the racial hierarchies on which rule was based.

Though local labour was cheap and plentiful for white colonists in most locations, the social hierarchies of colonial life often increased expenses considerably. Many of those who went to the colonies did not possess a private income and thus had to work for a living; colonial pay was seldom generous. Doctors in the colonial medical service, for example, were jealous of their right to engage in fee-paying private practice alongside their government duties. On occasions when that right was under threat, they pointed to their low salaries. In government service, promotion could be slow and often depended upon death or retirement to free up a position. Since men were expected to provide for wives and children as well as to keep a retinue of household servants, keeping up appearances could severely tax a family's income, and many juggled constant debt in their effort to lead a 'proper' colonial life. Goods imported from Britain, which always remained fashionable among and sought-after by colonials, were costly but socially necessary expenses for middle-class colonists. In the earlier years of the Empire, all this acted as a discouragement to marriage.

That it was men who governed the Empire is a well-established fact. But how did they do it? Few colonies supported a large contingent of British troops. Some have argued that because the British governed in a less violent fashion than their European rivals, they had the consent of local populations for their presence.[5] This benign picture of a kindly Empire is hard to sustain, however. Britain had no compunction about resorting to violence when necessary. And violence in the Empire took a bewildering variety of forms. In the first half of the twentieth century, for example, a significant weapon of colonial governments against political dissidents was incarceration. In India, in Africa and elsewhere, nationalists were in and out of jail, locked up for delivering rousing anti-colonial speeches or for urging disobedience against the government. Isolated penal settlements designed to hold non-white convicts housed political prisoners as well as common criminals. Colonial courts of law frequently meted out light sentences for whites convicted of violence against local peoples, but harsh punishments awaited the non-white offender convicted of violence against a colonist. In India in 1883, huge controversy followed the introduction of the Ilbert Bill, a law that would have permitted Indian judges jurisdiction over British subjects in criminal cases. The uproar from whites living in India was such that considerable modifications were made to the law before it was passed; the original provisions were much watered down by a new clause permitting whites to demand a trial by jury in which at least half the jurors were either British or American.

Overt violence was not uncommon. Colonial governments were seldom shy about sending military detachments to persuade obstinate and nominally independent rulers to back down on issues deemed critical by the British. British authorities were reluctant to use their armed forces against white insurgents in the tumultuous years of decolonisation, but much less fussy about deploying troops and police in non-white arenas (as we shall see in Chapter 11). Violence, in short, though not always visible, was nonetheless a central feature of colonial rule.

Yet there was far more to the success of the Empire than the gun and the sword, or even the navy frigate. The age of empire was also an age of collecting and of classifying, an age in which the very boundaries of knowledge seemed almost limitless, and the Empire played a substantial role in the intellectual confidence that bolstered these typically western views. Britain in the eighteenth and nineteenth centuries became an avid exponent, as did Europe more generally, of what we might call the knowledge trade. Changes in western scientific practice led to a new emphasis – in botany, in anatomy, in geography – on classification and ordering. As we have seen, scientists collecting data and specimens became common on eighteenth-century expeditions. For many colonists the lands and the peoples of the Empire were also specimens to be listed, categorised and labelled. Just as the poor in Britain became objects of official scrutiny in the age of reform early in the nineteenth century, colonies and colonial subjects were counted, described and classified. Some were seen as warrior-like, others as passive. Some were regarded as cruel, and others indolent. All, of course, were regarded as inferior to their British masters.

By the late eighteenth century, western opinion took seriously a quasi-scientific hierarchy that argued for a racial ladder of development that placed white northern Europeans at the pinnacle of reason and progress. Ideas about the developmental difference between black and white people found an especially fertile medium of culture in the self-congratulatory and dominantly Christian environment of Victorian Britain, thoroughly convinced of its moral and political superiority over not just its own colonised peoples but over its local European rivals. Newly developing disciplines such as anthropology, and sciences like physiology, emphasised racial difference rather than similarity, and it was a simple step from marking difference to equating it with moral development. Even in books aimed at British children, this difference was underlined. Agnes Baden-Powell, sister to Robert of Boy Scout fame, informed her young audience in 1912 that in Britain's 'magnificent Empire ... The territories are there, but the people are only coming'.[6]

Opinions about the effects of western education and western rule on colonial people went back and forth over time, and different interest groups clearly had markedly different stakes in this debate. North American colonists feared that Native Americans were degraded by exposure to whites, picking up only their bad habits and eschewing their better values. They moved to isolate Amerindians from contact with the west in order to preserve their 'noble savagery'. In the early 1830s, Thomas Macaulay made an impassioned plea – which nonetheless attracted a good deal of scepticism – for educating elite Indians in English ways in order to produce brown-skinned replicas of the 'superior' English through proper education. Evangelicals fervently believed in the civilising propensities of Christianisation, while others thought the changes brought about by empire and proselytising could never be more than superficial. These debates were, of course, the flip side of the concerns about colonists corrupted by exposure to lesser societies. Here, the terms of the thinking were all about measuring how far towards a western norm the colonised could be brought, and out of these concerns grew the new social sciences of anthropology and sociology, firmly rooted in the assumptions of imperialism.

Both in Britain and in the colonies, there were groups who saw a troubling gap between these rather fervent expositions of the moral good of empire and actual practice. The Aborigines' Protection Society (APS), which Thomas Fowell Buxton had helped found in London in 1836, constantly lamented the degradations visited upon Aboriginal peoples by British colonists. They too saw the colonised as weaker and inferior, and it was in imperialism's failure to protect the weak that their protests against colonialism lay. The APS argued that 'in proportion to their inherent feebleness is the strength of their claim to the paternal care of the Government'.[7] It was the actions of those living in the colonies, they argued, which required control. Humanitarians mostly failed in their efforts to control the course of colonisation, but their voices form nonetheless an important part of the landscape of imperialism. Their work influenced the creation of offices of protection in many regions. India and the Straits Settlements established Protectors of Immigrant offices to oversee migration while in the Australian colonies Aboriginal Protectorates were common by the late nineteenth century. Their work was firmly in a paternalist tradition that assumed the vulnerability and weakness of their charges.

In reality, all such concerns were as much class-specific as they were palpably racial. The larger mass of the people, whether in Egypt or Singapore, India or the West Indies, were faceless, and in this reckoning, irrelevant or irredeemable. It was the elites within colonial societies to whom colonisers turned much of their attention, and who they worked hard both to control and to accommodate. Lord Lugard's policy of indirect rule in early twentieth-century Africa looked to tribal chiefs to maintain stability and keep the colonial state ticking. In British India, the landowning classes had been steadily strengthened since the days of the EIC as a bulwark against rebellion. The rulers of independent states in India were carefully monitored

Figure 7.5 'A Group of Hausa', 1901: a typical turn-of-the-century photograph. The one white figure stands out against a seemingly impersonal mass of Africans

by British officials. The Chinese merchant class in Hong Kong and in the Malay peninsula were accorded a limited measure of participation in local government to ensure their loyalty to the British state. When they did as they were told, all remained pleasant; if they took on their colonial masters, they were liable to lose the tenuous privileges they had acquired.

Technology was another growth area vital to Britain's conduct of the Empire, for new and deadly weapons such as the Gatling gun were hard to counter. Technology was not limited, however, to military purposes. The development of extensive railway systems allowed the swift movement of goods as well as of soldiers, and while the impetus for building the rail networks was as much military as it was economic, as a passenger and goods service it changed the face of the Empire profoundly. In India, some 24,000 miles of track had been laid by the end of the nineteenth century; in British East Africa almost 600 miles of track. The huge Trans-Pacific Canadian railway was completed in 1885.

The development of telegraphy was another major factor in colonial success. Wars against the Ashanti in Africa (1873–4) and at Perak in 1875 were directed in large part by the telegraph. By the 1870s, the telegraph had become the standard mode of communication between the Colonial and India Offices in London and far-away governors; secret codes were developed for transmitting sensitive materials, and quicker decisions than had previously been possible became standard. Throughout the Empire, the application and introduction of western technology was always a piecemeal affair, designed more to serve the colonial state than those it colonised, despite the persistent rhetoric of munificence. Recall, for example, how eighteenth-century sugar production was strictly divided between the West Indies and Britain, the bulk of the refinement done after shipping to the United Kingdom. The colonies were restricted, in this case by mercantilist considerations, as to what they could undertake without British consent. The same was true in the Indian textile trade, for the British state would not countenance serious colonial competition with the fragile but important textile industries in Britain. The needs of the colonised remained in all such instances subservient to those of Britain, at the centre of the Empire.

Science, technology and medicine were routinely depicted as the beneficent bringers of modernity and prosperity to the colonies. They were also seen as above the fray of politics, as neutral ideals with invariably positive results. In 1924, at the newly built Wembley Stadium in northwest London, a huge British Empire Exhibition celebrated the enterprises of empire. A two-roomed 'pure science' display at the exhibition boasted of the benefits that western science and medicine offered Britain's Empire. The various items on display illustrated how medical and scientific knowledge was changing the face of colonies, making them healthier and more productive environments. The political message was not hard to read in this celebration of a technology-driven western model of development.

Policing was another important facet of colonial rule, although numbers were often quite small especially beyond urban areas. Police forces in the colonies tended to be more military in character than those in the British Isles. Not insignificantly, colonial policing was often modelled on the Royal Irish Constabulary, a body created specifically to quell nationalist unrest in Ireland. Unlike British constables, colonial police officers carried guns and were organised into military garrisons. There were two kinds of colonial police: a higher paid and more senior white rank and a 'native' force under their command. In many colonies beyond the white settler domains, it became standard practice to import police from other parts of the Empire. By the mid-nineteenth century Sikhs from British India were commonly employed as police officers in Hong Kong, Singapore and Perak. Barbadians were brought into the Trinidadian police force. As outsiders to the communities they policed, they were thought to be more intimidating to the local population and less corruptible. In times of crisis the colonial police forces, with their quasi-military background, were liable to be called upon as part of the defence services alongside the full military. This was common in India and during the Kenyan Emergency in the 1950s as well as in the treaty port of Shanghai during the 1930s. In the 1950s, especially in Africa, police numbers increased as the likelihood of protest escalated.

The colonial military, like colonial police forces, was frequently divided along racial lines. Senior military ranks were reserved for whites, although the larger proportion of white military men in the colonies were working class. A spate of substantial British military reforms in the 1870s allowed men to sign up for shorter periods of service, making military service a more practical and attractive option. In a colonial posting, a working-class recruit from Britain was amazed to find himself no longer at the bottom of the social pecking order. Still subject to military discipline, he could nonetheless lord it over native men who did his bidding. He might also feel quite wealthy for he was likely stationed somewhere where even meagre military pay went a long way.

The soldier and the sailor were regarded by many as the ultimate line of defence, the bulwark against colonial insurrection. Year after year, when the military budget was debated in parliament, this was the rationale offered to those who protested the high cost of defence. In 1867, the Indian commander-in-chief, W. R. Mansfield, described the British troops in India as the Empire's 'bullion deposit', vital for security and continued colonisation.[8]

Figure 7.6 Colonial troops of the British Empire in England for the Diamond Jubilee celebrations of Queen Victoria, 1897. In keeping with the Jubilee themes of unity and solidarity, soldiers from very different British colonies were carefully staged together to create an idealised view of a co-operative Empire

Source: Hulton Archive/Getty Images

The soldier, at least, was in the field unlike the staff of the Colonial Office, about whom there was often a great deal of resentment. Those living in the colonies regarded as unwarranted and certainly unwanted any interference from the imperial centre. It was common for colonists to argue that London officials could not properly appreciate local conditions and that they should therefore cede decision-making to those who lived and worked in the colonies. Colonists argued that officials stationed in Britain could not begin to understand local peoples as well as they, the colonists, could from years of observation and interaction. The Colonial Office returned the compliment, frequently scornful of the work done by colonial officials on the ground. After a series of reforms in the 1850s and 1870s, jobs in the British civil service became competitive, based in large part on examination scores but in the colonial service family ties and personal connections still aided recruitment. Clearly, those in the colonies and those at Whitehall saw expertise and qualification for the job in profoundly different ways. The brief tenures of most colonial governors and colonial secretaries – the most senior of the Colonial Office positions – fuelled all of these mutual suspicions. It was rare for a secretary of state for the colonies to serve more than a two-year term, and colonial governors seldom stayed more than six years in any one colony, although they often moved from colony to colony in the course of their careers. During Joseph Chamberlain's unusually long tenure as colonial secretary (1895–1903), selected Colonial Office staff were seconded to a colonial setting for a year to learn first-hand about the colony and about the conditions of work there. Officials from the colonies were simultaneously sent to London to fill the positions left vacant. The principle was that each would learn to appreciate the other's work and responsibilities. Despite Chamberlain's best efforts, the constant tension, not only between those with local experience and those without, but between the potential for continuity and the need to respond to changing politics in Westminster, made imperial governance a sometimes unwieldy and unpredictable business. While there were over-arching rhetorics (and sometimes even principles), much of what happened in the Empire was a pragmatic response to current conditions. When Sir Augustus Hemming, head of the West African department of the Colonial Office, asked permission for an official visit to the Gold Coast the request, he recalls, was 'refused on the ground that there appeared to be no necessity for the visit'.[9]

A substantial and important group of Britons living and working in the Empire was the missionary contingent; by the end of the nineteenth century there were some 10,000 British missionaries dotted across the globe. It was in the late eighteenth century that British missionary work in the Empire began to grow in earnest. Each of the major Christian denominations in Britain founded missionary societies in the 1790s. The missionary enterprise was, however, neither exclusively nor originally aimed at the colonised. In the early North American colonies, missions worked largely among the settler populations. It was in his missionary work in the 1730s in colonial

Georgia, North America, that John Wesley garnered the ideas that would lead to one of the world's most successful branches of Christianity, Methodism. In British Canada, missionaries were mostly concerned with the wanton behaviour of the miners, prospectors, loggers and trappers who had emigrated from Britain and who lived – and drank – hard in frontier communities. Even when attending to colonial populations, missionary work began with the intent of converting ruling groups, and not the lowly. The emphasis on non-settler colonies came, thus, quite late in missionary history, burgeoning towards the end of the eighteenth century and dominating missionary activity thereafter.

In these early years, colonial officials in both London and the colonies were often suspicious of the missionaries, who had to fight for permission to work in the colonies. They often faced suspicion and resentment not only from those they sought to convert, but also from colonial officials, for the missionaries were frequently critical of colonial practice and expert at making public their unflattering opinions of colonial governments. Missionaries had been in the forefront of anti-slavery protests and were vocal about what they saw as colonial exploitation of indigenous peoples. In the nineteenth century, missionaries spread across the colonial globe and could be found in the West Indies and the Pacific, in Africa and in India, in South-East Asia and the Chinese treaty ports and in North America. Over time, governments and missionaries came closer together, but missionaries nonetheless often had a quite complex role in the colonial world, promoting western values through conversion, but often critical of imperial policy and practice. Colonial governments often shared information about the whereabouts, travel and activities of missionary activists to minimise any political damage that might ensue from their work.

Yet at the same time securing a Christian foothold was often a necessity from the point of view of administrators. The spread of Islam in Africa was unwelcome to the British for Islamic states were frequently hostile to colonial rule and spawned nationalist protests. Some saw the Mahdist revolt in the Sudan in the 1880s as signalling an Islamic resurgence, which would undermine British influence throughout the region. Bishoprics sprang up in colonial cities from the 1840s to formalise the Anglican establishment.

Missionaries, perhaps more than any other class of colonisers, lived and worked among local peoples, building schools, hospitals and shelters, all designed to bring the gospel of Christianity to Britain's colonial subjects. Yet despite their distance from the state, and despite the disapproval and hostility they often experienced from the colonial bureaucracy, missionaries were nonetheless a part of imperial conquest for they mostly saw the populations among whom they worked as children in need of saving from their own ignorance and moral poverty. This is not to suggest that missionaries could not make a material difference to the lives of their charges. As mentioned earlier, they were often the only conduit for western health care and for education in remote areas, and mission schools improved literacy rates in many places. But the price was, in some ways, steep for embracing Christianity to the full meant adopting a new way of life. Converts were often given 'Christian' names to emphasise their social and cultural distance from the unconverted. They were often unable to maintain close links with their families and communities, and missionary disapproval of local customs often stood in the way of converts making good marriages or partnerships in their own communities. It was not imperialism as a philosophy that missionaries criticised; their disapproval was reserved for imperial politics that to them did nothing to consolidate and extend Christianity into non-Christian environments.

The missionary success rate, overall, was spotty. Many converts did not sustain the change long term, not least because missionary practice, despite a rhetoric of equality, could be rigid, hierarchical and unforgiving. Equality remained more a theological principle in the missionary world than a social practice. There was also a very significant trend among converts in adapting Christianity to a variety of colonial customs and traditions, an unexpected and, to the missionaries, mostly unwelcome outgrowth of their efforts (as we shall see in Chapter 8).

Unflattering portraits of missionaries dot the pages of Victorian novels: the unbending St John Rivers in Charlotte Brontë's *Jane Eyre* and Charles Dickens' redoubtable Mrs Jellyby who ignores her grimy and hungry children in her zeal to collect tracts and bibles for the 'savages' abroad. Imperial themes, characters and backgrounds were common, not only in nineteenth-century literature and art but in earlier periods too. Satirical cartoons and popular comedic dramas in the late eighteenth century constantly poked fun at *ingénues* made wealthy by the Empire and at the antics of those who desired to part them from their new-found wealth. By the late 1800s satire, as well as nineteenth-century realist novels, yielded in popularity to colonial romancing and the Empire was transformed into a place of adventure and secrecy, of bravery and individualism. Henry Morton Stanley's *In Darkest Africa* was an instant bestseller when it appeared in 1890. This new genre of what was effectively a literary and visual form of imperial propaganda coincided with political efforts to drum up imperial support and interest in the British population at large. The introduction early in the twentieth century of Empire Day (24 May) as a celebration, the increasingly colourful pageantry in Britain around Empire (as well as in the Empire itself) and the concerted effort to turn the school curriculum into an education for imperial longevity all mark a new centrality for the Empire around the start of the twentieth century. Shifts such as these are useful reminders of the way in which the Empire had different meanings in different eras, with distinctive and time-sensitive political resonances that cannot be lumped under a single heading. And just as ruling a colony was nuanced by time and place and form, so too were the reactions, responses and experiences of those who lived under British imperial rule. It is to their concerns and interests that we next turn.

Notes

1 J. Hight, *The English as a Colonising Nation* (Christchurch, Wellington and Dunedin: Whitcombe and Tombs [1903]), pp. 19, 20; J. H. Parry, *Trade and Dominion: The European Overseas Empires in the Eighteenth Century* (New York: Praeger, 1971), p. 40, quoting Lepel Griffin.

2 Alfred Milner, *Imperial Unity: Two Speeches delivered at Manchester (December 14, 1906) and Wolverhampton (December 17, 1906)* (London: National Review Office, 1907), p. 18.

3 Quoted in John Flint, *Cecil Rhodes* (London: Hutchinson, 1976), pp. 248–9. The grammatical omissions are in the original.

4 John Strachey, *India: Its Administration and Progress* (London: Macmillan, 1903), p. 432.

5 A good example of this genre is Niall Ferguson's *Empire: The Rise and Demise of the British World Order and the Lessons for Global Power* (New York: Basic Books, 2003). David Gilmour's *The British in India: Three Centuries of Ambition and Experience* (London: Allen Lane, 2018) does much the same for the British in India.

6 Agnes Baden-Powell, *The Handbook for Girl Guides, or How Girls Can Help Build the Empire* (London: Thomas Nelson & Sons, 1912), p. 405.

7 *The Colonial Intelligencer; or Aborigines' Friend*, New Series, vol. II, no. XXIV (April 1850), p. 408.

8 W. R. Mansfield to John Lawrence, 21 January 1867, British Library, India Office Private Papers, Mss. Eur. F.90/30, no. 91.

9 Augustus W. L. Hemming, 'The Colonial Office and the Crown Colonies', *The Empire Review* 11, no. 66 (July 1906), p. 504.

Further reading

In *Colonizing Nature: The Tropics in British Arts and Letters, 1760–1820* (Philadelphia, PA: University of Pennsylvania Press, 2005) Beth Fowkes Tobin demonstrates not just the interest generated by colonial expansion but the kinds of celebratory superiorities which accompanied the growing expansion of the Empire. V. G. Kiernan's now classic study, *The Lords of Human Kind: European Attitudes to the Outside World in the Imperial Age* (Harmondsworth: Penguin Books, 1972) details the attitudes of colonisers towards those they colonised, while in *Racism and Empire: White Settlers and Colored Immigrants in the British Self-governing Colonies, 1830–1910* (Ithaca, NY: Cornell University Press, 1976), Robert A. Huttenback reveals the racist attitudes that shaped the forms of settler colonialism in its most expansive era. In *Human Encumbrances: Political Violence and the Great Irish Famine* (Notre Dame, IN: Notre Dame University Press, 2011), David P. Nally shows how colonial rulership made Ireland more vulnerable to famine. Aidan Forth follows the logic of how colonial crises such as famine and disease led to what he dubs an 'empire of camps' and a culture of detention: *Barbed-Wire Imperialism: Britain's Empire of Camps, 1876–1903* (Berkeley, CA: University of California Press, 2017).

There is much good work on missionaries and the Empire including Hilary M. Carey's wide-ranging study, *God's Empire: Religion and Colonialism in the British World, c.1801–1908* (Cambridge: Cambridge University Press, 2011). *Missionary Writing and Empire, 1800–1860* by Anna Johnston (Cambridge: Cambridge University Press, 2003), Jeffrey Cox, *Imperial Fault Lines: Christianity and Colonial Power in India, 1818–1940* (Stanford, CA: Stanford University Press, 2002) and Andrew Porter's *Religion versus Empire? British Protestant Missionaries and Overseas Expansion, 1700–1914* (Manchester: Manchester University Press, 2004) all offer fresh perspectives on the missionary mind. A useful collection of essays on missionaries is *Missions and Empire* (Norman Etherington (ed.), Oxford: Oxford University Press, 2005). Consult Elizabeth Prevost's *The Communion of Women: Missions and Gender in Colonial Africa and the British Metropole* (Oxford: Oxford University Press, 2010) and Emily Manktelow's *Missionary Families: Race, Gender and Generation on the Spiritual Frontier* (Manchester: Manchester University Press, 2013) for British women missionaries.

Marjory Harper and Stephen Constantine's *Migration and Empire* (Oxford: Oxford University Press, 2010) is a comprehensive overview of colonial migration. Adele Perry's *On the Edge of Empire: Gender, Race, and the Making of British Columbia, 1849–1871* (Toronto: University of Toronto Press, 2001) wonderfully evokes the rough-and-tumble nature of developing white settler colonialism and the anxieties it produced. Harald Fischer-Tiné, *Low and Licentious Europeans: Race, Class and 'White Subalternity' in Colonial India* (New Delhi: Blackswan, 2009) confronts the issue of poor whites living in the colonies. Brian L. Blakeley's institutional history, *The Colonial Office, 1868–1892*, explains the administrative complexities of imperial government in Britain (Durham, NC: Duke University Press, 1972). Ronald Robinson and John Gallagher's *Africa and the Victorians: The Official Mind of Imperialism* (2nd edn, London: Macmillan, 1981) likewise emphasises those who ran the government offices responsible for the Empire. C. A. Bayly's study of intelligence networks in India reveals the workings of a complex imperial bureaucracy: *Empire and Information: Intelligence Gathering and Social Communication in India, 1780–1870* (Cambridge: Cambridge University Press, 1996).

8   Being ruled

Freedom has always been a cherished idea within British politics and culture, and the vision of Britain as a nation devoted to, and a champion of, freedom has a long history. In the years of imperialism, the concept of civilisation was often yoked to that of freedom, as colonising Britons imagined themselves preparing colonial subjects for their eventual freedom. The sentiment that colonial peoples required careful nurturing and proper education such that they might one day enjoy the benefits of freedom was a commonplace of journalists, politicians, explorers and travellers, and a good portion of Britons overall (as shown in Chapter 7). The Central Office of Information, created in 1946, issued books of photo cards on all aspects of British life and politics. The introduction to their 1948 publication, *Colonial Empire: Introducing the Colonies*, defined the colonies as 'those units of the Commonwealth which still need guidance and help from colonial Britain'.[1] Central to that argument was that freedom was some distance off, a future dream towards which colonial peoples might aspire and towards which they were expected to work. It was an elaborate justification not only of colonial rule but of colonial unfreedom, and its effect on all aspects of the existence of those who lived under colonial rule was huge. What, then, did it mean to live as a subject of the British Empire? Were the daily lives of Malays, Andamanese, Tamils, Zulus or Creoles directly affected by a distant if powerful country that claimed so much power over them? While the consequences and experience of people in different places, and of different ranks, were rarely the same, the effects of imperial rule were nonetheless potent, affecting every aspect of people's lives, livelihoods and relationships. Where one might live, job opportunities, property ownership, marriage laws, religious practice, education, entertainment: all these and more were affected by the presence and impact of colonialism.

In political terms, the colonised experienced radically different forms of government from those which would emerge in Britain during the era of colonial expansion. By the late 1920s all adults in Britain were entitled to a vote in national as well as local elections, while Crown Colony and Protectorate administrations were appointed from the top. The key roles in government were held by Britons, not local peoples, a pattern repeated in other official arenas such as the courtroom and among the police. This top-down and undemocratic rule played a large part in fuelling anti-colonial nationalist movements across the Empire.

As noted earlier, in the white settler colonies the principle of responsible self-government had given settler men over the age of 21, and who owned property, the right to vote for legislative assemblies. Other than in New Zealand and at the Cape, indigenous non-settler locals were denied these rights of political participation, their lives being much closer to that of colonial subjects in the Crown Colonies and Protectorates. In New Zealand, four seats in the legislative council were reserved for Māori from the 1860s. At the Cape the 1910 Act of Union reconfirmed the vote for male Africans and Cape Coloureds who met property and education qualifications; Africans lost even that right in 1936. For a brief period from the mid-1880s, Canadian natives living east of the Great Lakes were entitled to vote; that right, too, was withdrawn in 1898. The pattern for indigenous peoples was routinely one of loss rather than gain.

In Jamaica, as we have seen, governance went in a reverse direction from local representation and decision-making to dependent status. Though the shift to non-elective government came only after the 1865 rebellion at Morant Bay, Jamaican politics had been significantly affected by the abolition of slavery. As early as 1839, soon after abolition, parliament had considered suspending the Jamaican constitution for five years. The ensuing controversy forced the resignation of the prime minister, Lord Melbourne, and the plan was abandoned. Though it would be more than two decades before Jamaica lost its political independence, parliament's earlier consideration of the change illuminates how differing colonial situations could shape the debate over political representation, and how far Britain's needs rather than those of the colony dictated such decisions.

Colonial policy generally sought a degree of collaboration with those who the British regarded as the local elites (as suggested in Chapter 7). This tactic helped preserve conservative traditions as these elites recognised that their invitation to a limited form of power-sharing depended on their acceptance of Britain's ultimate power. Both Britons and colonial elites manoeuvred such liaisons to maximise their own power. In India princes who, in the days of the EIC, had been criticised as wilful, spoiled and tyrannical metamorphosed under direct rule to become close associates of the British Indian authorities. Co-operation with the British ensured a local prince's power. The same was so in twentieth-century Africa where the growing use of indirect rule looked to local chiefs and rulers to do much of Britain's work for it. The effect was often to make local rulers more responsive to the needs of the colonial government than to their own people, especially since the British rewarded such alliances with land and wealth as well as power. The British also cultivated wealthy merchants and traders. In the Malay peninsula Chinese businessmen enjoyed the ear of colonial officials, a favouritism much resented by indigenous locals and by poor Chinese. These favoured elites were anxious to distinguish themselves from their poorer compatriots whose labour built such economically successful cities as Singapore.

Politics aside, the economic needs of colonialism led to huge changes in landscape, land use and building. The urbanisation that had so drastically and yet so unequally altered the British Isles in the late eighteenth and early nineteenth centuries had similarly striking consequences in the colonies. Port cities became critical for the Empire, for through them people, manufactures and material were shipped to and fro. As in Britain, cities, whether inland or on the coast, offered new job opportunities and in the nineteenth and twentieth centuries mass urban migration was commonplace, producing new classes and communities, new styles of buildings and a more urgent attention to questions of sanitation and public safety. Kingston on the south-east coast of Jamaica was, in the eighteenth century, an affluent and bustling city occupied mostly by white planters and merchants and their retinues. After the abolition of slavery, and as former slaves moved there in search of work, the white population diminished dramatically and Kingston became a black and a much poorer city. In South Africa it was rich veins of gold and diamonds that prompted the founding of the cities of Kimberley and Johannesburg in the nineteenth century. The commercial importance of these areas led to the transformation of ragged, poverty-inflicted mining camps into major metropolitan areas in just a few decades. When Māori began to move in significant numbers to New Zealand's cities in the second half of the twentieth century they tended to be crowded into poorer, less attractive neighbourhoods that rapidly became associated with danger, squalor and poverty.

Colonial cities strictly segregated 'native' and 'European' residential areas. India's urban centres had long had separate 'white' towns and 'black' towns. Delhi, which displaced Calcutta as British India's capital in 1911, is a good example of how urban development mirrored the broad inequalities of colonialism. Old Delhi, which pre-dated British rule considerably, was 'local' territory. The buildings reflected Asian living styles in which shared dwelling space was common, and with no strict divisions between residential and commercial usage. By contrast New Delhi, designed by British architects Edwin Lutyens and Herbert Baker in the early twentieth century, was an area where fenced-off single-family bungalows, wide streets and a strict division of functions gave the city a wholly different feel than the crowded lanes of the old city. Increasingly, the areas where local people lived came to be seen by colonial officials as spaces of criminality, disease and political dissent. In many colonies, urban curfews restricted the movement of locals after dark, and those found in European areas of the city were subject to challenge and surveillance. In Victoria in western Canada, for example, from the 1860s Aboriginal Canadians were forbidden access to the city at night.

Curfews were just one way in which the changes wrought by a colonial presence constrained the mobility of colonial subjects. In Canada and in Australia especially, Aboriginal peoples were increasingly encouraged, if not forced, to live on reservations. Aboriginal Protection Ordinances in the

Australian colonies gave the office of the Protector of Aborigines widespread powers to dictate the contours of Aboriginal lives. Throughout southern Africa, black Africans were required to register with local authorities and to carry identification certificates; pass laws in many colonies allowed the prosecution of those found away from their locale without an employer's permission. In East and South Africa, black Africans were crowded into rural reserves. In Indian military towns (cantonments), Indian women were often banned from work that brought them into contact with soldiers, for fear that they would prostitute themselves and disease the soldiers. The rules, which assumed widespread prostitution among Indian women, narrowed both women's freedom of movement and the range of jobs open to them.

Wandering and nomadic peoples became a particular target of colonial scrutiny. In the early years of imperial rule, mobile peoples had served an enormously important purpose in helping the British understand and control unfamiliar terrain. Whether it was learning how to trap animals for their pelts, or to find waterholes in the parched Australian desert, indigenous peoples had been invaluable guides to the local terrain in the eighteenth century. In later years, however, whether through isolation on reservations or through criminal legislation, the lifestyles of nomadic peoples came under fire. From the 1820s onwards, governments in India moved increasingly against nomadic groups. Drastic 'criminal tribes' legislation in the 1830s sought to domesticate and settle them, mostly on land unappealing to white settlers. Similar policies affected nomadic peoples in Malaya and Sarawak. They were regarded as lacking proper systems of rule or land usage, a judgement used to justify their exclusion from lands they had traditionally exploited, and to deny them any prospect of ownership of such lands.

These distinctive and often impoverishing changes in land use and landscape were intimately linked to massive upheavals in the pattern, as well as the availability, of employment. Menial household work that in Britain was done largely by women was, in the subject colonies, frequently dominated by local men, a peculiarity suggestive of the ways in which race and gender were entangled in hierarchical social structures. Cooks, servants and cleaners (all of whom in Britain would have been overwhelmingly female) were – in India, in the African colonies, in the Straits Settlements, for example – mostly indigenous men. The use of colonised men in household jobs was a highly visible means to demonstrate the powerlessness of subject men. Using men as servants in kitchens and in laundries embodied in daily life and routine the power of British colonialism. This did not mean that there were no jobs for colonised women, nor that labour opportunities did not remain gendered. On the contrary, the sexual division of labour, if differently applied, was critical in colonial settings: women's sexual labour – as prostitutes as well as bearers of children – had been fundamental to successful colonisation since the days of slavery. Manufacturing and building work in the colonies often employed women as well as men, even as women in Britain were increasingly pushed out of such jobs. There was a far larger female manual labour force in the colonies than would have been acceptable in Britain by the nineteenth century.

Urbanisation and the building of railways in Asia and Africa produced work opportunities for indigenous men, as did the growth of large-scale agriculture, the exploitation of mineral resources (diamonds in South Africa, a variety of gemstones in Ceylon, copper, gold and tin in Australia) and the development of manufacturing. Their wages were far lower than those of white workers, and they were frequently assigned to the nastiest and the most dangerous of the jobs available. Ports and shipping also created jobs, and much of this new work profoundly altered existing social structures by housing workers in male-only barracks close to their work and away from their kin. Railway work also forced men to live apart from their families for long periods, as they moved across a country laying track.

In British colonies, and especially in British Africa, master and servant legislation governed relations between white employers and their colonised employees long after the equivalent British legislation had been abandoned in 1875. These laws favoured employer over employee, on the grounds that Africans, unused to modern labour discipline, needed greater surveillance than British workers. Leaving a job 'without lawful cause', drunkenness, careless work or insulting a master could all lead to formal prosecution, with penalties ranging from the withdrawal of wages to imprisonment. In Kenya, registration laws formalised the prosecution of desertion from a job, since the identity certificate adult men were required to carry noted their current employment alongside name, fingerprint, ethnic group and even past employment details. Employers had to notify the police that they were letting a worker go before he could be hired elsewhere. Without this formality, men could be prosecuted for deserting their jobs. The key principle of master and servant legislation was a breathtakingly unequal one in which employers were liable merely to civil action, while their workers faced criminal prosecution. Labourers frequently ignored or challenged such laws, though they could pay dearly for such infringements. Passes and identity certificates were illegally altered, were shared to help others get around or find work and, of course, were constantly lost.

Colonial employers in Africa consistently used floggings and beatings to discipline their workforce. Courts could also impose whippings, a practice that declined in East Africa only in the 1940s. It was not uncommon for serious injuries to result from the beatings inflicted by employers, which helps explain the high rate of desertion. When their native workers died from such assaults, colonial employers might occasionally find themselves arraigned in court. It was rare, however, that they would be found guilty for the judge, the lawyers and the juries in such colonies were their peers and reluctant to punish or harm their own. The Colonial Office in Britain was not happy with the reports of cavalier brutality that every so often reached them. On occasion a governor or an official in London would intervene, as happened in Burma in 1899 when soldiers from the West Kent Regiment gang-raped a local woman, Ma Gun, on Easter Sunday. The viceroy of India, Lord Curzon, stepped in when it became clear that the colonial courts were disinclined to act. On his orders, the entire regiment was transferred to Aden, widely regarded as among the most unpleasant of colonial postings. Though the incident was condemned in parliament, Curzon faced hostility from the Foreign Office for his intervention.

Alongside direct physical violence, colonial peoples endured poor working conditions in the diamond and gold mines of southern Africa as well as in the coalfields of India. The work done by local men was enormously dangerous as well as poorly remunerated. Mining companies, many of which in the early years of the trade were small and lacked much start-up capital, were notorious for their lack of attention to safety measures. Accidents and fatalities were common, and miners risked a host of work-related respiratory and other diseases. These were risks they shared with miners in Britain, but colonial mine workers, unlike their British counterparts, lived in crowded compounds with inadequate sanitation, further exposing them to disease and disharmony as well as separating them for long periods from family and friends. While miners in Britain were among the most successful groups of workers forming unions, that option was not available to their colonial counterparts.

In Dominion colonies, mining was a very different business. It was still a dangerous as well as an all-male work area, but at the silver mines at Broken Hill on the New South Wales/South Australia border and in the copper mines of South Australia, labour was white and was often in the vanguard of unionisation, which forced better working conditions as well as higher wages. White workers mostly refused to work alongside indigenous people in settler colonies, so the range of jobs was often greater for local peoples in areas of sparse white settlement. Their situation was always tenuous and as white populations grew, all but the most arduous and unpopular of jobs were closed to the indigenous population.

In India, textile manufacturing attracted migrants from rural areas to work in factories. Owners and managers exploited existing divisions of language and religion to keep the workforce from uniting, often adding to the tensions that would spill over into communal (religious) violence in British India. Conditions were routinely poor and dangerous, and wages low. While master and servant legislation in Africa claimed that colonial workers needed to be trained into modern work habits and discipline, the factories in India instead played up what were seen as traditional Indian relations based on reverence for family authority (*ma-bapp*). Workers were expected to revere the manager as an authority figure who would have the unit's best interests in mind. It was a system which was often violently interrupted by workers' frustrations at the inequalities it attempted to obliterate.

Work experience and opportunity in the colonies also owed much to changing patterns of land ownership and land usage. Plantations in Ireland, the West Indies and colonial North America had been among the earliest large-scale reallocations and apportionings of land affecting work in immediate and significant ways. Intensive sugar cultivation radically altered the countryside of many Caribbean islands over the course of the eighteenth century. The Highland clearances in Scotland in the mid-eighteenth century, and the changing patterns of agricultural taxation in India in the same period, proved disastrous for the majority, for the shift to an English model of single (or corporate) ownership robbed small cultivators of a stake in the land, reducing them to tenants with very few rights. Demanding levels of taxation, even in years of crop failure and famine, denuded the assets of much of rural British India, forcing people to migrate in search of work or face starvation, as thousands did in famine years. In 1912, peasant landholders in parts of Malaya were prohibited from growing rubber for sale for fear they would undercut the larger corporations. In Kenya, the railway cut deep through the territory traditionally farmed by the Kikuyu people, adversely affecting their ability to earn a living from the land, yet the Uganda–Kenya railway line was routinely heralded as a modern benefit bringing wealth and efficiency to East Africa. The Kikuyu lost more than 60,000 acres of fertile land to white settlers, further impoverishing them and laying the groundwork for stiff anti-colonial resistance in the twentieth century. Since settler colonialism was primarily driven by export, its encroachment on indigenous lands was often formidable.

In Egypt, the consolidation of land ownership took its toll on an agrarian population unable to compete with large landowners. The emphasis on producing crops for the British market forced many small proprietors to sell their land, but rather than profiting from these sales, spiralling land costs impoverished many since renting land also became prohibitively expensive. Many were forced into low-wage labour in the cotton fields in the late nineteenth century. Large-scale cotton growing required constant irrigation of the land, resulting in a significant increase in the water-borne parasites that caused the blinding affliction, schistosomiasis (also known as bilharzia). Those who worked in the fields were the most vulnerable to diseases, produced in large part by changes in the environment related to economic demand. Irrigation schemes throughout the colonies, if unintentionally, created an easy environment for the spread of malaria, by providing good breeding grounds for its carrier, the *anopheles* mosquito.

In Australia, too, the landscape was profoundly altered by the coming of colonialism, changes that sorely reduced the ability of Aboriginal peoples to survive in the outback. The introduction of sharp-hoofed animals to the continent had an adverse impact on the soil, native plants were crowded out by English flora and many local animals were hunted, sometimes to extinction, regarded as pests to settled agriculture. The creation of pasturelands for cattle and sheep created fire and flood hazards as well as soil erosion. Aboriginal responses were increasingly desperate, and increasingly subject to severe punishment, but the ability of the indigenous people to live off the land was fast vanishing in the wake of a settlement not of their choosing.

As in India and in Egypt, it was colonists' idea of proper land management and ownership that prevailed in the Australian colonies. It would be 1889 before *terra nullius* (discussed in Chapter 4) was fully confirmed in law, but long before then it had resulted in a denial of Aboriginal rights to land. Aboriginal settlements and sacred spaces could be erased without obligation or repayment, destroying lives and cultures at a stroke. Indigenous Canadians also saw their traditional lands appropriated without consideration. White settlement pushed local peoples further and further to the margins. By 1911, indigenous Canadians made up less than 1 per cent of Canada's total population, down from about one-fifth only a century earlier. The disappearance of the buffalo from over-hunting affected the provision of food, clothing and transport. In Southern Rhodesia, as late as 1937, Africans without work on white-owned lands were required to move to reservations where overcrowding and insanitary facilities made life miserable, uncomfortable and often short-lived. In some areas indigenous farmers were prohibited from growing certain crops to prevent competition with settler farmers.

In both settler and dependent colonies the best and most attractive land was reserved either for European use or concentrated in the hands of the local elite whose profits and wealth depended on their co-operation with colonial demands. It was not only land devoted to commercial, agricultural and industrial use that was cordoned off in this way. Just as the European areas of Indian towns and cities boasted wider streets and larger dwellings, the new hill stations in India created a series of exclusive resorts where whites could escape the ferocious summer heat of the plains. Indians in hill stations meanwhile were employees, never vacationers. These 'little Englands' in the hills became the model for similar resorts in other tropical areas, and it was no accident that the highest portion of Hong Kong island, The Peak, was also the colony's most exclusive address. Likewise, the fertile, cool, hilly region of central Kenya, known as the White Highlands, was an exclusively white enclave, its name reflecting its racial demography as well as its geography.

Colonial populations in the earlier eras of colonialism had often turned colonial commerce to advantage. In West Africa, in New Zealand and in North America, trade between locals and colonials by no means always disadvantaged the non-Europeans, and European objects were often put to uses unforeseen by traders. Items considered utilitarian by western traders were folded into local religious rites or became fashion statements. Although British commentators liked to write off colonial trading transactions as a case of fobbing off 'primitives' with cheap baubles, colonised peoples often turned trade to their advantage and profited by it. Such opportunities visibly diminished as the large-scale economics of capitalist Europe took off across the imperial world. Mass production, manufacture and a growing attention to what were seen as universally applicable economic laws disadvantaged those who lived in non-capitalist economic systems.

These kinds of inequalities produced a significant movement of labour not just within colonies, but across them too. Penal transportation saw convicts moved forcibly across the globe, and slavery shifted huge numbers of workers. As those forms of labour waned, indenture was revitalised. In the nineteenth century plantation owners sought alternative sources of labour to replace their freed slaves, and looked not to Britain, but to the Empire. Half or more of those who migrated under indenture in the seventeenth and eighteenth centuries were European in origin, but from the 1830s indentured labour was overwhelmingly Asian. Between 1879 and 1920, some 60,000 South Asians worked under indenture in Fiji, while indentured Fijians were moving to Queensland and other Pacific destinations. By 1838 there were around 25,000 indentured South Asians working on the sugar plantations of Mauritius. Thirty thousand or so Indian workers built Kenya's railways in the late 1890s, over a third of whom were killed or seriously injured in the process. Altogether more than a million South Asians worked under indenture in the British Empire. Their numbers forced the Indian government to get involved: in 1871, the government licensed recruiters and instituted medical examinations and an emigrant protectorate office. Determined recruiters shipped their human cargo out of French ports to skirt the new rules, undermining the effectiveness of these reforms.

Though Indians formed the bulk of the colonial indentured workforce in the nineteenth century, there were many Chinese, Pacific Islander and Sierra Leonian labourers. Some 18,000 indentured Chinese mined phosphate, gold and copper and worked on sugar plantations in the Pacific between the mid-1850s and the mid-1880s, and a similar number arrived in the West Indies after abolition. After the South African War, Chinese indentured labour was common for a brief period at the Transvaal gold mines. Their presence was hugely controversial and anti-slavery activists accused the government of revitalising slavery, while white settlers in the colony opposed their presence, anxious to keep non-white migrants out of the country altogether. In 1913, South Africa imposed restrictions on non-white immigration, as New Zealand had done in 1899, Australia in 1901 and Canada in 1910.

Working conditions for this new generation of indentured workers were almost always poor, and regulation was mostly ineffectual, although there was good reason for its existence. When, in the 1860s, the western Pacific became an active ground for labour recruitment, Melanesians and other Pacific islanders were sometimes kidnapped for work on the northern Queensland sugar plantations, a practice known as 'blackbirding'. Britain and Queensland both implemented legislation to prevent such kidnappings, but poor and desperate workers throughout the Empire knew little of the conditions they would face under indenture even when they voluntarily agreed to go.

Employers favoured indenture because it guaranteed a stable labour supply, and fixed the rate of pay for the duration of the contract. This, of course, helped drive down the overall cost of labour anywhere indenture was common, and it tended to make those under indenture unpopular with locals. While some employers paid money wages, others paid in rations. Most had rigorous systems in place to punish absenteeism. In some colonies a day's sickness meant the labourer owed the employer a day's work; on the expiry of a worker's contract, she or he had to work off sick or absent days with no further pay. In some colonies, Mauritius among them, pass laws similar to those seen in Africa confined indentured labourers to permitted areas.

Mortality rates were high on the plantations. Crowded and unhealthy conditions spread disease easily, and violence was a constant feature of life. News that Chinese mine workers at the Transvaal were being flogged for infractions in the early 1900s by mine officials provoked a massive outcry in Britain. Lord Milner was censured for sanctioning the floggings shortly after he returned from South Africa to Britain. Workers everywhere were easy prey for violent overseers since they could not change jobs, and both murder and suicide rates were high among indentured workers. Tensions on plantations were not eased by the imbalance between the numbers of men and of women. Sexual jealousies flared easily in these conditions and women were vulnerable. Other than among the indentured Indian populations, there were few women labourers, and even in the Indian communities there were many more men than women. Among the licensing requirements demanded by the government of India was a quota of women; ships that did not meet the ratios required by the government were not cleared for sailing. Where Indians were not the major source of indentured labour, the workforce was overwhelmingly male. Accompanying the Chinese indentured workers to the Transvaal gold fields, about a fifth of whom claimed to be married, were only five wives.

Many workers chose not to return home when their contracts expired. Queensland forced indentured workers to leave, and in parts of Africa taxes and fees were employed to discourage Indians from staying on. Many nonetheless did settle, not just in Africa but in the West Indies, Fiji and Mauritius. Over 600,000 Indians were living in Malaya in 1930. In the 1960s and 1970s, the Indian presence in East Africa would become a political flashpoint. African anti-colonials resented the Indian populations as a colonial legacy, part of the diaspora of cheap labour that had sustained British imperialism. In Kenya and in Uganda, in particular, the process of 'Africanisation' led to the wholesale and hasty expulsion of South Asians from the former colonies. Many chose to settle in Britain rather than in India, which had ceased over time to be home. The impact of Indian indenture continued to be felt in Fiji in the late twentieth and early twenty-first centuries, as Fijian nationalists sought to concentrate government power in native hands. In 1933, leaders of the Fijian population asked to live apart from the migrant Indians, creating a racial and cultural segregation of these populations with lasting consequences.

Although both the British and some colonial governments intervened on occasion to regulate the worst excesses of the indenture system, colonial

Figure 8.1 An idealised depiction of the 'coolie' in the nineteenth century
Source: Mary Evans Picture Library

regulation tended to be light in the arena of economic control, allowing private investors, both corporate and individual, considerable freedom. In Fiji, the largest single employer was the Australian sugar manufacturer, CSR (the Colonial Sugar Refining Company, founded in 1855, and even now Australia's largest sugar company). In Africa, companies such as the African Lakes Corporation controlled literally millions of acres. Private investment was typical in colonial settings, leading inevitably to distinctive imbalances in the economy, as profit and shareholder demands rather than local need dictated development. Essential infrastructure such as transportation was privately controlled, giving private corporations enormous power. Land could be and was seen solely in terms of profitability in most colonies. The effect was often devastating for residents who did not share in the profits, and not only in terms of their labour opportunity. Changes in land use alongside natural changes in weather patterns often helped produce droughts and their grim relative, famines. From at least the late eighteenth century, famines and crop failures in India were intensified by the forms of agricultural taxation, and therefore crop cultivation, introduced under British rule. A famine in northern India between 1860 and 1861 killed around 2 million people. More than 6 million died in famines that spread through the country in the 1870s, and in the late 1890s famine took another 5 million or so lives. A serious famine occurred in East Africa in 1919 as droughts and a plague of locusts devastated the crops. In the 1930s parts of southern Africa, once rich in grain, were importing food to cope with severe shortages. Where famine struck, disease almost inevitably followed. The monsoon failures of 1896 and 1897 in parts of India brought severe famines exacerbated by a simultaneous outbreak of plague in 1897.

Disease was helped in its spread by the lack of medical facilities available to local peoples. Indigenous practitioners facing diseases they had never before witnessed were unable to cope, and cholera, plague, influenza and a host of other, often fatal, diseases swept through vulnerable populations. A cholera epidemic which devastated the West Indies in the early 1850s killed almost 50,000 people. Fiji hosted virulent epidemics of measles, TB and influenza in the years of indenture. In Hong Kong and in India, plague and cholera outbreaks in the late nineteenth century took a damaging toll. Smallpox was a major killer among Australian Aboriginal populations. These diseases affected local and colonising populations, but it was when they affected white populations that research and action to stem epidemics were initiated. Even where colonial authorities did act to reduce the spread of diseases their methods were frequently unattractive to their colonial subjects. European doctors complained frequently about the suspicion with which they were regarded by colonised peoples, and about the unwillingness of local populations to undergo western treatments, and especially hospitalisation. Given that diseases and doctors often arrived in the colonies simultaneously, such suspicions were not unreasonable. Nor was the resentment felt by practitioners of non-western therapies who were often regarded by their European counterparts as superstitious quacks when, in practice, the western medical arsenal was often not much better or indeed that different from local treatments. What did differ radically were the western practices of hospitalising the sick and isolating the infectious. The rise of compulsory isolation tactics in India and in Africa in the late nineteenth and early twentieth centuries severely damaged relations between British doctors and indigenous patients; medical practitioners encountered sturdy resentment and resistance to their approaches. Colonial medical authorities took a pragmatic approach, seeing such measures as practical responses to urgent public health problems, particularly in crowded environments that facilitated the swift spread of pathogens. They were frequently unaware of, or unsympathetic to, the effects such policies had on families, economically as well as psychologically. Their application of western ways of tackling problems, such as the disinfecting of houses and furniture shown in Figure 8.2, did not help persuade subject peoples of the benefits of colonisation. Neither did the differential treatment regimens, especially in mental health, which saw indigenous patients as biologically distinct from whites.

Figure 8.2 Colonial authorities disinfecting and destroying the bedding of plague victims in Poona, India, 1897, as local people watch

Source: The Getty Research Institute (96.R.81)

Doctors saw local patients not only as superstitious but also uneducated, but they usually failed to appreciate the huge difference in the education available to British and to colonial children. Most of the education available to colonised children was provided by missionaries, who were also the main purveyors of medical treatment other than during epidemics. The education the missionary schools offered was quite basic, producing for the most part limited literacy and numeracy. While Britain in the later nineteenth century moved slowly towards compulsory education for all children, at least at the elementary level, the only equivalent laws in the colonies were, not surprisingly, in white settler lands. In 1921, only 3 per cent of Indians were formally educated, and less than 1 per cent had been English-educated. The EIC had long supported education in Sanskrit and in Arabic, but in the reform era of the 1830s 'Anglicists' pushing for English-language training and in western subjects had the upper hand. For the sons of the urban elite, government schools provided a training for young men who would join the Indian civil service. By the 1860s, both in British India and in nearby Ceylon, English-language schools had their own overseeing body, the Department of Public Instruction. This English-style education was reserved almost exclusively for a male elite who recognised the benefits of an English-language schooling for their sons.

Schools and colleges devoted to maintaining the local cultures and languages drew on much the same affluent client base. In South-East Asia and in India, Muslim schools offered elite males an alternative curriculum to that of the colonial authorities. Nonetheless, over time English became not just the language of colonial power, but of economic and political success. The switch in modern Canada to a dual language system is a direct result of the colonial era, when French was the minority language of a non-dominant population in the British colony. Modern Canadian practice aims to redress the balance by putting Francophone Canada on an equal footing with Anglophone Canada, especially with respect to official documents.

Yet English, the language of power, also adopted vocabulary from the colonies, much of which has survived in modern speech. The Aboriginal 'boomerang' has supplied an English verb, while the Indian 'bungalow' has given us a distinctive architectural style now seen in many countries around the world. In the islands of the Pacific, local peoples developed a language for communicating with the colonists, sometimes known as 'pidgin', incorporating local and English vocabulary. It was the islanders who instructed the English in this highly adaptive language. In India, in the West Indies, in Australia, distinct forms of English emerged, significantly different from that heard in England. English was dominant but not by any means uniform, whether as a written or a spoken medium of communication.

This phenomenon of adaptation or syncretism, in which the customs, practices, and beliefs of the colonial power were altered in light of local knowledge and uses was by no means confined to language. We have seen how locals found unexpected and unanticipated uses for items they traded or received as gifts from colonisers, and it is equally visible in the uses to which mission-taught Christianity was sometimes put. The continued flourishing even now of varieties of Christianity in many former British colonies suggests that the missions enjoyed some degree of success in their work, yet the adaptation of western Christianity to non-western belief systems was common. Many saw the missions not as a source of spiritual inspiration but as a practical and often secular source of training and education, housing, and health care. Others reshaped their newly acquired beliefs into a more familiar mould. By the eighteenth century, Jamaican Baptists had forged a hybrid religion that horrified the missionaries who observed it. It combined Christian belief with West African myalism, involving communication with the spirits of the dead, often through dance ceremonies, as a means of exorcising harm.

After the abolition of the slave trade, it was common for recaptives rescued from slaving ships to be settled in and around Freetown in the colony of Sierra Leone. The governor, Charles MacCarthy, envisioned a community of African Christians who could help 'civilise' Africa, and thus encouraged missionary activity in the early nineteenth century. In many respects it was a highly successful conversion exercise, with many adopting not just a new religion but many of the trappings of British life: a Christian name, western clothing, and so on. Yet religious practices, as in Jamaica, took on an identifiably local flavour in a syncretism not always to the taste of the missionaries and the white colonists.

Further south, in 1862, the British bishop of Natal, John William Colenso, published *The Pentateuch and the Book of Joshua Critically Examined* in which he outlined his misgivings about prevailing interpretations of the Old Testament Pentateuch as a document written by Moses, and protesting the limitations imposed on ministers in preaching these first five books of the Bible. Colenso was unorthodox in his beliefs, and sympathetic to the Zulu peoples among whom he lived. His challenge to a literal reading of the Bible had been shaped in no inconsiderable measure by the questions posed by William Ngidi, a Zulu Christian who was Colenso's language teacher and who worked with him on a translation of the Bible for use locally in Natal. A huge furore followed its publication. More than 11,000 clergymen signed a petition condemning Colenso, and the bishop of Cape Town excommunicated him, though this action was overturned in London in 1865. Colenso was unusually outspoken for a man in his position, but his work shows how local opinions and challenges could have considerable effect in shaping the work of the missions. Colenso's collaboration with Ngidi continued, and together they wrote a number of school textbooks, a history of Natal and a primer on hygiene.

Colonial peoples used syncretism to their own advantage, and one unexpected but inevitable adaptation that emerged out of colonial rule was the emergence of what one early twentieth-century anthropologist, C. G. Seligman, called the 'professional primitive'. Anthropologists, explorers and officials as well as tourists all encountered colonial peoples who, increasingly familiar with what colonists expected of them, played up to the images of savagery and primitivism which were the bread-and-butter depictions of the colonial world. Exhibitions and books offered western viewers a snapshot of societies – especially African and Pacific – as composed of scantily clad and brightly ornamented 'primitives' squatting in front of mud huts, which primed such expectations, and locals quickly learned to act the part where necessary. It could be a lucrative performance on occasion.

Nonetheless, colonial assumptions could significantly alter social structure and the forms of identity that colonised peoples themselves understood. Where once there were people of different cultural groupings living in proximity, under colonialism there were 'Africans' or 'Native Americans', labels unknown in precontact times and reflecting how colonists saw both regions and peoples. In slave colonies, people from widely differing cultures and societies were thrown together and, finding more in common with other slaves than with their masters, a homogenised idea of 'African' cultures unknown in Africa developed from those encounters. The assumptions made by missionaries and officials (both civil and military) about leadership and authority patterns in other societies helped create new forms of rule and indeed of dissent. The British emphasis on caste distinction in India reinforced and often strengthened these social divisions. The British could not understand societies in which there was no leader with whom they could formally communicate. The East African Kikuyu and the West African Igbo were not societies with chiefs, but the British need for identifiable rulers on whom they could devolve certain duties made them set about creating tribal chiefs where none had existed. The massive changes wrought by such actions were often deeply disruptive to social and political stability. Part of that strategy also lay in creating elaborate rituals around imperial rule, in which local as well as colonial rulers were entitled to certain forms of dress and ceremonies. Durbars, borrowed from the Mughal court, became demonstrations of loyalty to the Crown in British India; their precolonial existence in West Africa made them helpful tools of the colonial administration there too. Coronations and jubilees, such as the huge procession shown in Figure 8.3, were lavish occasions where the British sought to stimulate a show of loyalty to the Empire.

The British Empire, then, was a place of deep inequality between coloniser and colonised. A few small elite groups, useful to the British, were encouraged and pampered but the vast majority of those affected by colonial rule were almost certainly worse off as a result of imperial rule. Their lands were appropriated, their access to employment limited and prescribed, their

Figure 8.3 George V Jubilee procession in Hong Kong, 1935

movement often restricted and their communities redefined and sometimes literally moved from their locations. Although many in Britain saw colonialism as a beneficent force, an exercise in enlightened development allowing the entire world to enjoy the benefits of western living, the reality was often one of limitation, constraint and oppression. The growth of anti-colonial movements (charted in Chapter 10) throughout the colonial world was critically fuelled by this uneven distribution of wealth, power and privilege.

Note

1 *Colonial Empire: Introducing the Colonies* (London: Central Office of Information, 1948).

Further reading

Equal Subjects, Unequal Rights: Indigenous Peoples in British Settler Colonies, 1830–1910 (Julie Evans (ed.), Manchester: Manchester University Press, 2003) looks specifically at the experience of indigenous peoples affected by settler colonialism, while the essays in *Empire and Others: British Encounters with Indigenous Peoples, 1600–1850* (Martin Daunton and Rick Halpern (eds), Philadelphia, PA: University of Pennsylvania Press, 1999), although also investigating the experience of the colonised, looks at a broader range of colonial experiences. Read together, they offer an excellent introduction to the topic. In *Masters, Servants, and Magistrates in Britain and the Empire, 1562–1955* (Douglas Hay and Paul Craven (eds), Chapel Hill, NC: University of North Carolina Press, 2004), leading scholars look at the foundations of labour law in both Britain and its colonial possessions. *Black Experience and the Empire* (Philip D. Morgan and Sean Hawkins (eds), Oxford: Oxford University Press, 2004) offers a set of interesting essays on the meaning of race and skin colour within the imperial framework.

The experience of indentured workers under colonialism in the Caribbean is the subject of Madhavi Kale's *Fragments of Empire: Capital, Slavery, and Indian Indentured Labor Migration in the British Caribbean* (Philadelphia, PA: University of Pennsylvania Press, 1998) and of Marina Carter's *Voices from Indenture: Experiences of Indian Migrants in the British Empire* (London: Leicester University Press, 1996). Verene A. Shepherd's *Maharani's Misery: Narratives of a Passage from India to the Caribbean* (Barbados: University of the West Indies Press, 2002) tells the story of a young indentured woman who died on board a ship bound for Guyana from Calcutta. David Northrup, *Indentured Labor in the Age of Imperialism, 1838–1914* (New York: Cambridge University Press, 1995) takes a global look at post-slavery indenture.

Peder Anker's *Imperial Ecology: Environmental Order in the British Empire, 1895–1945* (Cambridge, MA: Harvard University Press, 2001) looks at administrators and officials tasked with environmental matters. *Environment and Empire* (Oxford: Oxford University Press, 2007), by William Beinart and Lotte Hughes, offers a wide-ranging overview of the environmental issues affecting the colonised throughout the Empire. In *Cutting Down Trees: Gender, Nutrition, and*

Agricultural Change in the Northern Province of Zambia, 1890–1990 (Portsmouth, NH: Heinemann; London: James Currey, 1994), Henrietta L. Moore and Megan Vaughan suggest intriguing links between ecology, gender and health in the Empire. Dane Kennedy describes the exclusive enclaves where the officials who ran India went to cool off during the sultry summer months in *The Magic Mountains: Hill Stations and the British Raj* (Berkeley, CA: University of California Press, 1996).

The scholarship on colonial medicine and science is substantial. Among the best medical studies are David Arnold's *Colonizing the Body: State Medicine and Epidemic Disease in Nineteenth-Century India* (Berkeley, CA: University of California Press, 1993), Randall M. Packard's *White Plague, Black Labor: Tuberculosis and the Political Economy of Health and Disease in South Africa* (Berkeley, CA: University of California Press, 1989) and Megan Vaughan's *Curing Their Ills: Colonial Power and African Illness* (Cambridge: Polity, 1991). On science and empire in the early colonial period, see Londa Schiebinger's *Plants and Empire: Colonial Bioprospecting in the Atlantic World* (Cambridge, MA: Harvard University Press, 2004). For the later period, Helen Tilley, *Africa as a Living Laboratory: Empire, Development, and the Problem of Scientific Knowledge, 1870–1950* (Chicago: University of Chicago Press, 2011) and Omnia El Shakry, *The Great Social Laboratory: Subjects of Knowledge in Colonial and Postcolonial Egypt* (Stanford, CA: Stanford University Press, 2007) are both valuable case studies.

Challenges to colonial rule, and especially on the topic of land rights, are the subject of *Native Claims: Indigenous Law against Empire, 1500–1920* (Saliha Belmessous (ed.), Oxford: Oxford University Press, 2011) in which a number of the essays deal with the British Empire. Nandini Chatterjee provides an interesting study of how Christianity was shaped by local practices in *The Making of Indian Secularism: Empire, Law and Christianity, 1830–1960* (Basingstoke: Palgrave Macmillan, 2011). Catherine Hall's *Civilising Subjects: Metropole and Colony in the English Imagination, 1830–1867* (Chicago, IL: University of Chicago Press, 2002) does some of the same work for the Caribbean.

9 Gender and sexuality

It will be obvious by now that the Empire, throughout its long history, was dominated by the concerns of colonising men. In Britain, the Empire was represented as a place of masculine proving and of adventure in which white women and indigenous peoples were, at best, incidental, and more often than not detrimental, to good rule. This perception was grounded in a ruler-oriented view of the Empire that regarded it as a dangerous and difficult environment needing to be tamed.

In Britain, the Empire was depicted as populated predominantly by men, an image that frequently left local populations as well as women invisible and uncounted. It was among migrant populations that dramatic imbalances in sex ratios in the colonial world were mostly to be found. Among colonising whites and labouring groups such as slaves, indentured workers and convicts, men vastly outnumbered women. Permanent colonised populations, despite the severe losses from disease or violence they sometimes suffered, had gender ratios closer to those found in Europe. Local practices, particularly in relation to the disposing of unwanted children of one sex or the other, might skew the ratio slightly, but those populations where men massively outweighed women were artificial creations of imperial expansion.

In many colonies, British women were thin on the ground, but this was not the case everywhere. British America before the War of Independence had a more equitable gender balance than British India at the same moment. In the port towns of New England in the early years of American colonisation, there were more than a few households headed by women whose husbands were at sea for lengthy periods. The circumstance and type of colonisation as well as the period affected gender balance. In settler lands there were often far more men, especially in the early stages of colonisation. In 1861 there were 150 men for every 100 women among white settlers in Australia, and 160 men for every 100 women in New Zealand. In most of Africa and in the Malay archipelago, there were roughly twice as many British men as British women into the 1920s, and it was only after the advent of direct British rule in India in 1858 that the numbers of white women there began to climb in any significant way.

It was no surprise, then, that the most general impression of the Empire was of a man's world. This perception directly affected the shape and the history of the Empire for both coloniser and colonised. The numerical dominance of men was associated directly with imperialism, and this helped reinforce the idea of empire as a gendered and masculine domain. Some colonial jobs actually demanded that men remain single: men employed by India's Forest Service, for example, could not marry until they had completed their probationary period. Regions considered particularly dangerous were often off-limits to women; married men posted to such places had to be willing to leave their wives behind. It was not only men in government service who faced restrictions. Many trading companies required their employees to seek company permission before marrying, and in some sectors marriage was permitted only after a man had served a set number of years on the job and for that company. Doctors and others argued that women's natural frailty and delicacy made them unfit for the rigours of colonial climates, hot or cold, while others saw dangers at every turn, whether from wildlife with a taste for human flesh, from disease or from unfriendly locals.

Gender is, however, about far more than numbers. The desire espoused by imperialists to ready colonised societies for future western-style freedom drew strength from the belief that the social structures of the colonising power were superior. Colonial administrators, settlers and other Britons seldom left their values and beliefs wholly behind when they moved from Britain to its colonies. Although a few of those who moved to the colonies expressly rejected British attitudes and customs, many remained convinced of British superiority and were keen to extend British values. One of the most powerful and far-reaching of the ideas they brought with them was that men and women inhabited separate public and private worlds. It was in the eighteenth century that the gendered belief that men were best suited to the public and women to the private sphere grew influential, at much the same time as imperial expansion was high on the British political agenda. Though this principle of 'separate spheres' was always and everywhere unrealistic, it was nonetheless powerful as an ideal and as an organising social principle. Clearly, it reflected a highly specific – and privileged – class position in which there was sufficient money for women not to be engaged in paid labour, a luxury well beyond the reach of many in Britain. Within Britain and in the colonies, the effects of this thinking were significant. It became increasingly difficult in Britain for married women to find formal paid work, and sentiment followed practice, with men defining their masculinity through the stay-at-home wife.

This division of public and private also operated beyond the economic sphere. Behaviour, especially sexual behaviour, was increasingly regulated by considerations of what was proper in the different spheres. The respectable person understood the requirements and limits of these boundaries and acted accordingly. Sex was an entirely private business, not to be talked about in public; commerce and politics were public functions, better suited to male conversation. Child-raising was a domestic and womanly activity. The heterosexual family in which father paid the bills and mother raised the children and created a calming environment, in contrast to the hustle and bustle of the public arena, was at the heart of this vision of the separate spheres.

Colonists often found drastically different social and sexual arrangements when they left Britain. Frequently the distinction between the worlds of public and private simply did not exist in other cultures. Attitudes to family, women and sexuality were sometimes radically different. Among many African peoples, for example, the idea of sexuality as a private affair made no sense, because the key social group was not the nuclear family but a bigger and broader collective in which responsibilities and ties were not to a spouse, but to this wider kin. In South Asia, marriage was mostly a family business, and was certainly not centred on personal attraction between one man and one woman. In situations such as these, the roles occupied by men and women could be very different from those familiar to colonists, and colonists mostly found these variations discomfiting rather than seeing them as viable alternatives. The disapproving descriptions of native sexuality that dominated earlier colonial periods gave way in the twentieth century to apparently scientific explanations for the 'hypersexuality' now seen to define colonial peoples. Sigmund Freud, the renowned pioneer of modern psychiatry, argued that there was an identifiable difference in the psycho-logical make-up of Europeans and what were thought of in his time as 'primitive' peoples. In a 1908 essay he argued that Africans, Pacific Islanders and Australian Aborigines lacked the period of sexual latency he believed moderated sex drive among Europeans.[1] The logic was that non-Europeans were thus more highly sexed.

Gender relations became a mainstay of colonial criticism alongside a dis-approval (sometimes mixed with envy) of the sexual behaviours of colonised peoples. In particular colonised societies came, quite early on, to be defined by the apparently vast number of ways in which women were degraded and brutalised. Brushing aside the huge inequalities experienced by women in Britain, one of the characteristics seen to define colonial peoples and to rele-gate them to a lesser status was their apparent lack of respect for women. The mistreatment of women became definitive of primitive societies, and one of many reasons justifying the need for colonial authority. Colonial peoples, claimed colonisers, sold their daughters into prostitution or domestic ser-vitude, or married them off at alarmingly young ages without a qualm. In many places 'natives' were said to kill female children at birth, because the expense of rearing them was not worth it. Those girls allowed to live were often kept in seclusion, restricted in movement and education, forced to hide behind heavy clothing and barred windows. When married, it was often in polygamous arrangements, and if they had the misfortune to survive their husbands they might be expected either to commit ritual suicide or to live singly and modestly after his death and not remarry. Their genitals were said to be subject to mutilation, and their delivery of children was threatened by the use of unclean and untrained midwives. Colonial women led, by British reckoning, a miserable, brutal and wretched existence in the shadow of their menfolk, who thought nothing of bartering women's bodies as commodities.

All of these practices undoubtedly did exist among some groups in some places, just as in Britain itself women endured restricted access to education, arranged marriages, loss of property rights upon marriage, domestic violence, little control over their children, minimal right to divorce and virtually no political power before the twentieth century. These parallels were seldom recognised, and instead colonial female perils came to spell the problems that made British rule imperative. These evils pointed not only to the misfortunes of women but also to the misbehaviour of men. It was the failure of colonised men to do right by women that many in Britain saw as justifying the need for British governance.

Emphasis on the oppression of women often involved selective reporting too, ignoring instances in which women enjoyed freedoms beyond those of women in the west. Missionaries in eighteenth-century North America, for example, found the matrilineal practices of the Huron peoples disturbing; the birth of a girl was celebrated more than that of a boy. Instances such as this were, throughout the colonial period, played down while female oppression at the hands of men was seen as widespread and characteristic of what was wrong with colonised societies.

In many places the colonial state began in the early nineteenth century to curb practices seen as detrimental to women's well-being. Laws banning *sati* and female infanticide or regulating age of marriage were passed in nineteenth-century India (see Chapter 5), and in the twentieth century there were attempts to tackle the custom of female circumcision in parts of Africa. In some instances, the influence of westernisation led to changes in local practice, as was the case among the middle-class intellectuals of Calcutta and other urban areas of India who began to move away from *purdah* (the seclusion of women) in the mid-nineteenth century.

The dilemma – for local reform groups as much as for the colonial state – was that imposing the values of another society seldom sat well with a large portion of the population. In the case of reform groups and organisations, that problem was part of the wider question of whether wholesale westernisation was the right direction for the future (a point examined in Chapter 10). Colonial governments, on the other hand, had no such qualms. Officials might believe that local populations would resist change, but this did not on the whole make them doubt the superiority of the reforms they sought to enact. When things went wrong, as they almost always did, it was local resistance and not colonial policy that was invariably faulted.

As we have seen, colonial rule relied on collaboration with some portion of the indigenous population, and relying on (and often) creating local elites distorted colonial understanding of indigenous customs and practices. Yet the enforcement of laws addressing intimate behaviours was invariably difficult, not only because of local resistance or subterfuge, but because enforcement often specifically relied on western practices. Age of consent legislation, for example, which laid down the minimum age at which girls could be married (or have heterosexual relations), assumed that age could be definitively established, something that became possible only where and when birth certificates were routine. The absence of birth certificates affected campaigns against female infanticide too, and some of the earliest instances of birth certification in India in the 1860s were the result of the state's concern with the death of infant girls. In all these cases colonists blamed men: it was the perverted appetites of men that victimised young girls exposed too early to conjugality, and it was men's carelessness and faulty authority that allowed infanticide to occur. The critique of colonial masculinity offered an implicit and flattering comparison with the chivalrous masculinity of the colonisers.

Many of the practices abhorred by colonial observers were also targeted by local critics, although the colonial state only occasionally joined forces with these reformers. Locals were not unaware of their own problems, just as critics in Britain found plenty at home in need of reform. The rich literary tradition of Bengal contains many a tale of the lonely child bride torn from her parents and mistreated by a mother-in-law who now ruled her every waking moment. The *mui tsai* of China, girls sold into domestic and sometimes sexual service at a young age and often in perpetuity, were commonly pictured in Chinese literature as powerless and exploited victims. Yet colonists bent on reform seldom chose to work in tandem with concerned locals to improve conditions.

For the colonised, social reform was also bound up with questions about whether changes to women's lives would require westernisation, not always a popular option among colonised peoples. While some welcomed western influence, many in colonial societies were critical of the west, preferring the traditions with which they had grown up. There was no wholesale yearning for western ways, but rather a critical reckoning of the benefits and disadvantages the west might bestow.

If the colonised woman was most typically held up as epitomising all that was wrong with other cultures, the British woman in the colonial world has taken much of the blame for the intolerance and hierarchical nature of colonialism. Some historians argue that the increase in women living in the Empire radically altered the practices and routines of colonial life, introducing snobbery, rigidity and formality, and aggravating and even creating racial tensions. The biggest hindrance Kim, the eponymous hero of Rudyard Kipling's famous novel set in British India, and all about political intrigue, faces is not physical danger but being 'eternally pestered by women'.[2] Women did not belong in Kim's world and were simply a nuisance. They distracted men from the business at hand. They required protection. They demanded polite society and sexual fidelity. They drew sharp racial lines between whites and others, and poisoned the earlier harmony of colonial conquest.

The arrival in parts of the Empire of greater numbers of women certainly coincided with some distinctive social changes in colonial rule, but the growth in the female population generally came about because changes were already under way. The nineteenth-century expansion of Britain's colonial holdings, and the growing complexity of colonial rule, required a more settled British presence. Asking ever-larger numbers of British men to forego participation in family life was not feasible, and so instead family moved to the Empire. Most British women in the Empire were there because of family circumstances; they were the sisters, daughters, mothers and wives of men posted to, and living in, the Empire. There were solo British women too, but their numbers were far smaller, and many married soon after arriving. With the increase in married women, the previously widespread habit among British men of taking mistresses and concubines from among the local population began to recede, or at least fade from view. Marital infidelity was hardly unknown in Britain, and the mistress was neither a new nor a singularly colonial phenomenon, but since women were leaving their families behind and moving to strange and far-removed settings to be with their husbands, their tolerance for such behaviours within marriage may well have waned in proportion. With so many more married men living with their wives in the later colonial years, local non-marital arrangements now competed with, rather than substituted for, recognised marriages.

With the growing presence of British women in the Empire came also a greater number of young children living with their parents in the colonies. New living conditions emerged from that singular change. British residential communities began to develop more fully, making racial exclusivity (by no means a new phenomenon) much more visible. Women's presence was intended to soften and domesticate dominantly male environments. In the settler context, officials hoped that by encouraging single women to migrate to the Canadian and Australian colonies these tough, male-dominated pioneer societies would become respectable and conformist. The Indian government's insistence on a female quota on ships carrying indentured labourers paralleled the policy of encouraging women's migration to the prairies and forests of Canada or to the sheep and cattle runs of Australia. Officials believed that a greater female presence would help stabilise labouring populations and therefore increase economic productivity. In the mining camps that began to spring up in southern Africa in the late nineteenth century, the presence of women close by, selling food, sex and companionship to the male workers, was tolerated and indeed sometimes quietly encouraged as a stabilising force in otherwise volatile conditions. Worried about the restlessness of the Indian male convicts serving time in the isolated Andaman Islands, out in the Bay of Bengal, officials introduced family immigration schemes in the mid-nineteenth century designed to rehabilitate criminals. In 1890 the authorities took the extraordinary step of allowing husbands to require that, even if the women's own sentences had expired, convict wives remain in the penal settlement with them while they finished out their own prison terms.

The conception of the Empire as a man's world, for the colonisers at least, guaranteed that masculinity was always important, if also always beset by uncertainty. That Empire was an unsuitable environment for women was a tenacious maxim that continued well into the twentieth century, and it depressed opportunities within the Empire for women. When the colonial service began appointing women to colonial service positions (in tiny numbers) in 1937, many of their male colleagues were unhappy. Those women who did rise to the senior ranks recognised the barriers imposed by sex. Margery Perham was perhaps the most notable of the small group of women who, by the mid-twentieth century, had made a name for themselves in colonial policy work. Perham's expertise on Africa made her a respected figure in both political and academic circles, and she was sufficiently eminent that she was invited to deliver the British Broadcasting Corporation's prestigious annual Reith lectures for 1961. Yet crossing the Pacific as a young woman in 1929, she had remarked on the accidental and gendered good fortune of a fellow passenger on his way to take up the governorship of American Samoa. 'I envied him', wrote Perham, 'his job – and his sex.'[3] Though Perham never allowed gender discrimination to deter her, she recognised how the system of empire made working there easier for men than for women.

Even after the mid-nineteenth century when women's presence grew, the Empire was a world dominated by men, and this had considerable consequences for both ruler and ruled. Since colonialism involved some form of domination, whether by military conquest, economic power or cultural ascendancy, it was easy to imagine maleness in terms of authority and power. The subjugation of men from the colonies under British rule made the assumption of weakness an easy one; their submission, for the rulers, was proof of a lesser manliness, for the manly would never concede defeat. Yet at the same time there were groups among the colonised who Britons saw as admirably masculine: some of the African peoples, such as the Ndebele who had fought vigorously against colonial intrusion, and the north Indians who the British called the 'martial races'. Newspaper and journal articles often described such men in almost erotic physical terms, emphasising height, muscularity and gait. They likewise derided colonial men they regarded as effeminate and insufficiently manly. Descriptions of such men tended to focus on their unhealthy pallor, weedy frames and air of constant exhaustion. There was always an undercurrent of fear that colonial effeminacy, brought about by luxury and indolence, might transfer to British men. Cartoons of the returning 'nabobs' in the late eighteenth century often showed them bedecked with jewels more suitable for women, a clear sign of a corruption that was at once economic, moral, physical and cultural.

Effeminacy was not the only danger to beset manliness. Homosexuality loomed large as a concern, and it was a widely held British belief (based on very little evidence) that male–male sexual relations were prevalent in many colonised societies. Colonial Office memoranda carefully noted such proclivities among wealthy and influential colonial men, more proof in British eyes of colonial inferiority. Ignoring the considerable male homosexual activity in the metropolis – made visible by the trial of the playwright Oscar Wilde in 1895 – the assumption of widespread homosexuality in the colonial tropics 'proved' colonial inadequacy. Although some colonies did have more fluid sexual rules than Britain, attitudes to same-sex relations in many of the places the British colonised matched those in Britain. The tendency to lump non-white colonies together as tolerant of practices outside the contours of British sexual respectability allowed a wholesale condemnation of what was seen as typical of colonial sexuality.

In practice, of course, imperial environments were frequently homosocial for white men. In the early years of imperial expansion especially, white men lived, worked and socialised largely among men. Prostitution and concubinage, serviced by colonial women, flourished but men lived mostly among other men. Such profoundly male environments, in which a female presence was temporary, provided fertile ground for same-sex liaisons that, though frowned upon and frequently hushed up, were not uncommon among British men.

The most exclusively male of all colonial environments was the military. Below the officer corps, army and navy men were discouraged from marrying. Only a tiny percentage of the rank-and-file was permitted to marry, a decision prompted in part by a fear that marriage would divert a man's loyalties from his regiment to his family, and in part by economic concerns. Particularly as a bulwark against homosexuality, prostitution was seen as vital to army stability, and in many places informal regulation of military prostitution existed from an early date. In India, Lord Bentinck took an active interest in schemes that required women working in the sex trade to submit to frequent genital examination and to compulsory treatment for sexually transmissible diseases (STDs). Such schemes, funded out of municipal and company coffers, were operating in the Indian presidencies from at least the 1790s. These regulatory experiments identified women but not men as the source of STDs. In the mid-nineteenth century, more systematic attempts to regulate the sex trade criss-crossed the Empire, including a system of regulated brothels designed to protect soldiers and sailors from STDs. These 'contagious diseases' laws tried to stem the high levels of STDs among colonial soldiers and sailors by genitally examining women sex workers at regular intervals. For a host of reasons, the laws failed: women avoided and resisted regulation, men visited unregulated women, the pathology of these diseases was only poorly understood and the available treatments were at best partial. In addition, these laws attracted massive protests both in Britain and in the colonies in the late nineteenth century, especially from women outraged at a double standard that held women but not men responsible for transmission of disease. By the century's end, these regulations had been formally abandoned, though they often lived on in informal schemes seldom policed by the state.

Although they failed in their goal of reducing STDs, the contagious disease laws tell us much about both gender relations and about sexuality in the Empire. That Victorian politicians could so easily pass laws legalising prostitution, an activity regularly deplored as immoral as well as uncivilised in the press, in parliament, in churches and on the streets, is in itself significant. Soldiers, as we have seen, were regarded as the ultimate defenders of the Empire, the force which, if and when resistance erupted, was called upon: they were the face and the frame of imperial masculinity, the final enforcers of rule through brute force. Women – in this case, colonial women – were expected to service them, to provide the necessary sexual outlet that masculinity was understood to require. It was, even for the squeamish Victorians, preferable that a man visit a prostitute than he have sexual relations with another man. Colonised women as mistresses and prostitutes, and British women as colonial wives and companions, were vital components in maintaining a gender structure that allowed for a clear distinction between men and women, masculinity and femininity, proper and improper forms of sexuality.

It is for this reason that we see so much regulation of sexuality in the Empire, especially in the nineteenth and early twentieth centuries. Laws of this sort kept both sexual behaviours and the boundaries between manliness and womanliness properly distinct. It was, of course, also axiomatic among the British that those they colonised were sexually promiscuous and unheeding of the idea of moderation. There is also no question that explorers and other colonists often did encounter locales where sexuality was very differently viewed than in Britain. Needless to say, many among the British took advantage of freer sexual mores while simultaneously deprecating the societies that offered them these opportunities.

This contradictory and often hypocritical position demonstrates British ambivalence about the gender structures and social organisation encountered in the colonies. The imperial period was one of deep Christian orthodoxy, with its bifurcated understanding of sexuality as either sinful or procreative. There was already a long tradition in the Christian world of regarding women as dangerous temptresses, easily reinforced when British men encountered women unencumbered by the religious association between sin and sexuality. In such environments, there was inevitably a fascination with women who differed so palpably from the representations (though not always the reality) of British womanhood. This ambivalence often paired desire and disgust: descriptions of colonised women frequently veered between enthusiasm for their beauty and sexual freedoms and horror at their ugliness and promiscuity.

In the summer of 1810, Londoners who could afford the steep 2s/6d entrance fee could view in the flesh the woman the papers were calling the

'Hottentot Venus', shipped for display from the Cape of Good Hope. Sara (or Saartje as she was known in South Africa) Baartman was a Khoisan woman who had made the long and perilous journey from South Africa to London by ship. Displayed by white entrepreneurs in fashionable Piccadilly on account of her allegedly vast buttocks, breasts and labia, Baartman has come to symbolise the early nineteenth-century European obsession with an abundant and exotic colonial sexuality. The hugely popular exhibition of Baartman's body in London, and later in Paris, was a colonial act, a display which illuminates both the European fascination with what they saw as excessive African sexuality and the ways in which women, almost everywhere subordinate to men in this period, were a key element in the power relationship that defined the Empire.

The depiction of colonial women as animalistic and beastly, even if also sometimes comely and erotic, dates back at least to the early days of navigation and European travel in the sixteenth century. Descriptions of women's bodies were a standard element in early travel writings, and these descriptions routinely focused on sexual attributes, often remarking in particular on women's breasts. It was an article of faith that childbirth was inconsequential for these naked and primitive women, in stark contrast to the sufferings endured in labour by 'civilised' women. This was a belief with huge geographical spread. Observers claimed this enviable trait of easy childbirth for the women of the Americas, of Australia, Africa and the Pacific. It was one of the hallmarks of 'primitive' sexuality and served to differentiate the heathen from the Christian. According to the Old Testament, after Adam and Eve sampled the forbidden apple, God's punishment included the vow that 'in sorrow thou shalt bring forth children'.[4] Widely interpreted as visiting pain on women during parturition, Christian women experienced God's curse on Eve while the heathen remained untouched.

In the eighteenth century, when naturalists began in earnest to seek for the origins of humankind and Carl Linnaeus argued for a commonality between apes and humans, the theme of bestiality crept into writings about non-western peoples. Claiming a greater resemblance between Africans and apes, Edward Long, writing in the 1770s, suggested that the 'oran-outang' passion for 'Negroe women' was 'a natural impulse of desire, such as inclines one animal towards another of the same species'.[5] The African and the ape were thus elided into one species. Such musings – and Long was far from atypical in his lurid imaginings – allowed sexual behaviour, real or imagined, to become the sign of cultural and moral inferiority, bolstering the justifications for colonial rule.

It is within such a climate of disapproval and misunderstanding that the remarkable political attention paid to the regulation of sexuality is best understood. Britain also saw an increase, particularly from the late nineteenth century, in governmental incursions into these professedly private areas of life. However, in the colonies we see a wider range of such laws and much earlier than would have been acceptable in Britain. The contagious diseases laws discussed earlier were already operating in a number of British colonies in the 1850s, yet were not introduced into Britain until 1864, and the British legislation was much less comprehensive than the colonial laws. In the colonies, laws dictated not only the contours of paid sex, but also marriage, abortion, infanticide, non-marital sex, age of consent, interracial sex and more. Whereas it was a criminal offence in Britain to have sex with girls under the age of twelve for most of the nineteenth century, the age of consent law passed in India in 1822 set that age at eight. Always prominent was the tension between what the British considered proper behaviour and the behaviours of the peoples they ruled.

The western definition of marriage that came increasingly to dominate in the colonies was particularly influential, because it covered such a wide range of practices from age of marriage to the status of widows, from authority within marriage to what legally constituted a marriage and, of course, how many people one could be married to simultaneously. Christian ideology, which saw marriage as exclusively a covenant between one woman and one man, could not countenance many of the practices Britons encountered in their colonies.

Concubinage (the keeping of a mistress) was increasingly out of favour, not only because more women were moving from Britain to the Empire, but because of a growing concern about the mixed-race offspring such relationships produced. The children of mixed-race intimacies often experienced considerable discrimination. In the early years of North American settlement, they were mostly raised within native families. In India, Eurasian children were sent to institutions founded specifically to train and raise them, but their likeliest future was in the tightly knit Eurasian community, set apart from both Indians and the English. In the West Indies a large mixed-race population lived separately from the black community and the planters alike.

In the early twentieth century, colonial policy dictated that government employees involved in sexual relationships with colonised women could not expect promotion, though the effect was probably to push these arrangements further to the margins rather than to reduce their frequency. Women would have been forced to live separately from their male partners, but still expected to provide them with sexual and other services. The loss of income or housing would all have been, of course, on the woman's side. The advantages of concubinage were always almost all on the male and British side.

Yet for both free and enslaved women liaisons with colonising men could and often did spell some economic improvement in their lives, even if only temporarily. The security of these arrangements was always tenuous. Men ended such relationships at their own convenience, often because they were marrying a white women or had been posted to a new location. Most colonial concubinage was among the less well off, although the stories of glamorous liaisons with wealthy princesses are those about which we generally hear. Few women were kept by wealthy foreigners, most instead servicing men of modest means and always aware that their arrangements could end abruptly. Unlike formal marriages, there were no responsibilities or duties expected of the men; in practice, some did support children they had fathered or settled a sum of money on the woman. It was a rare man who would recognise a mistress as a legitimate wife, and the children of the alliance as his heirs. All the responsibilities were centred on the woman for whom concubinage was a form of paid work. These 'temporary marriages' so typical of the colonies are best understood as a type of gendered labour.

Work more broadly is another area where the operation of colonial gender divisions was often markedly different than in Britain. Poor women who had to earn a living worked outside the house for wages, whether they lived in Britain, on the African continent, in Hong Kong or in Egypt. The work they performed, however, could be strikingly different and, not surprisingly, we can trace the very substantial effect of colonisation on the gendered division of colonial labour. As in Britain, heavy manual labour was increasingly male. In India where a tradition of manufacture pre-dated heavy industrialisation, it was women workers who lost their livelihoods, echoing the changes in the British textile industries where, by the mid-nineteenth century, a predominantly female labour force had been replaced overwhelmingly by male workers. In Britain, women's removal from the factories was widely hailed as a social and moral reform that improved the family even though the loss of women's wages was often devastating to the family income. In India, rather differently, the insistence of British merchants that Indian textiles not compete with British ones led to the deliberate slowing of Indian textile manufacture, and the consequent loss of huge numbers of traditionally female jobs. Agriculture became increasingly feminised as women sought alternative means to feed themselves and their families. Plantation work in India, especially in tea and coffee picking, became an increasingly female world while, by the early twentieth century, men occupied around 90 per cent of industrial jobs.

Nonetheless, a British observer moving between the colonies and Britain would have been struck by how many more colonial women worked in jobs that at home would long have been reserved for men. Their numbers diminished over time but the observer would have found women in the factories and underground in the mines, in the building trade working at heavy manual labour and in many other industries long closed to British working women. Thomas Alva Edison, the early American film entrepreneur, shot a series of films in the British West Indies in 1903 that registered the amazement of a western onlooker at the heavy manual labour performed by women. Three of the five films in the series showed women coaling ships docked in the Caribbean harbours, the women carrying baskets of coal on their heads into the boiler room of the vessels; the other two depicted more traditional scenes, women washing babies and clothes.

Protective labour legislation that had begun to restrict women's manual work in Britain from the 1840s came late to India. As in Britain, these laws were focused largely on manufacturing and mining, skirting the main employment areas in which women now found jobs. In 1911 women working in Indian factories were prohibited from night work; in Britain that proscription dated back to 1844. In 1928, limitations were placed on women's participation in mining in India; similar restrictions took effect in Britain in 1842. The shift out of heavy manual labour thus came far later in the colonies than in Britain, although it everywhere reduced women's chance of economic independence.

The distinctive movement of women into agriculture was Empire-wide. African men were increasingly occupied in mining and manufacture, often far from home, leaving women with the immediate burden of providing for families. Subsistence agriculture became women's work while large-scale corporate cash-cropping made increasing inroads into the land available for such work, further impoverishing rural women. As a result, women began to move further afield in search of work though in smaller numbers than men. They worked on agricultural plantations or moved to the cities as petty traders, as domestics, as sex workers, often combining these skills to make ends meet. As opportunities arose they might sell cooked food to men living in barracks, brew beer or offer sexual services, combining these as necessary to maximise their earnings.

White women also worked in the colonies, both in the settler lands and in the dependent colonies. In white settler environments, they occupied much the same place as in Britain, working principally in domestic service in the nineteenth century and expanding into the sales and service sectors over time. The same domestic sentiments – that women, especially once married, belonged in the home raising children – restricted white women's labour opportunities. For indigenous women in settler lands, there was, of course, even less opportunity. Domestic and sexual services were their likeliest means of supporting themselves in the white colonial world, and they could expect even lower remuneration than white women.

In non-settler colonies white working women were unwelcome to officials, despite their small numbers. They were routinely suspected of working in the sex trade. A single woman working as a barmaid in a city such as Singapore may have been in a typically female if morally ambiguous job, but her obvious independence mocked the idea of the Empire as a man's world. Officials regarded such women as putting 'proper' white women at risk, and many white women in the colonies agreed. Most of the white women living in Southern Rhodesia signed petitions presented to the legislative council in 1915 calling for a prohibition on the employment of women in bars and hotels. The petitions were unsuccessful, but they demonstrate the intensity of feeling about the topic and about the unstable status of white women in colonial settings. Even nurses, so much more respectably feminine, and by the later nineteenth century a reasonably common sight in the colonies, were kept on a tight rein, their free time and leisure pursuits carefully policed.

While white women, however limited their opportunities, might find work in a British colony, it was far harder for a woman from the colonies to find work in Britain. There were colonised women working in Britain for returned colonial families mostly in domestic positions, but their numbers were small and there were few alternatives for them. In the colonies, women certainly experienced a huge increase in mobility as a result of imperial rule, but their work choices remained more constrained than those of men. They could sometimes move within the Empire, but it would have been under indenture or with families. For men from the colonies, residence in Britain was a little easier. Those who worked, as many did, on ships that docked at British ports were quite likely to stay on in Britain for periods of time, working mostly in manual labour. Further up the social scale, it was not uncommon for elite colonial men to visit Britain, even sometimes to live there for long periods, as did Dadabhoi Naoroji who was sufficiently integrated into British society to serve as the member of parliament for a London constituency in the late nineteenth century.

White women of wealth, meanwhile, could move reasonably freely around the Empire. Activist women often visited imperial sites to investigate social conditions, while in the nineteenth century something of a cult developed in which wealthy women travellers visited spots off the tourist trail, publishing accounts of their adventures, many of which sold very well indeed. Although such women travelled generally without white male companions, they did not travel alone. Like the European male travellers and explorers of the era, these women travelled in the company of carriers, cooks and guides with local knowledge. This was very much a pastime of those with money to spare, and some amassed major collections of colonial art and artefacts. Mary Kingsley, who travelled extensively in West Africa in the closing years of the nineteenth century, collected widely. After her death from fever in South Africa in 1900 her uncle, the novelist Charles Kingsley, bequeathed her considerable collection to the Pitt Rivers Museum in Oxford.

Women such as Kingsley always remained anomalous, however. Women's contribution to empire-building was much more commonly seen through the lens of domesticity, and this helps explain why so many people continued to see a fundamental disconnect between the idea of the Empire and the presence of colonial women. In the early years, life was anything but domestic in the Empire. Even in the twentieth century, there were still plenty of rugged frontier outposts (memorialised over and over in fiction and in film) seen as masculine territory. Representations of the Empire in Britain tended to play up this dimension; it was more newsworthy and more exciting. Reading late nineteenth-century accounts of the Empire would have conjured a world of camel-riding, jungle-clearing, back-breaking labour in intemperate weather and always with danger close by. It was, then, only a place suitable for women when men had first civilised and tamed both the land and those who lived on it. Women's part was to maintain this hard-won advance by rearing future colonists, by maintaining order and cleanliness and by setting a civilising example. Writing in 1905 in the *Contemporary Review*, Liberal politician T. J. Macnamara declared that 'Empire cannot be built on rickety and flatchested citizens'.[6] Fears of diminishing working-class health and hygiene in the early twentieth century stimulated a greater attention to women's role as mothers in the white settler colonies as well as in Britain. Declining birth rates also triggered alarm for the future of the Empire. Increasingly governments investigated schemes for infant welfare and for promotion of family life, aided by a willing press who painted a picture of women's purpose in life as one of selfless devotion to the higher causes of family and Empire.

Missions in particular worked hard to promote Christian family models, and by the early twentieth century more women than men worked as missionaries in the Empire. Evangelical support for the abolition of slavery had often stressed that emancipation would permit Africans to live more

Figure 9.1 Missionary's wife and child seated on a hippopotamus, Africa, c.1910–20. The practice of photographing white colonists astride a dead wild animal was a common one, typically showing a proud hunter holding a gun astride his captured prey. Here the domestication of the usually male-dominated hunting scene conveys the masculine power of the British Empire over its feminised colonies

Source: Council for World Mission archive/SOAS Library (CWM/LMS/Africa/Photographs/Box 3/File 13)

easily in western family formations where men would head households and women raise the children. Schooling for girls in mission schools frequently emphasised feminised skills such as sewing and homecraft, while missionary support for convert families could be swiftly withdrawn if the family stepped out of line. Missionaries often struggled with their colonial congregations over control of children, for the missionaries regarded an education in Christianity as vital for securing permanent conversion. In many Australian colonies in the nineteenth century, Aboriginal children were removed from their natal families to institutions at the whim of local authorities, an unsettling forerunner of the 'stolen generation' years of the mid-twentieth century when part-Aboriginal children were forcibly placed in residential schools hundreds of miles from their families. Child removal in twentieth-century Australia (and among Canada's First Nations peoples) has become one of that country's greatest political scandals; by the late 1960s, 18 per cent of Aboriginal children in the Northern Territory were in care, removed by the state from their parents.

The growing female presence in the Empire created in some instances an inflated alarm about sexual danger. The long-standing prejudices entertained about the sexual looseness of 'lesser' peoples fuelled a fear that colonised men would be unable to control their sexual appetite for white women. The attack by Indian sepoys on English women and children at Cawnpore in 1857 quickly became in the British press a narrative of rape and sexual abuse as well as disloyalty. Although the evidence for those charges is flimsy, more than a half century later, when Indian soldiers fought alongside the British in the First World War, those convalescing from battle wounds in Britain were barely allowed off the hospital grounds for fear they would seduce British women. The War Office fought strenuously to ensure that British nurses were not engaged in duties that necessitated their even touching these men, for fear this would inflame the uncontrollable passions of the Indians.

This exaggerated vision of uncontrollable sexual desire led in some places to punitive laws that made the sexual assault of a white woman a capital offence. The first such law was passed in Southern Rhodesia in 1903, and copied in 1926 in Papua New Guinea where the law was explicitly named the White Women's Protection Ordinance. The New Guinea law remained in force until 1958. In Southern Rhodesia, although it was an offence for white women to engage in sexual relations with African men, or even to invite sexual attention from them, it was nonetheless black men who were likeliest to find themselves in court on such charges. 'Black peril' scares, as these have come to be known, reflected colonial anxiety about sexualised dangers to white male power. The thought that white women might choose sexual liaisons with men of colour was, if anything, an even more alarming prospect than that of their being coerced by such men.

Fears that white women might willingly stray into this sexually charged territory affected both colonial and domestic arenas. In the First World War, newspapers as well as official documents revealed qualms not only

Figure 9.2 Indian rebellion (1857) memorial at Cawnpore. Memorials to the English dead were common in India

Source: The Getty Research Institute (96.R.84)

that Indian soldiers would fascinate British women but that impression-able teenagers were being sexually lured by Chinese men. The race riots that rocked many British cities shortly after the war in 1919 were at least partially precipitated by white male resentment over white women's relationships with men of colour. It was around the same time that the Home Office issued marriage registrars with a warning statement to be given out to women considering marriage to men of allegedly lesser races. In addition to advising women that they might be marrying into polyg-amous cultures, the warning informed women that such marriages meant abandoning any protection from the British state. When a 'Savage South Africa' exhibition opened at London's Olympia in 1899, there was con-siderable controversy over the fact that the Zulu actors shared the stage with white women actresses. When one of the Africans became engaged to a white woman, the show was forced to close its doors to women. Critics saw the mixing of black men and white women as itself productive of the 'evil' of mixed-race marriage.

The gendered dangers that attended colonised peoples were, if less enthu-siastically policed by the colonial state, a critical feature of the experience of the colonised. Conflicts and jealousies over women were endemic in frontier societies where men outnumbered women: in these instances local women were highly vulnerable to rape, kidnapping and sexual coercion, and the penalties for colonising men were minimal. In the Australian outback in the nineteenth century it was taken for granted that white men could have their pick of the Aboriginal women they encountered, a practice commonly justified by claims that Aboriginal peoples were in any case promiscuous. It was not uncommon for Aboriginal women to be taken against their will by white settlers and kept in chains to prevent them from running away. The huge number of mixed-race children resulting from decades of exploitation would become in the mid-twentieth century the subject of an attempt to 'breed white' in Australia by removing them from their Aboriginal mothers and raising them with western and Christian values in residential schools. Never equal to white Australian children, these mixed-descent children were trained for work in domestic service if they were girls, and as farm and station hands if they were boys. At the same time, however, Aboriginal men accused of sexual violence against white women in colonial Australia were unlikely to obtain a fair trial, for their actions were considered, as in non-settler colonies, a dangerous threat to the ruling white race.

In some cases it was the after-effects of colonial rule that heightened the incidence of sexual and gendered violence. When the British withdrew from India in 1947 (see Chapter 11), the resulting violence led to the rape, assault and abduction of some 100,000 women by men of opposing religious factions. In many families, as news of the sexual violence spread, women were killed before they could be abducted, as a means to save the honour of the family. Women became a symbol of the anxieties produced by Partition, and they died in huge numbers on a battlefield produced by colonial rule and not of their own making. White fears of sexual danger may have been grossly out of proportion to reality, but sexual violence and danger were common experiences for colonised women, subject to colonialism's sexual coercion and its tendency to dehumanise the lives of colonised peoples.

The likelihood of colonial violence should not, however, blind us to the considerable efforts made by women to promote gender equality. Women in the colonies fought similar battles to those of British feminists to extend women's rights. Women in the white settler colonies of New Zealand and Australia won the right to vote early (see Chapter 4), although the extended franchise did not bring with it greater employment opportunity or other major changes in women's lives. In Australasia, women's suffrage (achieved in New Zealand in 1893 and by 1908 in Australia) was intended to stabilise and conserve the status quo, since it was widely assumed that women would either vote as their husbands did or be 'natural' conservatives. It is no coincidence that women's gains in Australia came at much the same moment that governments there were looking for ways to reduce the political influence of the predominantly male labour movement.

The question of suffrage was, however, merely theoretical in colonies where legislative bodies were appointed and not elected. As this slowly changed, women showed themselves ready and eager for political participation. Indian women demanded representation when the Government of India Act offered a limited opening of the political system in 1920. These cautious reforms gave Indians a say in provincial (but not central) government, and India's first elected woman took office on the Madras legislative council in 1927. In 1935, Indian women over the age of 21 and qualified by virtue of property or an education gained the right to vote; it was largely a symbolic victory for it enfranchised only some 6 million women in India's vast population. Yet women used their new rights vigorously; women won 56 of the 1,500 seats in the provincial Indian legislatures in 1936 and 1937. In Palestine, Jewish women fought for political representation (though not for Palestinian women) during the British Mandate period, a right they gained in the mid-1920s. Women were also active in the fight against colonialism, especially in the twentieth century. In Kenya, a detention camp for women Mau Mau supporters opened in 1954. Everywhere, colonised women joined the struggles for freedom from colonial rule: in Palestine, in Africa, in South-East and South Asia, anywhere where colonialism met local resistance (Chapter 10 will return us to their efforts).

Despite this long history of women's activism, British feminists tended to portray women from the colonies as helpless and degraded, enslaved and in need of help rather than as partners in a broader enterprise aimed at equality. Western feminists frequently enunciated their role as one of rescue, not so different from the aims of missionaries and reformers. In the late nineteenth century, the feminist press ran innumerable articles on the 'downtrodden' Indian woman kept behind high walls and deprived of an education. In the 1920s and 1930s, women politicians in Britain pressed the government to intervene in colonies that practised female circumcision, or where girls were sold into domestic servitude. It was rare that these campaigners sought alliances with local women's groups. They saw themselves rather as pioneers in places where women were too brutalised to fight on their own behalf.

The tendency to view colonised women as needing guidance and protection was often the result of a pro-imperialist politics within feminism. Many feminist activists were, in the nineteenth and early twentieth century, committed imperialists and their critiques were aimed in large part at Britain's failure to improve the lot of women rather than at the principles of colonialism. Yet even among those identified as anti-imperialist, the tendency to assume that colonised women could not speak for themselves has remained common.

There were always, of course, women who rejected the idea that non-western and colonial women were subordinate or more oppressed than their western sisters. One woman who thought that gender systems in other countries were certainly no worse than in her native Britain was Lady Mary Wortley Montagu who, as wife of the British consul to the Ottoman emperor, lived in the eastern Mediterranean in the early 1700s. Montagu thought that the veiling of women, so widely regarded by Europeans as a sign of female oppression, had a liberating aspect since it permitted women to go about disguised and invisible to their husbands.

Masculinity and femininity, defined according to western norms, were central planks in the management of the Empire. This is not to suggest that the societies Britain encountered were gender-neutral. On the contrary, they had their own notions of what constituted gender, and as we have seen, it was common for the colonisers to deprecate those ideas. Gender, defined as the social roles differently imposed upon men and women, shaped the colonial world deeply and in myriad ways. The expectations and the values of the multitudes of peoples involved – whether by choice or by force – in the colonial enterprise frequently clashed in this critical but slippery arena. The imbalance in sex ratios so often produced by the demands of the colonial economy, the differing outlooks on sex roles and on sexual behaviours, on the definition of the family, on what men and women could and should do meant that gender considerations were always a point of negotiation and a critical issue within the colonies. This was no side issue, but a key and central organising principle by which colonial rule was shaped and maintained.

Notes

1 Sigmund Freud, 'Character and Anal Eroticism', in J. Strachey (ed.), *The Standard Edition of the Complete Psychological Works of Sigmund Freud*, vol. 9 (London: Hogarth Press, 1953), pp. 169–75.
2 Edward Said, *Culture and Imperialism* (New York: Alfred Knopf, 1993), p. 137.
3 Margery Perham, *Pacific Prelude: A Journey to Samoa and Australasia* (London: Peter Owen, 1988), p. 77.

4 Genesis 3:16.
5 Edward Long, *The History of Jamaica. Reflections on Its Situation, Settlements, Inhabitants, Climate, Products, Commerce, Laws and Government*, vol. 2 (London, 1776; reprint edition, Montreal and Kingston: McGill-Queen's University Press, 2002), p. 364.
6 T. J. Macnamara, 'In Corpore Sano', *Contemporary Review* (February 1905), p. 248, quoted in Anna Davin, 'Imperialism and Motherhood', *History Workshop Journal* 9 (1978), p. 17.

Further reading

Two edited collections – Clare Midgley's *Gender and Imperialism* (Manchester: Manchester University Press, 1998) and Philippa Levine's *Gender and Empire* (Oxford: Oxford University Press, 2004) – engage the relations between gender history and the history of the British Empire.

For the experience of African women under colonialism, *Women in African Colonial Histories* (Jean Allman, Susan Geiger, and Nakanyike Musisi (eds), Bloomington, IN: Indiana University Press, 2002), is an invaluable collection. The four volumes [*Women in the Middle East and North Africa; Women in Latin America and the Caribbean; Women in Sub-Saharan Africa;* and *Women in Asia*] in the Indiana University Press series 'Restoring Women to History' (1999) are immensely helpful introductions to the topic.

In *Married to the Empire: Gender, Politics and Imperialism in India, 1883–1947* (Manchester: Manchester University Press, 2002), Mary A. Procida details the lives of British women living in the Empire. Henrice Altink looks at the lives of Jamaican women after slavery in *Destined for a Life of Service: Defining African-Jamaican Womanhood, 1865–1938* (Manchester: Manchester University Press, 2011). Kate Law's focus in *Gendering the Settler State: White Women, Race, Liberalism and Empire in Rhodesia, 1950–1980* (New York: Routledge, 2016) is on the politics of white settler women in late twentieth-century Rhodesia.

Antoinette Burton's *Burdens of History: British Feminists, Indian Women, and Imperial Culture, 1865–1915* (Chapel Hill, NC: University of North Carolina Press, 1994) takes a critical look at the attitudes of British feminists towards colonised women in the high colonial era. Clare Midgley's *Feminism and Empire: Women Activists in Imperial Britain, 1790–1865* (London: Routledge, 2007) suggests a direct link between the Empire and the emergence of a feminist politics in Britain.

For discussions of colonial masculinity, see Mrinalini Sinha, *Colonial Masculinity: The 'Manly Englishman' and the 'Effeminate Bengali' in the Late Nineteenth Century* (Manchester: Manchester University Press, 1995) and Wilson Chacko Jacob, *Working Out Egypt: Effendi Masculinity and Subject Formation in Colonial Modernity, 1870–1940* (Durham, NC: Duke University Press, 2011). In *Martial Races: The Military, Race and Masculinity in British Imperial Culture, 1857–1914* (Manchester: Manchester University Press, 2004) Heather Streets compares Scottish and Indian military regiments in a study of military masculinity. In *May the Best Man Win: Sport, Masculinity, and Nationalism in Great Britain and the Empire, 1880–1935* (New York: Palgrave Macmillan, 2004), Patrick F. McDevitt looks at gender and masculinity through the growth of sporting events and new sports in the Empire.

Sexuality, and especially male sexuality, is the theme of Anne McClintock's *Imperial Leather: Race, Gender, and Sexuality in the Colonial Context* (New York: Routledge, 1995), while in *Prostitution, Race and Politics: Policing Venereal Disease in the British Empire* (New York: Routledge, 2003) Philippa Levine explores colonial sexuality through an investigation of venereal disease policy throughout the British Empire. In *Gender and the Making of Modern Medicine in Colonial Egypt* (Aldershot: Ashgate, 2010) Hibba Abugideiri shows how colonial attitudes to gender shaped the contours of medical training and provision. *Black Peril, White Virtue: Sexual Crime in Southern Rhodesia, 1902–1935* (Bloomington, IN: Indiana University Press, 2000) by Jock McCulloch details the laws which forbade interracial sexual relations in Rhodesia. Damon Salesa's *Racial Crossings: Race, Intermarriage, and the Victorian British Empire* (Oxford: Oxford University Press, 2011), though focused on New Zealand, underscores the significance of sexuality and especially interracial sexuality, for broader colonial concerns.

Family structure in the nineteenth-century Empire is the theme of Elizabeth Buettner's study, *Empire Families: Britons and Late Imperial India* (Oxford: Oxford University Press, 2004), while Emma Rothschild's *The Inner Life of Empires: An Eighteenth Century History* (Princeton, NJ: Princeton University Press, 2011) traces the imperial sites which shaped the lives of the Johnstone siblings in the eighteenth century. In *Colonial Relations: The Douglas-Connolly Family and the Nineteenth-Century Imperial World* (Cambridge University Press, 2015), Adele Perry traces the fortunes of a mixed-race elite family in the Empire over four generations.

ntesting empire

Britain's Empire was at its largest following the end of the First World War, augmented by the mandated territories ceded to it by the new League of Nations. Yet we might just as reasonably emphasise not growth but contraction as the most characteristic feature of the twentieth-century British Empire (see Chapter 11). Here, and as the backdrop against which to understand decolonisation, we will discuss the slow and patchy but nonetheless critical growth of resistance to British rule in the Empire. Nationalist movements devoted to wresting control out of colonial hands posed a significant threat to imperial rule.

Nationalism already had a lengthy history by the time it began to appear among colonised peoples. In the nineteenth century, significant changes in European boundaries created the modern countries of Italy and Germany, while the First World War redrew the map of central and of eastern Europe in significant ways. Much of this change was achieved as a result of military and imperial activity, but it was accompanied by a considerable groundswell of popular sentiment about consolidating national identities. Colonial versions of these nationalist leanings could differ radically from those in Europe, but they shared an emphasis on the distinction between legitimate and illegitimate rule. In an era in which western imperial powers were embracing ever more democratic forms of government, the profound lack of indigenous representation in the majority of the colonies looked more and more out of step with the political tenor of the age. This is not to suggest that the forms of nationalism that took hold in British colonies were purely western imports. There were certainly western influences at work, but shrewd activists were also skilled at reinventing nationalist sentiments in an idiom more likely to appeal in their own populations. As a result, we see a lively range of activity in different parts of the Empire: what linked them, for the most part, was that they increasingly challenged the validity of British colonial rule. Anti-colonial nationalism was a specific form of nationalism yoked to a critique of colonial governance, but though it often helped move the process of decolonisation along, it was by no means the only factor in that process. British officials took anti-colonial nationalism very seriously, and responses to it were often vigorous and punitive.

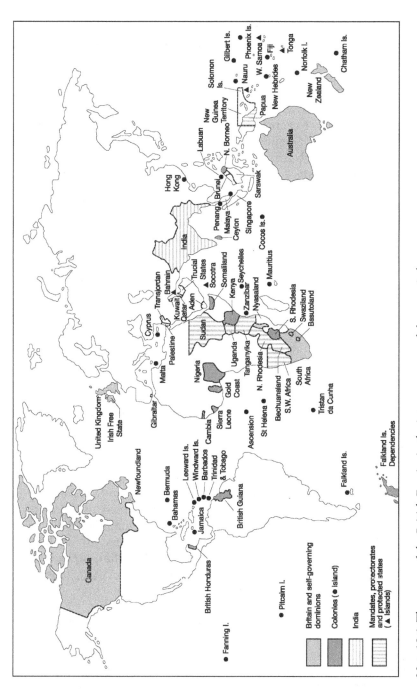

Map 10.1 The scope of the British Empire in the interwar years of the twentieth century

Source: *British Imperialism, 1750–1970*, Cambridge University Press (Smith, Simon c. 1988) p. 2, © Cambridge University Press, reproduced with permission of the author and publisher

To place a beginning date on anti-colonial nationalism is no easy task. Obviously it was a form of nationalist sentiment closely tied to the experience of being colonised by outside forces, and protests against such authority can be found early on in the history of the Empire. It was in the twentieth century, however, that protests spread – and spread quickly – such that very large segments of the Empire experienced sustained protest on a significant scale. The British had largely dismissed colonial resistance in the nineteenth century as local and tribal, but it became much harder to deny nationalist leanings in the twentieth century. Christopher Bayly has pointed out that the 'big' names in imperial administration at the turn of the century – Curzon in India, Milner in South Africa and Cromer in Egypt – prompted a rise in resistance to colonialism with the tactics they employed for 'heading off, diverting, or suppressing demand by the educated intelligentsia for greater freedom and political representation'. This was part of what John Darwin describes as the 'more aggressive and formalised imperial rule' in the face of increasingly stiff competition from other imperial contenders.[1]

At the start of the twentieth century, Britain's two major wars – the South African (or Boer) War of 1899–1902 and the First World War (1914–18) – shook loose a significant number of imperial ties. It had been by no means certain that Britain would win in South Africa, and it was only as the British endorsed increasingly ruthless tactics that they gained the upper hand against the Boers. The use of detention camps and of a 'scorched earth' policy to wreck the productivity of Boer farms did not boost respect for Britain around the world. There was a strong outcry against these tactics, yet they re-emerged half a century on when the British encountered resistance to their rule in Kenya and the Malay peninsula.

Trouble had been brewing in South Africa some years before war broke out. The new wealth provided by diamonds and gold had enriched the Boer states in the region and made them more confident of their political muscle. But the Transvaal president, Paul Kruger, had a formidable adversary in Cecil Rhodes whose expansionist aims did not sit well with the anti-British Boers. A decade of increasing friction resulted in the outbreak of war in 1899, and the settlement which ended it, by the 1902 Treaty of Vereeniging, began the slow unravelling of British control in the region. The South Africa Act of 1909 gave the Boers rights over their own internal affairs, but the three High Commission territories of Basutoland (Lesotho), Bechuanaland (Botswana) and Swaziland – which independent South Africa repeatedly tried to claim as its own – remained under British control.

The First World War likewise destabilised a number of imperial relationships within the Empire. Colonial troops were crucial, given how long the war dragged on. This was a highly labour intensive war requiring large numbers of troops in all theatres. Dominion and dependent colonies alike provided fighters and labour corps to bolster the British effort, but not without protest and dissension. Around 11,000 Boer soldiers mutinied when ordered to serve in late 1914. Australia twice rejected the policy of conscription, sending only a volunteer army. New Zealand (in 1916) and Canada (in 1917) introduced a military draft, although French Canada vigorously protested the Military Service Act. Canada led the Dominions in criticising British handling of the war, and demanded a greater role in determining wartime policy. The 1917 Imperial War Conference, made up of Dominion leaders and Whitehall politicians, was founded in response to the demands of the settler colonies, although the daily operations of the war remained firmly in British hands. The fledgling navies that Canada and Australia had so recently formed were brought under the authority of the Admiralty with very little consultation.

Dominion criticisms of Britain were seldom grounded in opposition to the war itself; both the leaders of the Dominion countries and their electorates mostly supported the war. Their frustrations concerned their own role in its conduct, and what they saw as British mismanagement. Among white-populated colonies, only Ireland boasted a strong anti-war faction, and it had the lowest rate of military recruitment. A mere 6 per cent of adult Irish men fought compared with 19 per cent of white New Zealanders and 13 per cent of white South Africans, Australians and Canadians (mostly Anglo-Canadians). Conscription, introduced in Britain in March 1915, was not applied in Ireland until April 1918.

India was invited to the Imperial War Conference, but the Crown Colonies and Protectorates were wholly unrepresented in wartime decision-making. Colonial troops from the dependent colonies were used as labourers, loading and unloading ships and transports, and were not issued weapons for fear they would turn them on their white masters. They enjoyed far less freedom than their white counterparts: their leaves were more constrained, and they were often not permitted to leave their camps except under escort.

Alone among the dependent colonies, India provided a significant fighting force for the British, including well over 100,000 on the Western Front in France. Indian soldiers had frequently been deployed in trouble spots around the Empire, but this was the first time they had been called upon to fight in Europe. When war broke out, nationalism was already widespread in India and activists expected that the help India afforded Britain would be repaid after the war with greater political representation and a move towards self-government.

Closer to home, in Ireland, nationalists continued to pursue their political goals during the war. 1912 saw the first measure of self government (Home Rule) for Ireland since the union of 1800, but the outbreak of war led to its suspension. By the time the war ended in 1918, plans for Home Rule were in tatters, and Ireland was on the brink of civil war. Taking advantage of the fact that military attention was focused elsewhere, a small cadre of Irish Republicans had proclaimed a provisional government in Dublin in 1916. In what became known as the Easter Uprising, some 1,600 Republican supporters occupied major buildings in Dublin, declaring a provisional government independent of Britain. Within a week troops brought in from

English garrisons had regained control of the city, but not before considerable damage had been done to public buildings. Around 3,500 people were arrested, about twice as many as were known to have been involved – the British government was anxious to send a stern message to Irish nationalists. In doing so, however, the government made a critical error that increased support for their nationalist antagonists: 80 rebels were sentenced to death for treason and in May 1916, shortly after the rebellion had been quelled, 15 were actually executed. Rather than quieting or frightening nationalist feelings, this quick and harsh response alienated the Irish public, pushing many who had not supported the rebellion closer to the nationalist camp.

The life of Roger Casement, also executed for treason in 1916, throws a revealing light on the close imperial connections of the era. Born in Dublin in 1864, Casement had as a young adult supported the British Empire, and worked as a British consul in various locations. He was well known in the early 1900s as a campaigner against human rights abuses in colonial and semi-colonial settings, and had broadcast the plight of workers on Congolese and Peruvian rubber plantations. By the time war broke out in 1914, Casement's disillusion with the Empire had led him along the path of Irish nationalism, and he had helped found the Irish Volunteers in 1913. His attempt to raise a nationalist brigade among Irish prisoners of war in Germany was what got him executed, though the deliberate circulation of his diaries (which revealed that he was gay) helped turn opinion against a man who had once been hailed as a great humanitarian. In 1965 his body was returned to Ireland from the grounds of London's Pentonville prison and Casement was given a state funeral in Dublin.

Ireland was not the only colony, however, where hostility and protest erupted during the war years. Serious uprisings in South Africa in 1914 and in 1915 demonstrated that the hostilities that had erupted there during the South African War were by no means contained. Britain also faced disturbances in Egypt, Turkey, Afghanistan and Iraq as well as in India soon after the end of the war. There were Buddhist revolts in Ceylon in 1915, peasant uprisings in Kerala in 1921, protests by the pan-Muslim Khilafat movement and jihads in Somaliland throughout the first two decades of the new century.

The forms that nationalism took in settler colonies and in dependent colonies were quite distinctive. The partial but considerable self-government enjoyed by the white populations of the Dominions, along with their strong sense of racial and cultural unity with Britain, deeply influenced their articulation of nationalism. Their elective political systems made their demands less far-reaching than those of colonies demanding independence from more autocratic systems of government. Largely uninterested in breaking away from the Empire, the white settler colonies were keen to consolidate the principles of self-determination. In 1917 the Imperial War Conference passed a resolution proposed by Jan Smuts of South Africa that called for a special conference at the end of the war to discuss full political and diplomatic autonomy for

Figure 10.1 Safe as the British Empire: War Savings Certificates, First World War poster. Despite the many colonial uprisings faced by Britain during the war years, posters such as this one emphasised that Britain's financial as well as political and global security were deeply tied to its Empire

Source: Private Collection/Photo © Barbara Singer/Bridgeman Images

the Dominions; Britain could no longer dictate policy without discussion and negotiation. At the Peace Conference in 1919 – where the former colonies of the German Empire were divided among the Allied powers – the Dominions insisted upon and won representation separate from the British. And almost as soon as Britain had formally acknowledged Dominion rights to negotiate treaties without imperial input, Canada signed a fishing rights treaty with the United States in 1923, completely bypassing Britain.

Ireland alone among the white-populated colonies took a different political path. Deeply divided at the end of the war, plans for Home Rule were all but impossible. Faced with nationalist agitation elsewhere, Britain was anxious to hold on to Ireland. Its secession from the Empire would clearly loosen more ties than merely those between Britain and Ireland. In 1918, the republican Sinn Fein party won 73 seats in the general election, and quickly set up its own assembly, declaring, as the nationalists had done in 1916, a republic that the British refused to recognise. In an effort to appease both separatist Republicans and Unionists (who wanted to maintain Ireland's ties with Britain), the 1920 Government of Ireland Act created two separate parliaments, divided broadly along Republican/Unionist as well as Catholic/Protestant lines. The six counties of Ulster in the north-east, largely Protestant and Unionist, were to become Northern Ireland, while the larger 26-county Catholic area would be renamed Southern Ireland. This plan for self-government failed, for while the Ulster counties had by 1921 embraced their new status, the Southern Irish activists refused to swear an oath of allegiance to the British Crown, a requirement upon which the British government insisted. Civil war and bitter conflict led finally to the granting in 1921 of Dominion status to Southern Ireland, renamed the Irish Free State. The partition of the country, however, spelled trouble. Fighting between disappointed Republicans and committed Unionists in Ulster disrupted people's lives long after the separation of the two Irelands.

The Dominion powers watched the Irish situation closely, for it raised critical questions about the limits of autonomy for self-governing entities within the Empire. The declaration of war in 1914 by the British monarch had been a declaration on behalf of the whole Empire: there was no need nor provision for consultation. During the war, Dominion leaders not only felt free to criticise British handling of the conflict but pressed for a greater and more influential role in policy-making. That push was maintained after the war, and the conflict in Ireland was in no small measure influential in applying that pressure. In 1931, the Statute of Westminster created the modern Commonwealth, formally acknowledging the Dominion (Commonwealth) countries as independent states no longer bound, other than by choice, by past or future British laws. Yet the dominant sentiment in these colonies remained pro-imperial. The majority did not seek to sever ties with Britain, but rather to approach equality within an imperial framework. This was in part an expression of a deeply held sense of British identity but it was also a shrewd assessment of military and diplomatic advantage. None of the Dominions seceded after 1931; complete separation was seldom their goal.

ADVANCED AUSTRALIA!

AUSTRALIA. "IF YOU PLEASE, MOTHER, I WANTED A LITTLE MORE FREEDOM, SO I 'VE HAD THIS
LATCH-KEY MADE. YOU DON'T MIND?"
BRITANNIA. "I 'M SURE, MY DEAR, IF ANYBODY CAN BE TRUSTED WITH IT, YOU CAN."

[Clause 74, "Australasian Federation Bill," abolishes appeal to Privy Council.]

Figure 10.2 Advanced Australia! *Punch*, 25 April 1900. The wry comments of the
satirical magazine, *Punch*, on the occasion of Australia's federation as
a single nation
Source: *Punch*, 25 April 1900

The significant changes in the relationship between the imperial centre and
the Dominions did not extend to Britain's other and more numerous colonial possessions, and in these, the aim of complete separation from Britain
was generally more developed. Though India had attended the Imperial War

Conference and the Cabinet, as well as the 1919 peace negotiations, its postwar history differed markedly from that of the Dominions. Nationalism was already a factor in Indian politics long before the war. The Indian National Congress (INC, known as the Congress) founded in 1885 was not the only organisation committed to nationalism, but its lengthy and influential history makes it prominent in any account of Indian anti-colonial nationalism. In its early days it drew largely from the same urban middle-class intelligentsia who had flocked to nineteenth-century reform societies. Its base of support would broaden considerably in the twentieth century, but it was in the cities, and especially in Calcutta, that its early promise was nurtured. But the INC was not unique and nor was nationalism always an organised force. For example, in 1913, Indian film-maker, D. G. Phalke, released what he called the first Indian film made for an Indian audience with an entirely Indian production team. His films, grounded in Hindu mythology, were hugely successful and often openly nationalist.

The resurgence of militant Hinduism in the late nineteenth and early twentieth century fed anti-colonial nationalism. The reassertion of non-western values and a strident critique of the west's role in India offered a non-western model of nationalism quite different from that promoted by the INC, and one that was sometimes productive of significant tensions between Hindus and Muslims. The British encouragement of the formation of the All-India Muslim League in 1906 as a counter to the Hindu-dominated INC was regarded by many in India as a deliberate manipulation of religious divisions designed to undermine the growth of a broader anti-colonial solidarity.

In the years before the First World War, nationalist challenges to British rule in India had been common, and both violent and peaceful tactics were employed. The concept of *swaraj* (self-government) was firmly in place among Indian activists by the early twentieth century. There were boycotts of British-manufactured goods, and from 1908 (at about the same time that militant suffrage activists in Britain turned to violent protest) radical nationalists resorted to bombings and assassination attempts. In 1906, the INC declared a formal commitment to self-government for India. Faced with these disturbances, the government offered some small measure of political representation in 1909 in the form of a limited electorate. This minimal concession was drastically undercut by a draconian press censorship act instituted a year later in 1910. This pattern of parallel concession and repression by the British authorities, each round of which sparked further anti-colonial militancy, would endure for decades.

The outbreak of war in 1914 further stoked discontent with colonial rule. The fiscal implications of the war were, for India, serious. Land revenue, the staple form of colonial government revenue, was augmented by customs and income taxes, the latter introduced in the cities in 1886. Indians found themselves paying for this distant war both with bodies and with taxes. By 1917 nationalism was once more growing in India, and political discontent among soldiers fighting in the war had the colonial authorities sufficiently worried that they carefully monitored the letters sent home to India by those fighting on the Western Front.

The protest movement known as *satyagraha* (truth-force or soul-force) began to gather steam in 1917. Its dual intent was to demonstrate Indian fitness for self-rule and to show respect for the enemy. Its most famous advocate was, of course, Mohandas 'Mahatma' Gandhi, who had returned to India in 1915 after 20 years abroad. Between 1915 and 1917 Gandhi travelled extensively in India, disseminating the principles of non-violent resistance, passive civil disobedience and a rejection of western values. Faced with growing unrest, the secretary of state for India, Edwin Montagu, announced in 1917 that Britain intended to move towards responsible self-government for India, but the actions of government did little to persuade Indian nationalists of the sincerity of this commitment. The INC had supported India's participation in the war, imagining that self-government would be the reward for participation. They were to be deeply disappointed by what Britain offered. 1919 in particular was a grim year for Indian anti-colonial nationalism. The Rowlatt Acts kept in place emergency measures usually reserved for wartime, which substantially curtailed ordinary civil liberties. Trial without jury and internment without trial led to widespread and serious protests across British India. It was at one such protest that one of the most notorious events in twentieth-century colonial history occurred. In the Punjabi city of Amritsar a large but peaceful crowd of protesters gathered in April 1919 in an enclosed area, the Jallianwalla Bagh. Without warning, the local military commander, General Reginald Dyer, ordered his troops to disperse the crowd by gunfire. Dyer sustained the firing for ten minutes as chaos and panic grew. Some 380 Indians were killed and more than 1,100 wounded. The firing came at a tense moment, shortly after the murder of a number of Europeans in and near the city, and after the assault of a white woman missionary. Dyer had not only ordered public floggings in retribution but had issued the notorious 'crawling order', forcing Indians to crawl on their hands and knees at the site of the missionary woman's beating. Relations between the British authorities in Amritsar and the Indian community were thus particularly tense when the firing occurred, and not helped by the reputation of the local lieutenant-governor, Michael O'Dwyer, who made no secret of his distaste for Indian political activism.

Dyer was officially censured and forced to step down from his position, but no legal action was ever pursued against him, and in some quarters he was treated like a hero. Reminiscent of the split in British opinion over Governor Eyre's handling of the Morant Bay rebellion in Jamaica in 1865 (see Chapter 6), Dyer attracted both ebullient support and fierce criticism in Britain. The British community in India wholeheartedly supported him. The House of Lords made clear its refusal to see Dyer punished in any significant way. On his return to England a sum of £30,000, raised by supporters, awaited him.

The failure of the British government meaningfully to punish Dyer's actions bolstered Indian anti-colonial nationalism and made Britain's claims to be a civilising coloniser seem rather hollow. By 1920, a major campaign of non-co-operation was in full swing, just as the British unveiled the latest round of political reform for India. The Government of India Act instituted a dyarchy in which both Indians and Britons served in ministerial offices. Three of the seven ministers on the executive council were to be Indian, and Indians would serve as ministers in the provincial councils. The law increased the size of the electorate, but the changes were largely cosmetic and nationalists knew it. Legislation from the provinces could be invalidated by the governor-general and the new Indian ministers were largely assigned to the 'softer' portfolios – education, health, agriculture – rather than being entrusted with sensitive and controversial issues such as revenue or policing. The Indian princes were brought into the new system via a chamber of princes which the British intended as a conservative counter to radical nationalism.

Discontent and nationalist activism, far from being quelled by these reforms, swelled in the 1920s and 1930s. Urban rioting increased as did the Gandhian tactic of civil disobedience. Calcutta suffered 40 riots in 1926 alone; there were assassinations and robberies as well as bombings. The response of the imperial authorities was increasingly military and punitive. Violence, despite Gandhi's pacifist stand, was common. The economic hardships of these years of rising prices and uncertain harvests also radicalised the countryside. Attacks on landlords and on property were common, and in the factories trades unions began to strengthen and grow. Class-based protests, urban and rural, added to the foment of unrest aimed in large part at colonial rule and its consequences. Congress boycotted the opening of the legislative assembly in 1929 and a new campaign of civil disobedience began in 1930.

Out of this crisis came the 1935 Government of India Act, which sought to placate nationalists, maintain cordial relations with the Indian principalities and sustain the support of the pro-imperialist wing within British politics. It failed on every count. The principle of dyarchy was extended to central government while the provincial councils were awarded full self-government. The electorate remained limited to about 30 million people (out of a population numbering more than 352 million) and defence and foreign policy were reserved to the governor-general. The Act nonetheless produced extraordinary election results in 1937, with the Congress Party securing an absolute majority in 6 of the 11 provinces and forming a government in 7 of them. The outbreak of war only two years later brought this political experiment to an abrupt end as Congress leaders resigned their posts in protest as the British once more declared war on behalf of India without any consultation. The contrast with the Dominions, where leaders had the right to declare war (or not) on their own behalf, hammered home the differential treatment of white settler colonies and of India. This inequality was deeply damaging. In 1942, the widespread 'Quit India' campaign led to the swift banning of Congress and the jailing of its leaders. These tactics fanned nationalist anger and the campaign spread from Bombay into the country-side and across the vast expanse of British India, leading to violent riots and attacks on government property and on the police.

The 'Quit India' campaign was only one of the wartime nationalist crises Britain faced in India. Led by Subhas Chandra Bose, a contingent of Indian soldiers, aided by the Japanese, formed the Indian National Army (INA) in opposition to British colonial rule. By 1943, Bose had some 11,000 soldiers ready, and was training another 20,000. Although Bose's campaign petered out, the INA demonstrated quite clearly that nationalist desires in many quarters far outweighed loyalty to the British. British efforts to court-martial some of the leaders stirred protest in India after the war, in much the same way that the execution of the Easter Rising rebels in Dublin made nationalist policies more attractive to many in Ireland. The British government, it seems, learned few lessons when it came to relations with their nationalist opponents. None of their actions suggest a state anxious to divest itself of its colonial possessions, and uninterested in its Empire. On the contrary, the reaction of British governments to nationalist protests suggests that neither Labour nor Conservative governments were ready to abandon the Empire. Among the most prominent of the pro-imperialists was Winston Churchill who had been vocal in his fears that the establishment of the Irish Free State and the prospect of a Dominion India would weaken Britain's hold on its Empire. Anti-colonial nationalism (in Ireland and in India especially) was, by this measure, successful: it forced the imperial centre to debate the very nature of the colonial enterprise.

By summer 1945, when Congress leaders were released from jail, it was clear that independence for India was inevitable. Growing violence between Hindu and Muslim Indians alongside nationalist agitation speeded the transfer of power, and the end result (detailed in Chapter 11) was the momentous partition of the former British India into India and Pakistan in August 1947, both as British Dominions. The subsequent violence was immense, but the two new states survived.

In the second volume of her autobiography, the white Rhodesian novelist, Doris Lessing, describes the moment in 1956 when she could no longer see Britain in a sentimental light. 'How very careless, how lazy, how indifferent the British Empire was, how lightly it took on vast countries and millions of people.'[2] Lessing's disappointment with what she saw as a cavalier and heartless Empire was unusual for a white African, but large numbers of black Africans shared her opinion. Colonised peoples could not but be aware of the growing gap between their own economic and political condition and those of the west; even during the years of the Depression when severe unemployment and considerable hardship affected many in Britain, the contrast between the developed and the colonial world was still stark.

In the West Indies, the suffrage was extended during the Second World War but the new constitutions granted only limited self-government. Moreover, labour conditions prompted the growth of trades unions which proved fertile ground for the development of nationalist leaders such as future Barbadian premier, Grantley Adams. In colonies where a wealthy white settler class lived in style while indigenous people found themselves on ever more marginal land, this visible disparity yielded growing resentment of colonial rule. Britain's decision in 1906 to allow a Master and Servant Ordinance in Kenya (which harshly punished Africans who violated labour contracts) and other legislation skewed to settler interests, fuelled deep resentment. It was to protect African land rights that in 1928 Jomo Kenyatta (first president of Kenya after independence) and Harry Thuku launched an organised political campaign among Africans in Kenya. Severe economic hardship in interwar Africa strengthened anti-colonial sentiment, and the labour migration that saw thousands of men moving in search of work enlarged urban populations, which were the earliest and most successful home for nationalist recruiting.

Throughout the Middle East, too, the British faced significant opposition to their influence and rule. Nationalists watched with concern when Muslim lands were given, without consultation, to the European colonial powers when the Ottoman Empire was broken up after the war. This new consolidation of European colonialism in the Muslim Middle East revealed that the voices of colonised peoples were of little importance and that the era of European imperialism was far from over. Self-determination was more theory and vision than practice. In Egypt, the British colonial authorities ruthlessly suppressed nationalism, tightly controlling what the local press could publish. When riots broke out there in 1919 (as they did that year in many British-controlled arenas), the British offered minor concessions to the nationalists. Despite bitter opposition from pro-imperial politicians such as Churchill, Britain declared Egypt independent in 1922 while still maintaining control of the Suez Canal and of foreign affairs. It was a situation guaranteed to raise ire among Egyptian nationalists, deprived of genuine control of Egyptian affairs. Britain also managed to upset the Dominion countries in that year, and along similar lines, expecting them – without consultation as in 1914–18 – to provide troops for a possible war with Turkey. The refusal of support by Canada and South Africa signalled a growing gulf between Britain and the Dominions. In the end, war was averted but the episode (known as the 1922 Chanak crisis) revealed that strains within and beyond the Empire were varied and deep. Russia had openly backed Turkey's claim for the return of former Ottoman territories, France had done so more covertly, leaving Britain diplomatically isolated.

Another area where British failure kindled nationalism was in Palestine whose administration (Mandate) Britain had formally acquired in 1920, but which had in practice become British in 1917 when military action forced the Turks out of the region. Zionist settlers in Palestine had been assured in 1917, in the so-called 'Balfour Declaration', that 'His Majesty's Government view with favour the establishment in Palestine of a national home for the Jewish people'.[3] Yet the British had also promised the Palestinians that their lands would not be compromised. These pledges were clearly incompatible despite a dividing of the territory at the River Jordan into Jewish and Arab zones. Britain's interest in Palestine stemmed, at least in part, from a desire to curb the ambitions of other European colonies. French influence in the Middle East was well established and the British hoped that Palestine would serve as a buffer between the Suez Canal and French-controlled Syria. They hoped that an overture to European Jews might help persuade the Russians to withdraw from the war and the Americans to enter it, both of which would help secure an Allied victory, by no means a foregone conclusion in 1917.

Growing Arab–Jewish violence resulted from continued Zionist migration to the region. In 1926 about 150,000 Jewish settlers lived in Palestine; by 1936, as fascism in Europe became more boldly anti-Semitic, those numbers rose to around 400,000, representing one-third of the total population of the area. The continued influx of Jews in the 1930s precipitated Arab attacks on both British troops and Jewish settlements. Serious rioting in 1929 resulted in more than 200 deaths. Until the Arab revolt of 1936 in Palestine, the British underestimated Arab nationalism. In the three years of this uprising, more than 5,000 Arabs died, and the British army burned villages and detained thousands of suspects. They were aided by armed Jewish police detachments. Arab Palestinians felt betrayed by the influx; Jewish settlers were frustrated by what they saw as Britain's dilatoriness in formalising a homeland. The restriction on Jewish immigration that Britain then imposed in 1941 could not have come at a worse time given the massive scale of the detention and killing of Jews that was now in force in parts of Europe.

In July 1946, 91 people were killed when the paramilitary Zionist organisation Irgun planted a bomb in the basement of the King David Hotel in Jerusalem (see Figure 10.3) that served as the Mandate headquarters. The result was the detention of some 800 suspected activists and a curb on civil liberties to which Irgun responded with further attacks. The majority of those who died were local Arabs, deepening the antagonism between Arabs and Jews in the region. In Britain anti-Semitic riots broke out in cities with large Jewish populations – just after the close of a war that had revealed the shocking depths of anti-Semitism in Europe. Both sides saw Britain as failing to fulfil promises.

In Iraq too, Arab rebellions against the British defined the 1920s, but the economic and strategic importance of the region took precedence over placating anti-colonial activists. It was only after the 1939–45 war that any substantive independence would come to the region (as shown in Chapter 11). Even after Iraq gained its independence in 1932, the British insisted on the use of Iraqi airfields for quick response in the region, and in return helped the new regime to quash Kurdish nationalism.

Figure 10.3 The King David Hotel, Jerusalem, after the bombing, 1946
Source: Popperfoto/Getty Images

Further south in sub-Saharan Africa, anti-colonial activities were also on the rise. In the 1890s, the West African writer Edward Blyden toured the USA and Britain, as well as West Africa, advocating African nationalism. What would become in 1925 the African National Congress (ANC) was founded in 1912 as the South African Native National Congress, adopting the passive resistance tactics of Indian nationalism. The South African Industrial and Commercial Workers Union organised successful strikes in 1919 and 1920, and the interwar years saw growing links between African-Americans, such as Marcus Garvey and his followers, and South African nationalists. Anti-colonialists learned from one another's struggles across the Empire.

Rioting and rebellion against British rule in Africa gathered steam in the early years of the twentieth century. Dissatisfaction over working conditions and economic inequality often helped fuel early nationalist sentiment. Violence broke out even before the First World War in British Guiana, Nigeria, Kenya, Natal and elsewhere in southern Africa, and though not all of this protest was explicitly anti-colonial, the widespread unhappiness with imperial rule spurred the growth of nationalism. A revolt among the

Nandi people in Kenya in 1905 over taxation and land had prompted a military sortie by the British that left over 1,000 people dead. Later nationalists claimed the Nandi leader, Koitalel Samoei, as Kenya's first freedom fighter for his resistance to imperial encroachment in East Africa. Death rates among local protesters were often high in these riots, although this did little to deter riots which, by 1918, had spread to Kenya and Northern Rhodesia, then to Aden out in the Red Sea and to Somaliland in the 1920s. Rail strikes crippled Sierra Leone in 1919 and again in 1926, and also Nigeria in 1921. Strikes hit the Rhodesian copper mines in 1935. Economic depression in the 1930s fuelled discontent, encouraging many political organisations in Africa to advocate for self-government. The Nigerian Youth Movement, founded in 1934, moved from promoting higher education to backing self-government.

The marked difference that indigenous peoples in colonies such as Kenya and Rhodesia witnessed between their own poverty and the privilege of white settlers kept anti-colonial resentment very much alive. While not all white settlers in these colonies were wealthy (many struggled to stay afloat in the interwar years), they lived on land appropriated from locals, and they employed black workers at low wages to do their bidding. These social and political inequalities produced impoverishment as well as social and economic disruption among displaced and relocated local peoples, that in turn encouraged the growth of nationalist organisations. Organisations such as the Kikuyu Central Association in Kenya (banned in 1940 as subversive) helped mobilise rural peasant populations and transform anti-colonial nationalism from a largely urban to a mass movement that incorporated rural peoples. This was an important dynamic, for Africa in the interwar years was still largely rural.

By the mid-1940s, African nationalism was far more than the collection of disparate regional dissatisfactions that British officials sometimes imagined it to be. Nationalist leaders in different colonies recognised similar goals, and in 1945 the fifth in a series of Pan-African Congresses, held in the northern British city of Manchester, pledged itself to a nonviolent socialist goal for the African colonies. The first of the congresses where a majority of the delegates were African rather than Caribbean, it was also the first to put African independence centre stage. The Pan-African movement had close ties to black liberation politics in the United States, and as the Cold War began to dominate world politics in the 1950s, its commitment to socialism would (as Chapter 11 discusses) have important consequences.

Despite the peaceable goals of the 1945 conference, politics in Africa were frequently violent. Rioting in the Gold Coast (the first British colony in Africa to gain independence in 1957) in 1948 resulted in 29 deaths. Buganda in eastern Africa witnessed anti-colonial riots in 1945 and again in 1949 and, as in the 1930s, the depression of the post-war years was a major catalyst. In the 1950s nationalism began to spread in earnest to rural Africa, and even harsh repression could not suppress its growth. By 1960 more than half of British Africa was independent: the press dubbed it 'Africa Year'.

Nationalism was also growing on the Malay peninsula where the nineteenth-century importation of non-native labour, and in particular the growth of a Straits Chinese community, had long divided the population. In the 1920s the nationalist Kuomintang, who had ousted the Chinese imperial family, had made considerable headway among the Straits Chinese population, as had their rivals, the Communists. Although neither ever exercised much influence outside the Chinese population, this non-western anti-colonial politics added a complex layer to the nationalist struggles of the region. In 1926 (four years before the establishment of the Malayan Communist Party), the Singapore Malay Union began to organise among indigenous Malay peoples. Anti-British strikes and risings erupted, intensifying after 1938, and met with severe repression from the British. Some 40,000 troops were sent to police the region in a futile attempt to stave off independence. One of the distinctive features of Malay anti-colonial nationalism was that there was never much common ground between the large ethnic Chinese population and the indigenous Malay population. It was, of course, imperial need that had created this diverse and divided population and that exploited the differences between the various nationalities, just as in India the British had encouraged divisions between Hindu and Muslim nationalisms, seeking to minimise the threat to British rule.

In Burma, too, colonial actions helped structure the particular form anti-colonialism took there. Nationalist organisations in Burma may not have shared a common vision of what Burma's post-independence future should look like, but they did have in common a desire for political separation from India. Shortly after the First World War, the exclusion of Burma from the political changes applied in India (from where the colony was governed), which had given Indians a greater if still limited role in governance, precipitated riots in Burma. Britain hastily extended the new system of dyarchy to Burma in 1921, but while Burmese nationalists shared an anti-colonial agenda the new system provoked markedly different readings of how nationalism should subsequently operate. Riots in the 1930s saw attacks on both Britons and Indians living in Burma.

In common with many other colonies, there were important differences in the goals of urban and rural activists, but it was perhaps the difference between those who emphasised Burma's Buddhist legacy and those who favoured a more westernised and secularised nationalism wedded to modernisation that ran deepest in Burmese nationalism. As in other colonial settings, there was a gulf between those embracing a western style of politics and those rejecting it. Rural rebellion, student strikes and riots were common in the interwar years, and the 1935 Government of Burma Act separated Burma from India, and considerably extended its self-governance. As elsewhere, the central policy areas of defence, foreign affairs and finance remained under British control, a move that encouraged and deepened anti-colonial anger. In the 1940s, some in Burma, as in India, allied with Japan in an anti-western political gesture.

These alliances with Japan highlight not only the anti-western element that was an inevitable by-product of imperial rule, but also the factors external to the specific rule of Britain. In particular, the two world wars had considerable repercussions. We have already traced the impact of the first of these conflagrations, visible perhaps most vividly in Egypt, India and Ireland. The Second World War was no less influential in sustaining, creating and sometimes transforming anti-colonial nationalisms throughout the Empire. Much of the war was fought on imperial soil and the Japanese occupation of much of the British Pacific in 1941–2, including Hong Kong and Singapore, as well as the war in Burma and the Pacific, exposed Britain's military and political vulnerabilities. Existing hostility to colonialism was certainly amplified by Britain's wartime failures. Just as Irish nationalists had seized the opportunity for rebellion in 1916 when British troops were occupied elsewhere, so in the 1940s did anti-colonial nationalists foment disturbances and seek allies against the British. The aftermath of the war did little to undercut these destabilisations of colonial authority. Britain's reliance after 1945 on American aid, and the growing division between capitalist and communist regimes worldwide, sharpened nationalist conflicts.

For subject peoples, nationalism spelled the prospect of independence and self-governance, free from colonial authority, but anti-colonial sentiment could also be found at the heart of the Empire and among those associated with the imperial power. In the nineteenth century critics attacked the greed and brutishness of British settlers, and in the late eighteenth century Edmund Burke had staked his career on his critique of a rapacious East India Company denuding India of its wealth. His contemporary Adam Smith, the influential Scottish economist, thought colonies an expensive drain on a country's wealth. The Radical Liberal member of parliament, cotton merchant Richard Cobden, opposed imperial expansion in the mid-nineteenth century as a path that would increase the national debt. Half a century later, J. A. Hobson published a slew of books including *The War in South Africa* (1900); *The Psychology of Jingoism* (1901); and most famously in 1902, *Imperialism* devoted to demonstrating that free trade, which he regarded as a capitalist imperative, was incompatible with imperialism. The greed and militarism he saw in imperialism were detrimental, he argued, to the colonies and Britain. Playwright George Bernard Shaw was another anti-colonial voice of the early twentieth century. Another literary figure of the period, Leonard Woolf, came by his opposition to imperialism via first-hand experience during his years in the civil service in Ceylon. Novelist George Orwell was likewise persuaded by his time in the colonial service in Burma of the bankruptcy of the imperial system.

Some western critics of imperialism were committed to ending it and others to reforming it. In the nineteenth and early twentieth centuries the Liberal Party had been publicly associated with opposition to the Empire, although its policies never reflected that position consistently. The Liberal Party sponsored the principles of Home Rule in Ireland but it was a compromise policy that won the party few friends either among Republicans or Unionists. These efforts led, moreover, to a major breach within the Liberal Party. Many Liberals who favoured union with Ireland switched political allegiance in the late nineteenth century when the Irish question dominated party politics.

In the twentieth century, the Liberal Party was eclipsed by the newer Labour Party, also for the most part associated with opposition to imperialism, but equally inconsistent in its practical approach to the issue once in government. In the nineteenth and the twentieth centuries, and perhaps especially in the post-1945 period (as Chapter 11 will show), the major political parties were often invested, whatever the tenor of their rhetoric, in holding onto the Empire. There were few other issues on which they could agree, but this often unacknowledged cross-party sense that the British Empire was important and worth saving shows that it remained a vital component of Britain's global profile. Torn as they often were by competing interests, the parliamentary parties overall believed in sustaining the Empire.

Anti-colonial organisations in Britain consistently questioned the ethics and politics of imperialism. In the 1950s, left-of-centre MP, Fenner Brockway, established the Movement for Colonial Freedom, protesting the repressive tactics employed by both Labour and Conservative governments to quell colonial rebellion. Brockway was particularly vocal, as was fellow Labour MP Barbara Castle, about the cruel tactics employed in the Kenyan emergency in the mid-1950s. Brockway, Castle and their supporters vigorously opposed detention without trial and protested the poor conditions of the detention camps hastily set up to contain Kenyan nationalism. The Africa Bureau, run by Reverend Guthrie Michael Scott, was founded to advise and support anti-colonial activity. Britain's Marxist parties, following Lenin's reading of imperialism as the 'highest stage of capitalism', all opposed imperialism, arguing that capitalism and colonialism were critically linked. During the Cold War many anti-colonial nationalist groups were aided and funded by the USSR as part of its broader anti-capitalist strategy. In 1927, the Anti-Imperialist League, based in Berlin, was created as a satellite organisation of Comintern, the Soviet office designed to promote communism internationally. European communist parties established organisations for colonial students.

Many anti-imperialists in the west were horribly disillusioned when the USSR embarked upon its own imperial quest. In 1956 and again in 1968, as Soviet tanks crushed rebellions in Hungary and in Czechoslovakia, membership of European communist parties plummeted. For nationalists on the ground in colonial arenas, however, the luxury of such principled dissociation was not possible. Just as some in Burma and India were willing to embrace Japanese fascism in the 1940s in order to oust Britain, in the Cold War years the aid offered to anti-colonial nationalists by the Soviet Union was often vital to a group's survival. Despite its own actions in eastern Europe, the Soviet Union continued to encourage and fund anti-colonial nationalist movements in regions where European colonialism was strong and where they could offer a thorough-going critique of the relationship between capitalism and imperialism, long a mainstay of Marxist economic and political analysis.

While Marxist readings of colonialism stressed class and economics, other divisive factors were also at work. The gap between rich and poor, between propertied and propertyless, was clearly critical in fomenting discontent in the colonies. Just as important, however, were racial distinctions. In the African settler colonies, whites generally owned the best land available, often employing the very people they had dispossessed to work it for them. In every colony, whites – even the working-class troops who at home had scant social standing – could dominate the local population, order them around, restrict their movements and demand obedience. This unmistakable and relentless division by skin colour was common throughout the Empire. Not surprisingly these characteristic colonial behaviours based on race shaped, in turn, a corresponding racialisation of anti-colonial nationalisms. Anti-Indian agitation in Burma and anti-Chinese attacks in Malaysia are good examples of how racial divides created by British rule could be translated into the practices of anti-colonial nationalism. Where outside groups were regarded as having benefited from colonialism to the detriment of the local population, frictions between these populations complicated the racial situation. In the wake of decolonisation (as Chapter 11 will discuss) such divisions often had dramatic as well as violent effects on migrant populations, even those who had lived for generations – and perhaps been born – in their new abodes.

Sexual divisions were sometimes less immediately apparent than racial ones in the strategies of anti-colonial nationalisms, yet the effects of nationalist activity on the role and position of colonised women could be profound. On the one hand, the increased levels of protest that were, by the mid-twentieth century, characteristic of nationalism in colonial environments often brought women into the political arena in larger numbers. Nationalist women's organisations encouraged political participation. Sarojini Naidu became the first woman president of the Indian National Congress in 1925. In the 1880s Anna Parnell's Ladies' Land League had played an important role in Irish politics. The United Malays national organisation had a women's branch, and the All-India Women's Conference was highly visible and active from the late 1920s. These organisations often focused on the specific issues most pressing for women within the broader national context.

Yet it was often the case that women were asked to put their claims on hold, to subordinate their needs to what male nationalists argued were the more urgent and larger issues at stake. Such arguments were often backed by claims that because of women's importance as child-bearers and child-rearers, they were thus the 'mothers of the nation' whose principal duty was to ensure the continuance of race and society through reproduction. This relegation of women to a narrow and domestic role within the nationalist struggle was common, and though many women accepted this as part of their commitment to nationalism, it did not always bode well for women's post-independence status. Gendered divisions were also central to how nationalisms invoked the all-important sentiment of sacrifice. Men, in effect, were called upon to be willing to sacrifice their life fighting for the cause, while women had to be willing to sacrifice husbands and sons. In that light, of course, the demand for women's rights could be made to seem deeply individualistic and somewhat selfish.

In many instances the power struggles associated with anti-colonial nationalism involved a politics of public space more readily occupied by men. Women in many colonised cultures, and certainly in imperial Britain, had long been expected to fulfil largely domestic roles as mothers and child-carers. Their future role was often part of the larger discussion of what the postcolonial nation might look like. As we have seen nationalist movements could be decisively anti-western, but they could also embrace some aspects of western culture and values. What to keep and what to reject was always a central concern, and the role and position of women was invariably a central component in this determination, even as women's rights were regarded as less important than winning independence. Some sought to define a proper and traditional role for women, others were open to changes in women's status. In all cases, however, gender was a central concern for nationalism, even where women were asked to put nationalism before gender reform.

The position of women within the politics of anti-colonial nationalism highlights the close connections between the political and cultural aspects of imperialism. These kinds of struggles over definition and role were critical both in shaping the nature of nationalist activity and what came after. They demonstrate very clearly the common tensions between embracing and rejecting western values, for as we have seen, it was a commonplace among colonists to represent colonials as cruel or at least indifferent to women. Did the liberation of women and a change in their social roles mean, then, that western ways had been adopted? In the controversy in the late nineteenth century over child marriage in India, this issue surfaced quite explicitly. The enforcing of an age of sexual consent upon child brides in 1891 set off a noisy protest among Hindus offended by the prospect of legitimate husbands liable to prosecution for conjugal relations, and by what they saw as a British misreading of Indian attitudes to women and to sexuality. Badly managed colonial rule in this instance led to a quickening of the pace of nationalism, another instance of Britain's seeming failure to learn from past errors, as well as a salutary reminder that nationalism could be quite conservative in its aspirations and attitudes.

Nationalism was never a single and unified movement. Inevitably there were competing ideas as to what (or who) a nation was within the colonial arena. The ways in which imperialism had redrawn political and cultural boundaries over the years and favoured some groups over others clouded and complicated what was already at stake: how was a nation to be defined, more especially after years of colonial rule had brought together hitherto separate peoples? In India, for example, differences in that vision were by no means confined to religious sectarianism, although the communal violence that erupted so dramatically between Hindus and Muslims in the 1940s was certainly a dominant factor. But we should remember that Gandhi, so frequently depicted in popular culture as the hero of twentieth-century Indian nationalism, had many detractors in India, and his rejection of class-based protest was not universally popular. B. R. Ambedkar who organised India's lowest caste, the *harijans*, in the 1930s criticised Gandhi for his failure to condemn the caste system, but nonetheless identified with a broader nationalist agenda. Equally, the racial tension between Malay and Chinese residents of the Straits Settlements revealed distinctive readings of how a postcolonial state might function. These were rifts created in large measure by the vagaries of colonial rule itself, which had blurred cultural, ethnic and religious boundaries with ruthless insensitivity. If decolonisation, to which we now turn our attention, did not always lead to a harmonious independence, the effect of colonial rule must be seen to play some considerable role in that result.

Notes

1 C. A. Bayly, *The Birth of the Modern World, 1780–1914* (Oxford: Blackwell, 2004), p. 233; John Darwin, *The Empire Project: The Rise and Fall of the British World-System, 1830–1970* (Cambridge: Cambridge University Press, 2009), p. 106.
2 Doris Lessing, *Walking in the Shade. Volume Two of My Autobiography* (New York: HarperCollins, 1997), p. 209.
3 Balfour Declaration, 1917. The text of the Declaration can be found online at www.fordham.edu/halsall/mod/balfour.asp.

Further reading

Benedict Anderson's *Imagined Communities: Reflections on the Origin and Spread of Nationalism* (London: New Left Books, 1991) remains the classic study of colonialism and nationalism. Although British colonialism is not his focus, the book is a key work in the area. Also of considerable importance is Partha Chatterjee's *Nationalist Thought and the Colonial World: A Derivative Discourse?* (Minneapolis, MN: University of Minnesota Press, 1998). *The Idea of Freedom in Asia and Africa*, (Robert H. Taylor (ed.), Stanford, CA: Stanford University Press, 2002) is a useful collection detailing the ideas that spread through colonial territories as nationalism gathered steam. D. A. Low's *Britain and Indian Nationalism, 1929–1942: Imprint of Ambiguity* (Cambridge: Cambridge University Press, 1997) details the intense fight for self-determination in interwar India and in *The Turning Point in Africa: British Colonial Policy, 1938–48* (London: Cass, 1982), R. D. Pearce discusses African nationalism and protest. Antoinette Burton lays out the vulnerabilities of the Empire in *The Trouble with Empire: Challenges to Modern British Imperialism* (Oxford: Oxford University Press, 2015).

Bernard Porter investigates how British radicals understood African colonialism in his *Critics of Empire: British Radical Attitudes to Colonialism in Africa 1895–1914* (New York: St Martin's Press, 1968). Mira Matikkala offers a broad overview of anti-imperial thought in *Empire and the Imperial Ambition: Liberty, Englishness and Anti-imperialism in Late-Victorian Britain* (London: I. B. Tauris, 2011). The growing connections between African-American activists and anti-colonial nationalists are the topic of Martin Staniland, *American Intellectuals and African Nationalists, 1955–1970* (New Haven, CT: Yale University Press, 1991) and of Susan D. Pennybacker, *From Scottsboro to Munich: Race and Political Culture in 1930s Britain* (Princeton, NJ: Princeton University Press, 2009). Martin Thomas and Richard Toye discuss the rhetoric around empire in *Arguing about Empire: Imperial Rhetoric in Britain and France, 1882–1956* (Oxford: Oxford University Press, 2017).

In *Gender and Nation* (Thousand Oaks, CA: Sage, 1997), Nira Yuval-Davis explores the links between gender and nationalism. So too do the essays in *Gendered Nations: Nationalisms and Gender Order in the Long Nineteenth Century* (Ida Blom, Karen Hagemann and Catherine Hall (eds), New York: Berg, 1996). Kumari Jayawardena's *Feminism and Nationalism in the Third World* (London: Zed Books, 1986) was one of the first studies to explore this critical link. One valuable case study of gender and nationalism is Cora Ann Presley, *Kikuyu Women, the Mau Mau Rebellion and Social Change in Kenya* (Boulder, CO: Westview Press, 1992). Paula M. Krebs *Gender, Race, and the Writing of Empire: Public Discourse and the Boer War* (Cambridge: Cambridge University Press, 1999) connects one of the major offensives of the colonial period with gender. Denis Judd's *The Boer War* (London: John Murray, 2002) is a thorough general history of that war.

The broadest assessment of the Empire and the First World War can be found in the essays in *Race, Empire and First World War Writing* (Santanu Das (ed.), Cambridge: Cambridge University Press, 2011).

11 Decolonisation

Anti-colonial nationalism in the twentieth century played a major role (as suggested in Chapter 10) in shaping the years of decolonisation that dominated the politics of British imperialism after the Second World War. Many other issues, however, were equally prominent. There had never been a time when global issues – who was allied with whom, where trade routes were centred, and the interactions between polities – did not play a significant role in imperial politics, and the process of decolonisation was no different in this respect. Like colonialism, decolonisation was a global phenomenon, and one with a long history. In the eighteenth century not only had Britain lost its 13 North American colonies but a slave revolt in French St Domingue resulted in the establishment of independent Haiti. In the nineteenth century, the Iberian empires of Spain and Portugal lost their dominance in the Americas as colony after colony rebelled and won independence. After the First World War, the map was redrawn as former Russian colonies became independent, as did satellites of the crumbling Austro-Hungarian and Ottoman Empires. Germany's Empire had been dismantled. By the early 1920s, most of Ireland had broken away from Britain. This patchwork of imperial loss and nationalist gain reminds us that empires fail and fall, sometimes piecemeal, other times wholly.

The post-1945 decolonisations, in which Britain lost the bulk of its Empire, took place in three distinctive periods: in the late 1940s, when colonies in South Asia, or governed from there, became independent; from the late 1950s to the early 1960s, when much of Africa left the Empire; and in the late 1960s and 1970s, when Britain decamped from its remaining colonies east of Suez and elsewhere, mostly as a result of its persistently weak economic position.

Decolonisation is a term used mostly by colonising nations, Britain among them, to signal both the period and process whereby former colonies gained political independence and the right to choose their own forms of rule and leadership. In former colonies it is also referred to, not surprisingly as liberation rather than decolonisation, reflecting the freedom to which anti-colonial nationalists aspired. In this chapter our emphasis is on understanding from the coloniser's perspective why such changes occurred, and so rapidly, investigating less how former colonies won their freedom than why Britain disgorged so fully its imperial possessions in the second half of the twentieth century.

In many respects, and in many places, the world after 1945 was fundamentally different than it had been prior to six years of global conflict. The war years had escalated technological gains, shifted political alliances and engendered radically changed economic structures. While Britain's palpable decline in economic and political muscle was not brought about solely by the hardships and costs of war, the war escalated and intensified a trend that had long been apparent in the UK. Britain's economy and industries had felt the pressure of stiff competition throughout the twentieth century, but it was still possible between the two world wars for Britain, in large part because of its huge empire, to see itself as a major figure on the world stage. After 1945, that image was a much harder sell, and the mantle of power, certainly in the political and economic realms, shifted across the Atlantic Ocean to the United States.

The rise of America to world prominence was one of the most distinctive changes of the post-1945 period. The popularity of American culture and products in Britain was visible as early as the 1920s; Hollywood films, jazz and American fashion were hugely popular in interwar Britain. But America's pivotal role in the Second World War from 1941, and its economic strength and dominance during and after the war, had a durable and powerful effect on the entire world. Without American money much of Europe, and Britain in particular, would have suffered severe economic hardship after the war. The USA made major economic gains during the war while Britain in 1945 faced a massive deficit as well as the need to rebuild many areas damaged by bombing raids.

American attitudes to colonialism, meanwhile, were complex. America had largely divested itself of its own imperial holdings, the Philippines gaining independence in 1946 while Alaska and Hawaii were folded into statehood. American rhetoric rejected colonialism and a State Department official paper, released in 1942, supporting national independence for colonies had angered the British. After the war, however, when the Soviets emerged as a potential rival on the world stage, American attitudes to European colonialism tended to be shaped principally by Cold War imperatives. Where colonialism was viewed as a bulwark against communism, the USA was happy to support it.

Although the USA was in profoundly better economic shape at the end of the war than any of the other industrial nations, it faced nonetheless a new and powerful enemy in the Soviet Union (USSR). Despite its own imperial ambitions, the USSR fostered and funded nationalist movements in colonies under western European rule. The Soviets were as cynical in their exploitation of imperialism and anti-colonial nationalism as were their American rivals, funding and fostering nationalism in the colonies of the capitalist world while extending the USSR's own hold in eastern Europe with considerable brutality and little regard for national sovereignty. The spirit of capitalism so key to American identity and success could not but regard communist Russia – and its imperial ambitions – as a threat. The Cold War, which would mould so much of the world's politics until the 1990s, forged new alliances as these two 'super powers' – the USA and the USSR – worked to secure their positions. Britain, heavily reliant on infusions of American cash to save its ailing economy, and itself identified with the exploitation of colonial resources (both labour and goods), was inevitably allied with the USA, while many of its colonies found in the USSR a generous benefactor of education, weaponry and advice in their campaigns for independence. The Cold War's deep embroilment in the politics and economics of imperialism had a profound effect on British decolonisation. As Britain would find out in the 1950s, moreover, the price of American friendship could be intensely humiliating. The colonial world throughout the years of the Cold War was a theatre in which the west and the USSR clashed, the USSR encouraging the destabilising effects of anti-colonialism in order to weaken the capitalist power bloc. The fear that prior colonies would turn towards communism rather than the free trade capitalism of the western world was a critical factor affecting the process of decolonisation.

Alongside Britain's unavoidable entanglement in the rivalries between the USA and the USSR, the principle of European co-operation emerged in the 1950s. This recognition of common European interests was rooted to some degree in a fear that communist Russia would turn its attention westward. Memories of foreign occupation were fresh in those parts of Europe where the Nazis had been successful invaders. Alliances across western Europe, which would also foster better trade agreements, were designed to protect these nations from the Soviet giant on its eastern doorstep. Britain, by the late 1950s, was anxious to play a part in this new alliance, more particularly when enhanced colonial trade proved unable to solve its economic slump, and unrest in colonial arenas was growing costly to control. Britain applied for membership of the European Economic Community (EEC) in 1961, a sign of disengagement from its close economic ties with its colonies. France, however, vetoed Britain's membership on the grounds that its ties to the Commonwealth and to the USA rendered Britain insufficiently European. Ironically Britain's application for membership was opposed by the very Commonwealth leaders whose ties to Britain had shaped Charles de Gaulle's scepticism about Britain's commitment to Europe. De Gaulle would veto Britain's next attempt in 1967 to gain membership, and it was not until 1973 (and a change in French leadership) that Britain finally gained entry to what is now called the European Union.

Britain's (now troubled) relationship to the EEC was not, however, the only way in which Europe helped shape the course of British decolonisation in the late twentieth century. De Gaulle's decision in 1960 to abandon French imperial claims in West and Equatorial Africa also helped accelerate British decolonisation in the region. In that same year, Belgium withdrew quite suddenly from the Congo, precipitating political tensions the British feared would spill over into neighbouring British colonies such as Uganda and Northern Rhodesia. Congolese radicals founded alliances with the USSR, and Britain potentially faced in this area of Africa both local turbulence and a potential Cold War threat. Moreover, 'Africa Year' in 1960 also saw 16 newly independent African states accepted into the United Nations (UN), an indication of where the sympathies of that body lay.

Anti-colonial nationalism, alongside these complex global relationships, created the conditions in which decolonisation occurred. The scale of discontent and of demands for self-direction clearly escalated after the Second World War. In 1954, Kwame Nkrumah, who in 1949 had founded a nationalist party in the Gold Coast colony in West Africa, issued his 'Declaration to the Colonial Peoples of the World'. Imperialism, he claimed, was an exploitative system. All peoples had the right to govern themselves. The Gold Coast subsequently became, in 1957, Ghana, the first African colony to gain independence from Britain. Nkrumah's defiant condemnation of the colonial system in 1954 was an important rallying call for anti-colonial nationalism in the region, for in profound ways, the post-1945 era was truly the coming of age of western notions of democracy. While the dispossessed in underdeveloped countries looked on, those in the western world experienced a bountiful economic democratisation in which property and consumer goods became more affordable and available, even in economically depressed Britain. Denied in many instances even a say in policy affecting their livelihood, their culture, their practices and laws, colonial activists turned increasingly to demands for complete independence. The Gold Coast's path to independence in many ways reflects the complexities of decolonisation. The colony had grown increasingly prosperous through cocoa production before the Second World War, and colonial officials approved the moderate African politics that seemed to dominate the colony until the late 1940s. The Gold Coast became a far more radical environment under the growing influence of the British-educated Nkrumah whose socialist-inspired politics alarmed officials sufficiently for them to jail him in the 1950s. This shift from model colony to problem child did not derail decolonisation; on the contrary, it may have precipitated the change, as in India. But the shift illustrates the kind of assessments made by officials around the question of a colony's suitability for independence.

In some respects, Britain's increasing economic presence in Africa in the late 1940s and 1950s had also fuelled resentment that was easily channelled by nationalists. Africa's importance during the Second World War was both strategic and economic. Its harbours and airfields were vital to the conduct of war in the region, and after the Japanese took Malaya, tin from West Africa became so crucial that the government conscripted local men into the mines. Britain hoped to use the riches of its African colonies to improve its economic situation at home. As a result, the British presence in remote rural as well as urban areas of Africa grew significantly after the war, as colonial development schemes were vigorously implemented. Many Africans who had hitherto been directly unaware of or unaffected by a colonial presence were now irked by this intervention; it was another fertile source for nationalist organising.

Greater economic intervention in the colonies pre-dated the Second World War. Britain's weakened trading status in the interwar period had made attention to imperial markets attractive. Agencies for colonial development began to proliferate: the Empire Cotton Growing Corporation dates from 1921 and the Empire Marketing Board from 1926. Yet neither these bodies nor colonial development were given the sustained funding needed to make the dream of a British-centred global economy a reality. It was a case of too little too late. The Colonial Development Act (1929), with its slender annual budget of £1 million, had minimal effect. The 1940 Colonial Development and Welfare Act, and the Colonial Development Corporation that followed in its wake in 1948, were broader and more ambitious in scope but projects were often mismanaged, emphasising modern technologies and management principles that did not always sit well with the local workforce. In colonies such as Southern Rhodesia and Kenya, development funding often favoured large-scale projects undertaken by white settlers (using African labour), and discouraged traditional small-scale local agriculture. Agricultural improvements designed to combat soil erosion and other problems sometimes led to the culling of herds owned by Africans who could ill afford the losses. These new intrusions into the local economy left many locals unhappy with the intentions of the colonial state. Development initiatives did not end when countries gained independence. Overseas aid and development programmes, as well as non-governmental humanitarian organisations, were a continuing presence in many former colonies and, while offering sometimes vital aid, they were also a reminder of the dependent relationships upon which imperialism had rested.

Britain's economic woes made her position an acutely difficult one. Reliant on American money and fearful of communism, saddled with the costs of running an increasingly fractious Empire, anxious to alleviate economic hardships and sustain popular welfare reforms at home, Labour and Conservative governments alike wrestled with whether the Empire was worth the money. This was no new concern; throughout Britain's imperial age there had been constant grumbles in parliament about how much the Empire cost, and indeed not all colonies were profitable, either for the state or for those investing or working in them. Things came to a head, however, after 1945 when a condition of the £3.75 billion loan Britain received from America was that sterling be made fully convertible with the American dollar. During the war, sterling earnings could be spent only in sterling-based countries, but the American loan was contingent upon opening up world markets without restriction. Britain rather cynically complied by greatly limiting the economic freedoms of its colonised peoples in order to improve its own domestic situation. Africa and South-East Asia, in particular, were far more intensively exploited than they had been before the war. It would be tempting to assume that this greater attention to, and exploitation of, the valuable commodities these colonies had to offer would have enriched the local peoples. On the contrary, the stringent rules Britain imposed were designed to enhance sterling and Britain itself, rather than spreading the wealth more equitably. Colonial currencies were required to maintain fixed exchange rates with sterling, to sell their currency earnings to Britain in return for sterling and to permit free sterling transfers. It was a plan clearly intended to get Britain out of economic trouble at the expense of its Empire, despite the fact that many colonies suffered economic and political losses as great as those endured by Britain during the war years. The often inflationary conditions that Britain's economic policies produced in the colonies further fuelled anti-colonial resistance.

These economic policies did not work, and demonstrated in every respect British determination to use the Empire in pursuit of domestic priorities. When it became clear that the convertibility with the dollar required by the Americans was proving difficult to achieve, the Labour government devalued sterling in 1949 without bothering to consult the Commonwealth countries. It was a slap in the face for the Dominions, once more ignored on policy affecting the Empire as a whole.

Resentment of Britain by its colonies was also exacerbated by the conduct of Britain during and even before wartime. The Australians, for example, harboured a deep sense of betrayal over the Japanese invasions in the Pacific. Popular Australian sentiment blamed the British for favouring the western theatre of war, leaving them vulnerable to attack. When in 1951, Australia and the USA signed a pact to protect one another from hostilities in the Pacific, the British were conspicuously excluded, as they had been after the First World War when Canada sought economic co-operation with neighbouring America. The Indian soldiers who fought with the Allies played a vital role in the war and, as had been the case in the First World War, anticipated that their efforts would be recognised by some further degree of Indian independence. Britain's failure to reward colonies for their wartime loyalties (as we saw in Chapter 10) angered many activists. Malta and Ceylon were made wartime promises of self-government, but although Ceylon was granted independence in 1948, Malta had to suffice with mere internal self-government in 1947. Malta was, after all, as J. D. Krivine of the Empire Information Section of Britain's Office of Information pointed out, 'a vital strategic point in the Mediterranean'.[1] British interests were put ahead of local ones. Direct rule was reimposed in Malta in 1959 when the British and Maltese governments failed to reach agreement on economic issues; Malta did not win complete independence until 1964.

Colonialism, on the eve of decolonisation, was a volatile and disparate phenomenon. The 1930s and even the war years had seen a good deal of unrest (as Chapter 10 detailed) in many parts of the Empire. The Palestine mandate had proven to be a diplomatic minefield, and the region was further destabilised by an army rebellion against the British in 1941 in the former mandate of Iraq. British rule faced labour protests across Africa, rebellion broke out in Cyprus in 1939 and in India wave after wave of protest panicked the authorities into arresting prominent Congress Party members. Such a hugely unpopular move compounded existing and serious tensions between ruler and ruled in India. Coupled with the wartime Japanese occupation of British colonies in South-East Asia, it was apparent even at Westminster that the colonial world was, in the 1940s, under threat from many directions.

The allied victory in the war in 1945 brought little relief on the colonial front. Hasty and ill-conceived decision-making and botched attempts at compromise characterised the 1947 partition of India and the declaration of the state of Israel a year later. The legacy of these earliest instances of decolonisation remain among the most intractable of the world's conflicts today, as Pakistan and India continue to feud over the disputed territory of Kashmir, and as people die daily in Palestine and in Israel from sectarian violence.

There is no question that in many instances, and not just in this first period of decolonisation, the British had their hand forced by circumstance. Expense, political turbulence and global diplomatic considerations all affected the speed and progress of the process, although both Labour and Conservative governments throughout the period of decolonisation kept up a firm rhetoric that emphasised Britain's control of events and of the overall process. While this was frequently little more than political posturing, it nonetheless revealed a salient element of both British imperialism and its dismantling. Britain always insisted that it would be the judge, and the best judge, of when a particular colony was ready for independence. This was an attitude that grew to a large extent out of that overwhelming justification of nineteenth-century empire, the 'civilising mission'. Such attitudes were not much dislodged when, after the First World War, the new League of Nations adhered to the idea of 'trusteeship' in dividing up Germany's confiscated colonies and those of the former Ottoman Empire. The hierarchy built into the classes of mandate that structured post-war colonialism conceived of Africa as less capable of independence than the Ottoman states of Syria, Lebanon, Iraq and Palestine. While the Middle Eastern states that made up the Class A mandates were to be advanced to independence, the B (German East Africa) and C (German South-West Africa and the Pacific territories) mandates were classified as territories to be governed well and humanely, but with no timetable for granting independence. The British, clearly, were not alone in adopting hierarchies which saw some peoples as more 'advanced' than others. Thus while the reality was often much messier, British rhetoric at any rate was that the time for decolonisation was something it alone would and could determine. The myth of the contented imperial subject persisted, as demonstrated in this photograph (Figure 11.1) of the royal tour of the West Indies at a late stage of decolonisation.

Figure 11.1 The 1966 Royal tour of the West Indies
Source: TopFoto

In practice, and though the British often put a brave face on their actions, the era of decolonisation was littered with humiliating defeats. The date for Indian independence was accelerated by some ten months as the British faced increasing violence between Hindus and Muslims that they feared would spread to the army. In 1946 there were police strikes and naval mutinies in India as well as violent protests in both rural and urban areas. Lord Mountbatten arrived in India in March 1947 to oversee the shift to independence, with a date of June 1948 set for the occasion. Circumstances were such that the handover came within five months of his taking office, in August 1947. Though the principle of partition had been rejected by the British as late as 1946, when independence came in the following year, Pakistan's claim to exist as a separate nation was nonetheless realised.

Four years later in 1951, the British-owned oil refinery at Abadan in Iran was nationalised. Although Iran had the largest oil reserves under British control, neither the UN nor the USA was prepared to sanction British military intervention to restore the refinery to British hands, yet two years later, the British and the Americans joined forces to topple the Iranian regime when they feared the growth of Soviet influence in the region. It was clear that the senior partner in this venture was the superpower and not Britain, and that the rationale for intervention was the Cold War rather than British oil interests. Indeed, some have argued that Britain's decision in 1956 to march into Egypt was influenced by its humiliation in Iran earlier in the decade. The record is unclear as to how far such considerations were at work, but what is not in doubt is the botched job Britain, along with France, made in Egypt in 1956.

The Suez Crisis has often been regarded as the turning point that accelerated the pace of decolonisation and ushered in its second phase, beginning just a year later in 1957 with Ghana winning its independence. But while Britain's showing in Egypt in 1956 vividly underscored its weaknesses and loss of world influence, the fiasco was not truly a catalyst for what would follow. Plans for Ghanaian and even Nigerian independence were already well advanced when the Suez débâcle occurred; it perhaps gave many in Britain pause for thought, but Suez was not decisive for the spread of decolonisation. Its principal importance in the imperial landscape is probably that it revealed so deeply that Britain was no longer a major political force.

The Suez episode does usefully highlight, however, the tangled connections that characterised the era of decolonisation. It was the Egyptian abandonment in 1951 of an Anglo-Egyptian treaty that set off the events leading to the 1956 invasion. A 1936 treaty had exempted the Suez Canal Zone from Britain's guarantee to withdraw its troops from Egypt, but on the outbreak of war in 1939 that withdrawal was postponed. Even after the war, no effort was made to leave Egypt and in 1952, Gamal Abdel Nasser led a coup to unseat King Farouk, widely regarded in the region as collaborating too closely with the British. Pressure for British military withdrawal intensified in the early years of Nasser's rule, and the last British troops departed in June 1956. This phased withdrawal, 20 years after the guarantees of the Anglo-Egyptian treaty, left a void that Britain was anxious to fill for this was an oil-rich region that the west was anxious not to lose to the Soviet sphere of influence. To replace Egypt, Britain first sought out Iraq as its closest ally in the Middle East, having advanced that territory to independence in 1932. But when Britain wooed Jordan to enter the 1955 Baghdad Pact it had created with Iraq and Turkey, Nasser set about organising anti-British protests in Jordan's capital and, as a mark of his power, nationalised the Suez Canal, still a hugely important thoroughfare for British shipping. Though upset by Nasser's actions, the USA was unwilling to use force in the region. Rebuffed by the Americans, the British held secret negotiations with the French and the Israelis, devising a plan that in retrospect seems little short of absurd.

The Israelis were to attack Egypt, and the British and the French would issue an ultimatum for a ceasefire knowing that Nasser would refuse. This would give them an 'excuse' in turn to attack Egypt. And this was exactly what ensued between 29 and 31 October 1956. The condemnation of the

Franco-British attack was instant and unbending; the USA, the UN and the Commonwealth all decried the action as did the Soviet Union and the Arab states, and by 7 November British forces were forced to withdraw under enormous international pressure. The economic effects of the episode brought home to Britain just how dependent the country was on American goodwill. The Suez Crisis precipitated a run on the pound, weakening sterling in the exchange market considerably. It was only when the British agreed to leave Egypt unconditionally that the USA and the International Monetary Fund agreed to bail Britain out of this sterling crisis. If the British learned anything from Suez, it was not that decolonisation was a necessity, but that new power structures meant that the meaning and muscle of its Empire had shifted radically and had been irretrievably weakened. The Suez Crisis did not usher in or even accelerate decolonisation; instead it exposed the fact that the Empire was no longer a source of political strength for Britain.

Britain would face a further major incident that vividly demonstrated its drastically reduced powers when, in 1965, white Africans opposed to black African rule in the colony of Southern Rhodesia, declared their independence (UDI – Unilateral Declaration of Independence) from the Empire under the leadership of Ian Smith. Though Britain protested and even implemented economic sanctions, apartheid South Africa, welcoming a fellow white supremacist regime close by, ignored the sanctions, ensuring supplies to Southern Rhodesia. The imperial blow was, of course, a double one for not only had a colony rejected imperialism and unilaterally claimed its independence, but its closest ally, South Africa, was a former British colony that had withdrawn from the Commonwealth in 1961, when new member countries objected to its racially based system of governance that denied black Africans basic human and political rights. Britain and the white settler lands of Australia and New Zealand were willing to allow South Africa into the Commonwealth despite its apartheid rule. It was South Africa itself, faced with criticism from former colonies, that withdrew its application for membership.

Southern Rhodesia, which in 1923 had opted to remain a self-governing colony rather than join the South African Union, did not back down, and its stand proved a deeply embarrassing example of British weakness, both economically and politically. In some respects, the situation there was farcical. In a veritable display of the British stiff upper lip, the colonial governor – with neither salary nor telephone communication – continued to entertain guests as if nothing untoward had occurred, while the Rhodesians, intent on independence, refused to recognise his legitimacy. The UN, recognising the illegality as well as the racist intent of Smith's regime, condemned the Southern Rhodesian action and called on UN member countries to repudiate the new leadership. The British prime minister, Harold Wilson, was reluctant to respond with military intervention. In non-white colonies such as Kenya and Malaya and, of course, in Egypt, the use of force had been quickly deployed when nationalism erupted in violence, but Wilson was a shrewd politician and knew that military action against a white colony would be political suicide. These racially motivated considerations went deeper, however, for Wilson knew that neighbouring South Africa would be a major conduit in the event of economic sanctions, and applying pressure to as critical a trading partner as South Africa at a time of economic distress was out of the question; economics trumped any principles around racial equality, even for a Labour government.

In the end, Smith forced the British prime minister's hand, withdrawing from negotiations that would – in British eyes – have legitimised an illegal regime. Faced with Smith's intractable position, economic sanctions were the sole option left to the British, and they were, as expected, a miserable failure. In subsequent years the death toll from guerrilla warfare in the country rose alarmingly. It would be 1980 before the newly named Zimbabwe, with a black majority, emerged from the ruins of a bloody civil war.

The UN was not always as supportive of Britain as it had been in this case, and its position on Southern Rhodesia was guided critically by its disapproval of the minority white rule that Smith championed. Five years earlier, the UN's General Assembly had passed its Declaration on the Granting of Independence to Colonial Countries and People. It was, of course, by no means the first death knell sounded for European colonialism, but the UN's lending of its name and its legitimacy to post-war criticisms of colonialism was an important statement of a changed political climate.

One strategy explored as a means to knit the Empire together was the introduction of regional federations akin to those which had produced the nations of Canada in 1867 and Australia in 1901. The federal principle was revived in the post-war period, particularly by Conservative administrations, in the West Indies (1958), Central Africa (1953), East Africa (1955), South Arabia (1959; 1963) and Malaya (1963). All failed within a short time. This was not, in retrospect, all that surprising for they brought together disparate groups with competing objectives, often ignoring significant power differentials between member colonies.

In reshaping and reorganising the Commonwealth, Britain also hoped to foster goodwill and continued relations with former colonies in a world that no longer found full-scale colonialism acceptable. The Commonwealth was often little more than a public relations exercise; Britain had seen no reason to consult Commonwealth countries over Suez or over its bids for EEC membership. Yet money and effort went into making this body seem an important and mutually respectful and beneficial one. The term 'Commonwealth' had been chosen by the newly federated Australia in 1900 as one that did not imply colonial domination. The Balfour Report of 1926 defined Commonwealth countries as characterised by a common allegiance to the British Crown, and in 1931, as we have seen, the Statute of Westminster legally embodied their status as equal partners, confirming the full independence of member states whose acts could not be invalidated by the Westminster parliament. At this juncture, of course, Commonwealth membership was limited to those settler colonies where self-governance was already a fact. In the 1940s, the British envisaged a two-tier Commonwealth in which the non-white colonies of Asia and Africa would occupy a lesser form of membership.

Commonwealth eligibility required reconsideration when the newly independent republics of South Asia were born. Constitutional experts regarded allegiance to the monarch as incompatible with the republican nature of these new nations. Republics – as far back in British imperial terms as 1776 when the American colonies broke away – specifically rejected monarchical loyalty, and it was republican refusal in Ireland to pledge such loyalty that had wrecked the 1920 Home Rule plans there. However, Britain wanted to foster continued ties with India and Pakistan, if mostly to ensure that they would not be brought within the Soviet sphere of influence. As a result, in 1949 the Commonwealth was redefined to allay republican doubts and to make full membership of the new South Asian nations possible. But though the make-up of the Commonwealth changed considerably after the war, it was never a body with any real power, and its representativeness of the Empire was, at best, spotty. None of Britain's former Arab or Middle East colonies ever joined the Commonwealth, and as we have seen, South Africa withdrew its application for membership in 1961. Burma left in 1948, and Eire in 1949, unwilling to accept the British monarch as head of state.

The Commonwealth, then, was an idea more than a functioning reality, but its rhetoric – however unreflective of the actual situation – is a useful guide to the complex mechanisms at work in the disbandment of the Empire. In particular, the palpable fact that, for all the talk of equality, there was no way in which to ensure that Britain consult Commonwealth nations suggests that the gap between principle and reality was always important. Britain wanted to hold on at least to an idea of its continued global importance in the face of shrinking influence and economic decline. The Empire was, to all intents and purposes, the only place where such a posture was at all possible and even there, as we have seen, compromise was frequently forced upon Britain. Still, British politicians maintained a rhetoric of power and self-determination. Labour foreign secretary, Ernest Bevin, dreamed in the post-war 1940s of the Empire providing precious economic resources that would be the envy of the superpowers, an extraordinary vision for a country so wholly dependent on foreign aid. At the start of the 1960s, and in the wake of serious nationalist violence in many parts of the Empire, Bevin's colleague and former prime minister, Clement Attlee, claimed that Britain stood out among imperial powers in history as the only empire that had 'voluntarily surrendered its hegemony over subject peoples'.[2] The events of the 1950s belie his statement: Britain fought nationalist uprisings in Malaya, Kenya, Cyprus, Iraq, the Gold Coast and Egypt, and often with considerable violence.

Yet, as we have seen in the case of Southern Rhodesia, the use of force was sometimes not an option, and the key determination of this was clearly race. Britain was reluctant to take up arms against white societies, reserving military intervention and police action in the main for its dealings with peoples of colour. Cyprus may be the exception here but the rising level of terrorism on the island in the 1950s, coupled with its 'easterly' associations with the former Ottoman Empire, singled the colony out. Elsewhere it was almost always against Asian, African and Middle Eastern peoples that force was employed. This racial consideration consistently influenced the decolonisation process, and was a legacy that affected not only Britain but the Dominion nations for whom white settler identity was a key identification. Australia from its birth as a nation had prevented non-white immigration (and would do so until 1966), and during the First World War it was the white settler colonies who protested Britain's insistence on making India a member of the Imperial Conference to which the self-governing colonies had been invited. The idea of trusteeship, as we have seen, was applied only to predominantly non-white colonies regarded as not yet ready for independence. Such thinking also shaped the timetable of decolonisation.

In the late 1940s Britain saw India and the Middle East as far more suitable candidates for independence than supposedly 'backward' Africa. It was a view that conveniently ignored Britain's own unwillingness over the years

Figure 11.2 Strong words in Cyprus
Source: Central Press/Getty Images

to fund and promote economic development and better health and education practices in its African colonies. Britain's colonial reckoning was always a hierarchical one in which some races were endowed with superior power and control. It was the Aryan racial characteristics of Indians that elevated them in imperial eyes above the Africans. In African settler contexts, Britain not only avoided the use of force wherever feasible, but until quite late in the decolonisation process worked hard to avoid black African majority rule, so tenacious was the belief that such peoples were unready for political responsibility. Alan Lennox-Boyd, Conservative colonial secretary from 1954 to 1959, publicly decried Africans as too backward for independence. More bizarrely, proponents of ethnopsychiatry (the study of the psychology and behaviour of non-western peoples) argued that many of those who sought independence in Africa were motivated not by politics but by mental illness manifested as a demand for freedom from colonial rule.[3]

Yet there was little real surprise for Britain when demands for independence grew in the 1950s. In 1939 Lord Hailey, an experienced colonial administrator, was commissioned to examine British governance in Africa with a view to ultimate self-government there. Hailey's views were pessimistic; he saw little prospect of goodwill towards British rule among Africans. His report was buried as economic development issues took precedence at the Colonial Office, prompted by Britain's economic anxieties. Nonetheless, its commissioning, as well as its conclusions, suggests that some far-sighted officials saw the prospect of decolonisation looming even as war broke out in 1939.

Anticipated or otherwise, there were innumerable instances in which the prospect of cutting a colony loose was weighed overwhelmingly in terms of its implications for Britain. Cyprus, for example, was a strategic foothold that linked the Mediterranean and the Middle East, and was British Middle East HQ for the Suez Canal Zone. Singapore's importance as a port was unparalleled and, of course, there were fears that, like the Malayan mainland, it was vulnerable to Chinese communism. These political and economic considerations with ramifications for Britain generally overrode local wishes.

Africa was on the agenda once again after the war ended, this time in connection with ensuring that the Middle East did not fall under Soviet influence, and that the USSR did not claim territory in Africa. Ernest Bevin supported a consolidation of defence forces to protect the Middle East, the Mediterranean and Africa. His idea for a 'Lagos-Mombasa line' became part of a broader strategy in the late 1940s to develop Africa as a bulwark against communism and as an economic boom for Britain. These plans show a great deal more concern with British than with African prosperity and security.

The Middle East, where the economic importance of oil and a very different colonial history afforded the region some political purchase, became increasingly important to Britain's imperial goals. It was only late in the nineteenth century, and mostly after the First World War, that Britain acquired much of a foothold (other than in Egypt) in the Middle East. Prior to the insatiable thirst for oil so characteristic of the twentieth century, Britain's principal interest in the region had been as a route through to India and other colonies, both overland and by sea. However, the mandates created by the League of Nations after the First World War made the region increasingly important. Britain's interest and stake in the Arab world came at a time of growing Arab nationalism and increased Zionist migration to Palestine. Moreover, by the late 1940s, almost two-thirds of Britain's oil originated in the region, a percentage predicted to grow in the 1950s. British businesses thus had major investments in the Middle East, and energy policy was increasingly dependent on the uninterrupted flow of this oil.

As we have seen, the Suez Crisis was not truly a catalyst for decolonisation, but it certainly served as an illustration of the growing force of Arab nationalism, and Britain's handling of the situation there had not made it any friends in the Arab world. Even earlier, in 1947, Anglo-Arab relations were strained when Britain, cognisant of the risk of sending the Arabs in the direction of the Soviets, turned the future of Palestine over to the UN for resolution. Britain found itself in an impossible situation, bound by Balfour's 1917 promise to protect a Jewish homeland but faced with vigorous Arab opposition. The pro-Zionist stand of America was not insignificant, given Britain's need for American aid, yet imperial concerns, as well as British oil interests, relied on Arab goodwill, for Britain was the largest western presence in the area. Complicating matters was that in 1945 many European Jews were clamouring to move to Palestine after experiencing the genocidal anti-Semitism of the 1930s and 1940s. Britain was assailed on all sides: Palestinians made it clear they wanted the country to retain an Arab majority; Jews in the region took up increasingly violent tactics to force their desire for a Jewish state. Even in Britain there was no unanimity on the issue. The Colonial and the Foreign Offices, who shared administration of the territory, favoured different solutions. Britain resigned the mandate after the UN recommended separate Arab and Jewish states at the end of 1947. Israel subsequently declared its independence in May 1948, an action which precipitated the immediate outbreak of a conflict still burningly alive today.

The crisis over Palestine was one of the two major colonial problems Britain faced in the immediate post-war years, the other being the partition of India. The 1950s brought little relief from this sense of colonial crisis. Cyprus, Malaya and Kenya all erupted in violent opposition to colonialism. The defeat of the French in Indochina in 1954 and in Algeria in 1962 were reminders to the British that anti-colonial nationalism had roots both deep and broad.

Less than two years after its humiliating defeat in Egypt, Britain's power in the Middle East was further eroded by the Iraqi revolution of 1958, in which a Soviet-backed regime toppled the ruling pro-British party, jeopardising Britain's capacity to maintain military bases in Iraq. There can be no doubt that one factor in the Iraqi coup was the pro-British stand of the ousted monarch, just as had been the case in the 1952 coup in Egypt.

With the loss of Iraqi co-operation, the mess surrounding Suez and Britain's earlier expulsion from Iran, it was to the colonial port and Protectorate of Aden, now part of Yemen, that the British turned. A huge new oil plant under construction there was intended to replace lost British refineries nationalised by Iran. Aden became the British military headquarters in the Middle East for the Arabian peninsula from the late 1950s. From here, the British despatched troops to shore up the Jordanian regime in 1958, to Kuwait to stem Iraqi hostilities in 1961 and to Yemen in 1962 to quell nationalists there.

Aden would see its own share of instability in the 1960s, when the civil war in southern Yemen (secured by the 1934 treaty of Sana'a and Britain's last colonial acquisition – though it had been ceded to Britain by Turkey as early as 1839) spilled over into the territory, fanned by active Arab nationalism. Aden's constitution was suspended and direct rule reimposed in 1965, but the violence did not stop. Britain ultimately withdrew from the colony in November 1967, a decision that would have a considerable effect on the final major phase of decolonisation. It was in the wake of that decision that the larger policy of withdrawing from the Empire 'east of Suez' was made by a Labour government weighed down by economic disintegration. In 1967, following another currency devaluation, the British government announced its intention to withdraw from the Persian Gulf and the Malay archipelago by 1971, the so-called 'east of Suez' arena. Simultaneously, large tracts of the British West Indies and of British island colonies in the Pacific secured independence, including Fiji, Dominica and the Bahamas. The pace of decolonisation in the late 1960s and 1970s was rapid and, since virtually all of British Africa had gained independence by the time this new policy of withdrawal was announced, the Empire as a formal entity was, certainly symbolically, becoming a relic with only a few small colonies and dependencies remaining. Fourteen self-governing territories remain, at the time of writing, under British control; they have been officially known as British Overseas Territories since 2002, and though under British jurisdiction, they do not form part of the United Kingdom. A good number are in the Caribbean (Anguilla, Bermuda, British Virgin Islands, Cayman Islands, Montserrat and Turks and Caicos islands) and others are dotted around the South Atlantic, Pacific and Indian Oceans. The Channel Islands (Jersey and Guernsey) and the Isle of Man are Crown dependencies; they have the right – with the consent of the Crown – to pass legislation affecting their own islands.

One small island chain experienced the full force of colonial rule when in 1965 the UK purchased the seven atolls of the Chagos Archipelago from the self-governing colony of Mauritius and created the British Indian Ocean Territory. A year later the US and the UK executed an agreement giving the US the right to use the islands for defence purposes. Citing the Colonial Boundaries Act of 1895, Britain forcibly removed the entire population of the archipelago to facilitate the US military base at Diego Garcia. As recently as 2016, the United Kingdom reiterated that it would not support Chagossian resettlement and the case has been in litigation since 2010. In May 2019, the UN General Assembly overwhelmingly voted to condemn British occupation of the islands, although the government remains unmoved by the stunning 116–6 vote (56 countries abstained).

The Chagos debate is part of an interesting postscript to the story of nationalism, illustrating that decolonisation was by no means a capstone that secured success or rendered nationalism redundant. In white settler colonies, the last half of the twentieth century witnessed considerable lobbying from indigenous groups fighting for recognition of indigenous rights to land as well as advances in political, cultural and social equality. Aboriginal rights organisations in Canada and Australia, for example, have argued for the return of territory to indigenous peoples, a strategy based on recognition of the distinctiveness and autonomy of ethnic groups with claims to land and property. The similarities with earlier nationalist claims and demands against the colonial government suggest that the forms of nationalism peculiar to anti-colonialism are also capable of successful transformation, and that decolonisation should not be considered in any way an absolute ending.

If the beginnings of the Empire may be said to lie with the migration of white settlers, the end of the Empire might likewise be characterised by the phenomenon of migration, but a reverse migration in which, after the Second World War, colonial subjects arrived in increasing numbers in Britain. Earlier colonial migration into Britain had been mostly Irish and Australian but following the war, the situation changed considerably, as would the law. The effects on British culture and society have been, over time, dramatic.

The earliest immigration restrictions in Britain, the Alien Acts of the early twentieth century designed principally to slow Jewish immigration, did not apply to citizens of British colonies. The first restriction specifically affecting colonial subjects was the 1925 Coloured Alien Seamen Order that required black sailors who could not prove British nationality to register as aliens. It was a doubly cynical move: as an Order-in-Council rather than a bill debated in parliament, there was no public scrutiny of its contents, and officials also knew full well that few sailors would be able to produce the requisite documentation. The Order was renewed in 1938 and again in 1942.

The pre-war restrictions were more race-conscious than colonial-conscious, but in the years after the war the two factors would come together in sometimes explosive ways. The British Nationality Act of 1948 gave equal right of entry to all subjects of the Empire, at a time of considerable labour shortage when active recruitment of overseas workers, mostly in Ireland and Europe, was taking place. In the late 1940s, a trickle of West Indian migrants – mostly young men – began to arrive in Britain in search of a more prosperous future. Between 1948 and 1952 the total number of colonial migrants arriving each year was between 1,000 and 2,000. Numbers climbed in the 1950s and into the 1960s, peaking in 1961. By the late 1950s, there were some 10,000 Indians and Pakistanis migrating alongside West Indians and whites from both the Dominions and Ireland. West Indian immigration increased when, in 1952, the USA implemented restrictions on Caribbean immigration. In the 1950s various British transport companies and the National Health Service, among others, also actively recruited in the area, keen to expand their workforce.

Black and Asian migrants in these years often received a hostile reception when they arrived in Britain. They often faced difficulty finding housing in an era when a 'no coloureds, no Irish' letting advertisement was permissible and far from uncommon. New migrants frequently knew more about the country they were entering than Britons knew about the colonies from which they had come, since education in the colonies had traditionally focused more on Britain than on local history and geography. In his memoir of arriving in Britain from Uganda in the 1970s, Mahmood Mamdani tells us that 'To the colonial child, England was the rainbow on the horizon'.[4]

White colonials sometimes experienced a degree of condescension; it was British and not New Zealand or Australian history that formed the bulk of the curriculum in those colonies, and Christmas cards in the Antipodes bore winter scenes of snow and red robins despite the fact that December was

Figure 11.3 Jamaican immigrants at Victoria Station, London, 1956. When immigrants arrived from the Caribbean, they were often given temporary housing in shelters and underground stations

Source: Haywood Magee/Picture Post/Hulton Archive/Getty Images

summertime there. But white colonials in Britain were not targets of racism and fear, as were the West Indian and South Asian migrants who also sought a new life in Britain after the war. Sporadic racial violence throughout the 1940s and 1950s culminated in race riots in London's Notting Hill and in the Midlands town of Nottingham in 1958, and in the 1960s more than a few Asian households were fire-bombed. From the late 1960s a series of Race Relations Acts began to tackle institutional discrimination, but the task was immense. Black and Asian Britons remained disproportionally unemployed and imprisoned, and vulnerable to attack as racially inflected riots blazed through Britain's major cities in the 1980s, and most recently in 2011.

Following the quickening migration of the early 1960s, the Conservative government implemented a new and far more restrictive immigration policy in 1962. The Commonwealth Immigrants Act drastically reduced migrant numbers by distinguishing between skilled and unskilled workers as well as by favouring those who came with jobs in hand. On the face of it, the law was in no way directed against immigrants from the non-white colonies, yet the home secretary, R. A. B. Butler, confidently maintained that 'its restrictive effect is intended to, and would in fact, operate on coloured people almost exclusively'.[5] The non-white population in Britain at the time was 0.7 per cent, and economists at the Treasury had indicated that there were no economic grounds for exclusion. Race was clearly a major factor in the passing of the law.

Though the Labour Party protested the 1962 law, they would themselves further restrict Asian immigration in 1968, and indeed a group of Labour MPs had, in 1948, complained to the Prime Minister about what they regarded as 'excessive' immigration even as Britain desperately needed workers in many occupations in the aftermath of war. Labour's new rules in the late 1960s were precipitated by the arrival of Indians not from the sub-continent, but from newly independent African nations who had embarked on a policy of 'Africanisation' designed to expunge the colonial past. Although formal expulsion would not come until a little later, Indians living in Kenya and Uganda – many of whom had been there for generations – faced increasing discrimination from resentful Africans encouraged to see them as greedy beneficiaries of British colonialism. Many looked to England as a safe haven, and it was these entry seekers at whom the 1968 Act was aimed. Kenyans of European descent had been guaranteed entry into Britain under a special Nationality Act of 1964, but Indian Kenyans seeking entry now qualified only if they had a parent or grandparent born, adopted, registered or naturalised in the United Kingdom, a policy which severely limited who could qualify. When Idi Amin peremptorily expelled all Indians from Uganda in 1972, the Conservative government made an exception to the rule, allowing 30,000 to enter, and setting off a racist firestorm among anti-immigration activists. Just the previous year another Immigration Act had further separated the rights of Dominion and other colonial migrants, easing the burden on the former considerably. British subjects were now divided into patrials and non-patrials, categories defined such that white settler populations would more easily qualify. These were years of high tension in Britain over both immigration and race. Enoch Powell's famously inflammatory 'Rivers of Blood' speech, delivered to a Conservative Association audience in Birmingham in 1968, spoke of immigration as 'a national danger'. His eyes were on the civil rights movement in America, and he painted a picture in his speech of a traditional England under siege from alien populations.

Further refinements followed in 1981 when Margaret Thatcher's radical Conservative government redefined British nationality into three categories: British citizenship; British Dependent Territories citizenship; and British Overseas citizenship. The right to live in Britain was now restricted to British citizens unless they were subjects of the old Dominions. In the debate on the law in the Commons, Conservative MP Ivor Stanbrook argued, in a fascinating acknowledgement of the effects of decolonisation, that 'we have no duty – moral or legal – to the inhabitants of those countries that were formerly in the British Empire, and which threw off our sovereignty and repudiated their allegiance to the Queen'.[6] Stanbrook was no novice when it came to Britain's imperial history. He had spent ten years in the colonial service in Nigeria in the 1950s and, after retiring from politics, pursued a doctorate on the topic of British nationality. His view that independence nullified close relations with Britain, other than the former Dominions, was common in the era of decolonisation.

Perhaps the most extraordinary of the immigration practices developed in post-war Britain was the gynaecological testing of women from India and Pakistan, both at the point of entry into Britain and at British high commissions in South Asia. The rationale behind what the press quickly dubbed 'virginity testing' was that it would catch women who falsely claimed they were entering the country already betrothed, the assumption being that an unmarried woman from South Asia would invariably be a virgin. Uncovered in 1979, evidence suggests the practice had begun overseas earlier in the 1970s; it was only with reports of a case on British soil that protests ensued. When the incident was raised before the UN Commission on Human Rights in February 1979, one angry representative claimed the practice 'reflected the persistence of racism and colonialism in a disguised form'.[7]

As part of the Conservative government's 'hostile environment' policy aimed at deterring illegal immigrants, a new immigration law in 2012 required documentation for work, housing and benefits. This stringent requirement fell hard on many of those who had arrived in Britain before the early 1970s; with a legal right to enter and live in the UK, they neither needed nor were given any documents. The law granted those who had arrived in the UK from a Commonwealth country before 1973 an automatic right to remain permanently, unless they left the country for more than two years. But from 2012, challenged at hospitals and clinics, in workplaces and by landlords, by workers at local benefits offices to furnish evidence of their legality, many of these migrants, and especially the elderly, found themselves targeted as illegal immigrants. In six London boroughs, vans emblazoned with the slogan 'Go Home or Face Arrest' operated under a short-lived pilot scheme to discourage illegal immigration in the summer of 2013. Only 11 people left the country as a direct result of this strategy, but at least 83 have been deported and many others have lost their jobs, their benefits and even their homes. After a pause in deportations as the scandal broke in 2017, the government announced their resumption in February 2019. At the time of writing, the scandal had not dimmed and the futures of more than 50,000 continue to be uncertain. Some 60 years after the arrival of the first Jamaican immigrants aboard the *Empire Windrush* in 1948, the politics of colonial immigration endures.

Despite the hardships faced by colonial migrants, the changes that have ensued in British culture as a result of this changing demographic have been remarkable. Music, art, film and literature have been shaped since the 1950s by migrants from all over the colonies. British supermarkets now sell samosas and curries alongside pork pies and Marmite. Musical styles combining different cultures, such as 2 Tone, bhangra, Asian Underground and grime, have exerted considerable influence on the British music scene as have calypso, ska and dubstep among others. Visual artists such as Sonia Boyce, the Singh Twins and Yinka Shonibare, and novelists such as Andrea Levy, Onyeka and Zadie Smith, are widely acclaimed. Zines such as *Burnt Roti* and *Yellowzine* offer a platform for Britain's black and Asian communities. From at least the 1930s and well after the war, London especially became a focus for black activism and culture. Recent work has also demonstrated the ways in which the radical changes to health care, social services and housing accessibility across the nation occasioned by the post-war welfare state were shaped by decolonisation and new immigrant communities. The National Health Service, with its long history of active colonial recruitment, currently boasts a far higher percentage of BAME (black, Asian and minority ethnic) workers than other service sectors. Almost 20 per cent of NHS staff (and 42.9 per cent of doctors) are from BAME backgrounds compared with 6.6 per cent of the police force, 7 per cent of court judges and around 8 per cent of teachers. 1987 saw the first post-war MPs from non-white backgrounds elected to parliament; that number had risen to 52 (around 8 per cent) by 2017.

The controversial place of immigration to Britain is an integral part of the story of decolonisation, for the issue at stake was always about the status of those whose histories were linked to Britain's imperial expansion, and who among them could truly be regarded – and why – as British. It is a story about racial difference, differentials of power and of economic and political muscle. And alongside the women and men who hoped to find a better life in Britain, there were also those who had left Britain to live and work in the colonies and who did not relish the prospect of return. A good few stayed on in non-settler colonies, some in retirement, others doing similar work for new employers in agricultural development, in administration, in business and commerce. Their numbers were not huge, and few are left today, but theirs is a story mostly still untold and yet a signal element in the broader tale of decolonisation.

Their continued presence in former colonial territories usefully reminds us that the end of empire was by no means the close of a chapter, for the long-term impact and consequences of British imperialism are with us still, and resonate in the acrimonious debates over Brexit since 2016. Many of the most intractable and violent of contemporary political trouble spots share a colonial British legacy. Whether we seek to understand the stand-off between Palestinians and Israelis, the rise of the Ba'ath party in Iraq, the violence in Kashmir or in Northern Ireland, in all these instances British influence has been central. Much of the inter-ethnic violence that has followed and still follows decolonisation – in Iraq, Uganda, Nigeria, Fiji, Zimbabwe and elsewhere – is also part of the legacy of colonialism. Not only was the uneven, rapid and often panicked withdrawal of British rule in many places a necessarily destabilising factor in itself, with new nations economically ill-placed for success and survival, but in many instances the British grouped together, for administrative convenience, peoples with very little in common beyond geographical proximity, practically guaranteeing future strife.

The massive upheaval that followed the clumsy partition of India in 1947 should have alerted the colonists to such problems, but the lesson remained unlearned. In South Asia, millions of people found themselves virtually without warning in potentially hostile territory – Muslims in Hindu territory and vice versa. The bloodbath of communal violence that overtook newly independent Pakistan and India forced many to cross the border and begin anew in what was, religion aside, now a foreign country. The turmoil and damage of the early post-partition years left a lasting scar on the region. Yet when Nigeria was created as an independent nation just over a decade later in 1960, the authorities did not look back and take stock as they might have done. This was not an easily or obviously definable country or, indeed, one in which an obvious group of leaders had emerged. Critical cultural and linguistic as well as political and religious divides were well known to British authorities, and were in place at the very birth of the Nigerian nation. Civil war – almost inevitably – ensued within a decade. It was a story that would be repeated over and over again. In Fiji, violence has divided the immigrant Indian community brought over by the British as indentured plantation labour from indigenous Fijians. In Kenya and Uganda in the 1960s, South Asians were forcibly expelled in a wave of 'Africanisation'. In Malaysia, there has been chronic tension between the Chinese, encouraged by the British to migrate there in the nineteenth century, and indigenous Malays. In the Sudan, there has been little peace between rival factions since independence in 1955. And the list goes on.

But if this rather grim list suggests that decolonisation *produced* violence that the British had formerly kept in check, it is worth bearing in mind the violence with which the British often met anti-colonial nationalisms in their Empire. Violence was not the exclusive characteristic of colonial peoples. As decolonisation rapidly advanced, the British fought bloody campaigns around the globe to stem the rising tide of nationalism. For most of the 1950s, troops were stationed in Malaya to combat a strong and disciplined communist-nationalist guerrilla force. In Kenya the British spent the 1950s attempting to quell the Kikuyu-led Mau Mau, detaining thousands of suspects in internment camps and enclosed villages. It was not lost on angry locals that by the end of the Mau Mau emergency, the white death toll was around 70 and the black death toll around 10,000, that villages and houses had been destroyed wholesale, and that thousands had been detained, often on flimsy grounds, in camps where violence was casual and routine. Whether in Africa, India or even Cyprus, the British never hesitated to incarcerate nationalist leaders, often on insubstantial charges. In Malaya, compulsory resettlement of village Chinese thought to be potential supporters of the guerrillas was a heavy-handed piece of coercion, part of a vast clampdown on civil rights designed to isolate and oust the guerrillas. Britain, it might be said, was fighting for its imperial life, and was more than willing to employ violence in selected contexts to secure that end.

In the spring of 2011, the British High Court instructed the Foreign Office to release documents, brought from Kenya when the colony became independent, but never made public, and which detailed attempts to crush the Mau Mau rebellion. The documents revealed that British politicians and high-ranking officials not only knew of, but frequently authorised, the harsh treatment of detainees. The presiding judge in the case noted: 'There is ample evidence even in the few papers that I have seen suggesting that there may have been systematic torture of detainees during the Emergency.'[8] Also in April 2011, a judicial review in Malaysia led to the release of documents showing that the Foreign Office had in the 1990s worked to prevent a criminal investigation into the 1948 killing of unarmed Malay villagers by British troops, and the burning of their village, and that investigations into the action in 1970 had also been suppressed. While these documents clearly show that violence was an acceptable method for British colonial administrators, what is most remarkable is that such documents survived into the twenty-first century. Documents showing Britain in a bad light were routinely destroyed before British officials departed the colonies. In 2013 the government settled more than 5,000 claims but a second wave of litigation resulted, in August 2018, in dismissal in the British courts.

The last military conflict in defence of a colonial possession was also perhaps the oddest, for it occurred after almost the entire Empire had broken up, and when few in Britain really saw the nation as still defined by its Empire. In 1982, just months after the naval presence at the Falkland Islands was withdrawn as part of a cost-cutting exercise by the Conservative

Figure 11.4 Mau Mau captives lined up prior to being transported to detention camps
Source: Popperfoto/Getty Images

government, this obscure surviving outpost of the British Empire was invaded by neighbouring Argentina, which had long clamoured for sovereignty over the territory. Margaret Thatcher, the British prime minister, countered by sending troops to regain the islands. The whole affair was over in three months and British rule restored. Some of the popularity of this adventure can be explained by the fact that the Argentinian leader was a widely reviled and brutal dictator, but there was also a substantial element of imperial sentiment in the affair. Popular opinion saw British success as a reminder of past glories and strengths, of a time when Britain ruled the seas and a hefty portion of the globe. In practical terms, the British in the years after the Second World War may have deemed their colonial possessions not 'worth' the expense or too burdensome to maintain, but the image of empire as epitomising British power and glory nonetheless remained a strong undercurrent in national self-reckoning. Whether it was reliance on America in the late 1940s, humiliation in the Middle East in the 1950s or continued and long-term economic decline – and really a potent brew of all these and more – that led to Britain's abandonment of its idea of itself as politically prominent, the idea of empire remains even now palpable.

Some argue that imperialism has successfully survived the mechanics and process of decolonisation, and continues to operate today. Inequities in wealth, in the ability to use resources, in education and in literacy, in health care and any number of other critical factors keep previously colonised nations in thrall to the wealth of developed countries, many of them former colonising powers. If Britain's Empire is but a shadow of its earlier and massive presence, its legacy indubitably lives on.

Notes

1 J. D. Krivine, 'Malta and Self-Government', *World Affairs* 111, no. 2 (1948), p. 113.
2 Clement Attlee, *Empire into Commonwealth* (London, 1961), p. 1.
3 See, for example, J. C. Carothers, *The Psychology of Mau Mau* (Nairobi: Government Printer, 1954).
4 Mahmood Mamdani, *From Citizen to Refugee: Ugandan Asians Come to Britain* (London: Frances Pinter, 1973), p. 79.
5 Wendy Webster, 'The Empire Comes Home: Commonwealth Migration to Britain', in Andrew Thompson (ed.), *Britain's Experience of Empire in the Twentieth Century* (Oxford: Oxford University Press, 2012), p. 132.
6 House of Commons Parliamentary Debates (Hansard), 28 January 1981, vol. 977, c.1983.
7 Commission on Human Rights, 35th session, 23 February 1979, para. 27, quoted in Evan Smith and Marinella Marmo, 'Uncovering the "Virginity Testing" Controversy in the National Archives: The Intersectionality of Discrimination in British Immigration History', *Gender & History* 23, no. 1 (2011), p. 157.
8 *Mutua & others* v. *Foreign & Commonwealth Office*, EWHC 1913 (QB), 21 July 2011, para. 125. The full judgment can be accessed online at: www.bailii.org/ew/cases/EWHC/QB/2011/1913.html. For the 2018 case, see www.bailii.org/ew/cases/EWHC/QB/2018/2066.html.

Further reading

Helpful overviews of the process of decolonisation include M. E. Chamberlain, *Decolonization: The Fall of the European Empires* (Oxford: Blackwell, 2nd edn, 1999), Raymond F. Betts, *Decolonization* (2nd edn, New York: Routledge, 2004) and Nicholas J. White, *Decolonisation: The British Experience since 1945* (London: Longman, 1999). In *The End of the British Empire: The Historical Debate* (Oxford: Blackwell, 1991) John Darwin surveys the different rationales that historians have offered for why decolonisation occurred when and how it did. Peter

Clarke offers an exhaustive survey of *The Last Thousand Days of the British Empire* (London: Allen Lane, 2007).

A much longer perspective colours D. George Boyce's views on decolonisation in his *Decolonization and the British Empire, 1775–1997* (New York: St Martin's Press, 1999) where he analyses eighteenth-century dissatisfactions with imperial rule alongside the more typical concentration on the events of the twentieth century. A. N. Porter and A. J. Stockwell straddle the divide of the Second World War in *British Imperial Policy and Decolonization, 1938–64* (Basingstoke: Macmillan, 1987) while John Springhall sees the post-war years as more critical in *Decolonization Since 1945: The Collapse of European Overseas Empires* (Basingstoke: Palgrave, 2001). While Mark Mazower's *No Enchanted Palace: The End of Empire and the Ideological Origins of the United Nations* (Princeton, NJ: Princeton University Press, 2009) is not specific to British decolonisation, it offers a helpful backdrop against which to understand the politics of the day. Sarah Stockwell examines institutions within Britain which she sees as central to the unfolding of decolonisation in *The British End of the British Empire* (Cambridge: Cambridge University Press, 2018).

C. A. Bayly and Timothy Harper offer a pair of books that consider the damage wrought to Britain's Asian colonial presence during the Second World War: *Forgotten Armies: The Fall of British Asia, 1941–1945* (London: Allen Lane, 2004) and *Forgotten Wars: The End of Britain's Asian Empire* (London: Allen Lane, 2007).

Stephen Howe offers an overview of left-wing anti-colonialism in *Anticolonialism in British Politics: The Left and the End of Empire, 1918–1964* (Oxford: Oxford University Press, 1993). The connections between Indian and Irish nationalists has been explored by many historians. See, for example, Kate O'Malley, *Ireland, India and Empire: Indo-Irish Radical Connections, 1919–64* (Manchester: Manchester University Press, 2008).

There is a considerable body of work on the partition of India. Notable books in this field include Yasmin Khan, *The Great Partition: The Making of India and Pakistan* (New Haven, CT: Yale University Press, 2007) and Gyanendra Pandey, *Remembering Partition: Violence, Nationalism, and History in India* (Cambridge: Cambridge University Press, 2001). On the experience of women at Partition, two thorough accounts are Ritu Menon and Kamla Bhasin, *Borders and Boundaries: Women in India's Partition* (New Delhi: Kali for Women, 1998) and Urvashi Butalia, *The Other Side of Silence: Voices from the Partition of India* (New Delhi: Penguin Books India, 1998).

David M. Anderson's *Histories of the Hanged: Britain's Dirty War in Kenya and the End of Empire* (London: Weidenfeld and Nicolson, 2005), Daniel Branch's *Defeating Mau Mau, Creating Kenya: Counterinsurgency, Civil War, and Decolonization* (Cambridge: Cambridge University Press, 2009) and Caroline Elkins, *Britain's Gulag: The Brutal End of Empire in Kenya* (London: Jonathan Cape, 2005) are important works on the Mau Mau rebellion. The essays in *At Home with the Empire: Metropolitan Culture and the Imperial World* (Catherine Hall and Sonya O. Rose (eds), Cambridge: Cambridge University Press, 2006) consider the effects of empire on Britain itself, while Jordanna Bailkin's *The Afterlife of Empire* (Berkeley, CA: University of California Press, 2012) discusses how ideas about welfare provision were shaped by decolonisation. A burgeoning literature explores the close relationship of empire to humanitarianism: a good introduction to the issue is Michael Barnett's *Empire of Humanity: A History of Humanitarianism* (Ithaca, NY: Cornell University Press, 2011).

On the culture of British migrants, Paul Gilroy's *There Ain't No Black in the Union Jack* (Chicago, IL: University of Chicago Press, 1987) argues that the forging of a black British identity in the 1970s and 1980s revealed the colonial racism that continued to structure white British attitudes. Paul Rich's *Race and Empire in British Politics* (Cambridge: Cambridge University Press, 1990) covers some of the same ground over a much longer period, although from the point of view of policy-makers. In *Black London: The Imperial Metropolis and Decolonization in the Twentieth Century* (Berkeley: University of California Press, 2015), Marc Matera tells the fascinating story of black intellectuals in inter-war London.

On British immigration policy, key works include Kathleen Paul, *Whitewashing Britain: Race and Citizenship in the Postwar Era* (Ithaca, NY: Cornell University Press, 1997), Colin Holmes, *John Bull's Island: Immigration and British Society, 1871–1971* (Basingstoke: Macmillan, 1988), Paniko Panayi, *An Immigration History of Britain: Multicultural Racism since 1800* (Harlow: Longman, 2010) and Randall Hansen, *Citizenship and Immigration in Post-War Britain. The Institutional Origins of a Multi-Cultural Nation* (Oxford: Oxford University Press, 2000). In *Imagining Home. Gender, 'Race', and National Identity, 1945–1964* (London: Routledge, 1998) Wendy Webster links gender, colonialism and immigration. In *London Is the Place for Me: Black Britons, Citizenship, and the Politics of Race* (Oxford: Oxford University Press, 2015), Kennetta Hammond Perry explores how black Britons negotiated the fraught race relations of the postwar era. A. James Hammerton's *Migrants of the British Diaspora Since the 1960s: Stories from Modern Nomads* (Manchester: Manchester University Press, 2017) explores white migration from Britain to the former Dominions from the 1960s on.

Chronology of British Empire

1480
Ships sent out from Bristol to explore Atlantic lands

1494
Columbus reaches Jamaica

1497
John Cabot and his son Sebastian reach Newfoundland

1549
Matthew Cabot seeks a north-east passage to China

1562
Sir John Hawkins' first English Atlantic slave voyage
English and French Huguenots establish a settlement on the Florida coast,
    destroyed by the Spanish in 1565

1564
Hawkins' second expedition establishes slaving as a commercial operation

1576
Martin Frobisher attempts to find a North-West Passage to the Pacific
    Ocean

1577–80
Francis Drake circumnavigates the globe, claiming the west coast of North
    America as New Albion

1578
Humphrey Gilbert secures patent from Elizabeth I to found colonies in lands
    'not actually possessed of any Christian prince or people'

1580
Tobago claimed as British

1581
Levant Company founded

1583
Newfoundland proclaimed English

1584
Walter Ralegh attempts to establish a colony at Roanoke

1586
Colonists abandon Roanoke, sailing with Drake
Spain introduces *asiento* system

1587
Second attempt to found a colony at Roanoke fails

1588
Defeat of Spanish Armada
Charter granted to a River Gambia trading company

1591
James Lancaster reaches India and Malay archipelago

1595
Walter Ralegh secures patent to open up Guiana between the Orinoco and
   the Amazon

1600
Establishment of English East India Company under royal charter

1601
First East India Company voyage to the Spice Islands

1602
First exploration of New England coast by Bartholomew Gosnold

1605
George Waymouth explores New England coast

1606
Virginia Association founded

1607
First permanent English settlement at Jamestown, Virginia
Plymouth Company establishes Popham Plantation settlement near
   Kennebec River; lasted only a year

1610
Company of Adventurers founded to explore Newfoundland

1612
Development of tobacco in Virginia; first importation of slaves
British defeat Portuguese off Surat, India

1613
First British factory established at Surat

1615
Somers Island Company receives charter to colonise Bermuda
Mughals grant the British permission to trade in India

1617
Attempted settlement of Avalon Peninsula, Newfoundland, fails
First commercial export of tobacco from Virginia

1618
Start of Thirty Years' War
English fort built at Constantyne, Gold Coast

1619
First sale of blacks in Jamestown, Virginia
Establishment of elected assembly (House of Burgesses) in Virginia

1620
Mayflower, headed for Virginia, blown off course, landing at Cape Cod and
    founding Plymouth

1621
James I grants Sir William Alexander the Acadian peninsula of Canada
    (Nova Scotia)

1623
Powhatan Indians attack tobacco plantations along James River ('Virginia
    Massacre')
Massacre of Amboina, Dutch murder in Spice Islands of 10 English and 9
    Japanese

1624
Virginia becomes a royal colony
St Kitts becomes first English settlement in West Indies

1625
British settle Barbados
Charles I establishes a Commission of Trade to administer the colonies

1627
Barbados Company founded to settle the island
War between Britain and France

1628
Settlement of Nevis in West Indies
First colonists arrive in Salem

1629
Massachusetts Bay Company founded, charter confirmed by Charles I
Puritan Providence Company establishes a settlement at Santa Catalina
    Island off the coast of Nicaragua
Quebec captured by the English
Settlement of the Bahamas

1630
First settlers arrive in Massachusetts

1632
Antigua and Montserrat settled
Lord Baltimore obtains grant of land at Chesapeake Bay to settle Catholics;
    establishment of Maryland as a Catholic colony
Treaty of St Germain-en-Laye restores Quebec and Acadia, and cedes Nova
    Scotia, to France
Establishment of slave depots on coast of west Africa

1633
First East India Company factories established in Bengal

1634
Commission of Trade renamed the Commission for Plantations

1636
Rhode Island founded by Puritans fearful of religious intolerance elsewhere
    in the American colonies

1639
Francis Day establishes station at Fort St George, Madras
Unsuccessful settlement at St Lucia

1641
Spanish drive settlers off Santa Catalina Island as well as out of the Bahamas

1644
Rhode Island chartered

1648
End of Thirty Years' War; Spain recognises Dutch independence

1650
East India Company permitted to establish a trading base on the Hugli River in eastern India

1651
Annexation of St Helena, South Atlantic, by the East India Company

1652
First Anglo-Dutch War provoked by trade restrictions (until 1654)

1654
Surinam Company founded (British Guiana)
Nova Scotia restored to the British

1655
Cromwell attacks the Spanish in the West Indies, capturing Jamaica

1657
Bahamas recolonised
East India Company granted a charter to govern St Helena

1660
Navigation Act requires English and colonial ships to be used for export and import to/from British colonies

1661
East India Company settles St Helena
East India Company charter confirmed; re-confirmation required every 20 years
Bombay and Tangiers given to Charles II as part of dowry of Catherine de Berganza
Barbuda settled by the British

1662
Connecticut chartered
Jamaican constitution provides for a Governor, a nominated council and an elected assembly

1663

Anguilla, Antigua, Barbados, Montserrat, Nevis and St Christopher [St Kitts] brought under Crown rule

Settlement of Carolina

Staple Act requires goods for British colonies be shipped only from English ports

New charter for Rhode Island

Company of Royal Adventurers formed for African trading, including slaves

1664

Settlement at Jamaica begins

Settlement of Delaware and New Jersey

British take Dutch North American colony of New Netherlands on the Hudson River, and some Dutch settlements in West Africa

French seize Montserrat

Second Anglo-Dutch War (until 1667)

1667

Treaty of Breda ends the Second Anglo-Dutch War dividing West Indies between French, Dutch and English. Dutch relinquish New Amsterdam (New York), New Jersey and Delaware estuary. British relinquish Dutch Surinam and Acadia

Nova Scotia returned to French rule

1668

Montserrat restored to Britain

Bombay given to the East India Company

1669

First British fur trading posts established at Fort Rupert and Fort Albany in Canada

1670

Spain cedes Caribbean Cayman Islands, administered from Jamaica

Dutch re-occupy New York after Treaty of Dover allies Charles II and Louis XIV against the Dutch

Treaty of Madrid confirms Jamaica as a British possession

Hudson's Bay Company chartered

1672

Royal African Company incorporated to control British slave trade

Third Anglo-Dutch War in the West Indies (until 1678): France and England allied against Holland

1673
First major slave revolt, Jamaica
Dutch capture of St Helena

1674
Treaty of Westminster restores New York to English possession

1675
War between Native Americans and settlers in Massachusetts (until 1678)

1678
Settlement of Turks and Caicos Islands

1680
New Hampshire chartered

1681
Settlement of Pennsylvania

1684
Bermuda becomes a Crown Colony

1685
East India Company establishes a trading centre and garrison at Bencoolen
   (south-west Sumatra)

1687
Bombay supersedes Surat as western headquarters of East India Company

1689
War of the Grand Alliance (also known as King William's War; until 1697) in
   West Indies. English, Iroquois and Dutch allied against French

1690
English trading port (Fort William) at Calcutta founded

1695
Company of Scotland established for trading to Africa and the Indies

1696
Establishment of Board of Trade and Plantations

1698
Attempted settlement at Darien by Company of Scotland
Slave trade opened to private traders

1699
Second Darien expedition fails
Colonies forbidden to export manufactured woollens
Formation of Presidency of Bengal by East India Company

1701
War of the Spanish Succession: Dutch and English trying to stop Spanish
 territories from falling to the French (until 1713)
Founding of the Society for the Propagation of the Gospel in Foreign Parts
 (Church of England)
Company of Scotland goes bankrupt

1703
France and Spain seize Bahamas from the British

1704
British occupy Gibraltar
Dissenters and Catholics excluded from public office in Ireland

1705
British colonies in America opened to direct trade in linen with Ireland

1707
Act of Union between England and Scotland

1708
British occupy Menorca

1709
East India Company reformed

1711
Incorporation of South Sea Company

1713
Treaty of Utrecht ends War of the Spanish Succession: confirmed British
 acquisition of Acadia (Nova Scotia) and Newfoundland, Hudson's
 Bay, Anguilla, Nevis and St Kitts, and retention of Gibraltar and
 Menorca
British Virgin Islands brought under Crown rule
Treaty confirms British possession of Gibraltar
Right to supply slaves to Spanish colonies (*asiento*) shifted from French to
 British

1717
Bahamas brought under Crown rule
First South Sea Company voyage
First importation of slaves to Boer territory

1718
Penal transportation introduced

1719
Colonies forbidden to export iron

1720
Declaratory Act empowers Westminster to make law for Ireland; denies appellate jurisdiction of Irish House of Lords

1729
Royal governor appointed at Newfoundland

1730
First Maroon War, Jamaica (until 1740)

1731
Colonies forbidden to export hats

1732
Settlement of Georgia

1733
Molasses Act imposes sugar duties in American colonies

1734
Systematic settlement of Cayman Islands begins

1739
War of Jenkins' Ear: trade war between Britain and Spain (until 1741)

1740
War of the Austrian Succession (until 1748)

1744
France declares war on Britain

1746
Madras captured by the French
Irish Parliament bans marriages between Catholics and Protestants

1748
Treaty of Aix-la-Chapelle ends War of the Austrian Succession. Britain exchanges Louisbourg for Madras

1750
African Company of Merchants founded

1751
Robert Clive's victory at Battle of Arcot, capital of the Carnatic, India

1753
Georgia becomes a royal Colony

1756
Seven Years' War (to 1763)
French seize Menorca
British capture Dominica
Siraj-ud-Daula (Nawab of Bengal) captures Calcutta

1757
Defeat of Siraj-ud-Daula at Plassey – replaced by Mir Jafar (Bengal)
Robert Clive takes Chandernagore, India

1758
British drive French out of West Africa

1759
British occupy Gorée and Guadeloupe
Quebec surrenders to the British
British take Masulipatam, India; Nizam of Hyderabad agrees to support the British

1760
Montreal falls to British
Slave revolt in Jamaica (Tacky's revolt)

1761
Capture of French settlement at Pondicherry (India)

1762
Alexander Dalrymple recommends colonising Balambangan in Sulu archipelago (Borneo) to improve the China trade
Grenada conquered from the French
British capture Martinique, Havana, Manila, St Vincent and Tobago

1763

Defeat of France in Seven Years' War; Treaty of Paris cedes all French territory east of Mississippi River to Britain (Grenada, Dominica, St Vincent
& Tobago)

Creation of East and West Florida, and of Quebec (all by royal proclamation)

Annexation of Dominica, Grenada, Tobago and St Vincent as well as
Senegal

Annexation of Prince Edward Island as part of Nova Scotia

France regains Pondicherry, Martinique, Guadeloupe, Gorée and St Lucia

Havana and Manila/Philippines returned to the Spanish

Proclamation Line sets limits of British colonisation in America at the
Alleghenies

1764

Defeat of Mir Kasim at Buxar

John Byron declares the Falklands (off the coast of Argentina) British

Plantation Act (Sugar Act) reinstitutes sugar duties in the American
colonies

1765

Stamp Act rejected by American colonists

Robert Clive returns to India as Governor of Bengal

Treaty of Allahabad guarantees East India Company control of *diwani*
(Bengal)

1766

First British garrison at West Falkland

Stamp Act repealed after rioting in America

Declaratory Act asserts British rights to govern in colonies

Annexation of Turks and Caicos Islands, administered from Jamaica

Establishment of West Indian free ports

Virgin Islands (Caribbean) seized from the Dutch

1767

Revenue Act, America

First English ship (*Dolphin*) to visit Tahiti

1768

Establishment of Colonial Department (abolished after American
Revolution)

Captain Cook's first voyage

1769

Cook claims North Island of New Zealand for Britain

Prince Edward Island (Canada) becomes a separate colony

1770
Cook claims South Island of New Zealand

1771
Britain's claims to the Falkland Islands ceded by Spain and France

1772
Mansfield judgment ends slavery in Britain by ruling that enslaved persons landing on English soil were free
Cook's second voyage
Balambangan settlement recommended by Dalrymple founded

1773
Tea Act in the American colonies prompts the 'Boston Tea Party'
Regulating Act establishes Governor-Generalship and Supreme Court for British India
Robert Clive accused of financial misconduct
St Vincent and the Grenadines surrender sovereignty to Britain

1774
Quebec Act restores French civil law and gives Catholics political and religious equality
Massachusetts constitution rewritten
First Continental Congress of the American colonies
Coercive Acts, America
Britain withdraws from Falkland Islands

1775
Initial battles of American-British War at Lexington, Bunker Hill and Quebec City

1776
Second Continental Congress of the American colonies
American Declaration of Independence
Cook's third voyage

1778
Capture of St Lucia from French
France enters American War of Independence

1779
French capture St Vincent and Grenada
Cook killed in Sandwich Islands
Spain enters American War of Independence
First Kaffir War between Boers and Bantus

1780
Defeat of Madras armies by Haidar Ali of Mysore, India
British send a Superintendent to Belize

1781
French capture of Tobago
Bahamas surrenders to Spain
Cornwallis surrenders to Washington at Yorktown, ending Revolutionary War

1782
French occupation of St Christopher and Montserrat
Menorca returned to Spain
Colonial affairs moved to domain of Home Office
Irish Declaratory Act repealed

1783
Peace of Versailles marks American independence and Britain's loss of the
    American colonies
End of French occupation of St Christopher and St Vincent, Montserrat and
    Grenada
St Lucia returned to the French
Zong case: insurance claim for 131 slaves thrown overboard from a
    Liverpool slave ship in 1781
Bahamas returned from Spanish to British rule as a Crown Colony
House of Lords rejects India Bill (authored by Fox) which would have seen
    British government assume direct responsibility for India
Rights of British over the Gambia River estuary (Africa) recognised

1784
India Act (authored by Pitt) passes, giving Crown greater control of British
    India and establishing a supervisory board of the East India Company
    in London.
Asiatic Society of Bengal founded
Loyalists settle in Canada
New Brunswick becomes a Canadian province

1785
Impeachment of Warren Hastings

1786
Leasing of Penang by East India Company; first British settlement on
    Malay coast
Decision to establish penal colony at Botany Bay
Spain abandons claims to British Honduras

1787
Establishment of Sierra Leone as settlement for freed slaves
Society for the Abolition of the Slave Trade founded

1788
First fleet arrives at Botany Bay, establishing the first Australian penal colony
Regulation of slave trade
Trial of Warren Hastings
African Association founded

1789
Mutiny on HMS *Bounty*
Penal colony established in the Andaman Islands

1790
British expelled from Nootka Sound (Vancouver Island) by Spain
Mutineers from HMS *Bounty* arrive on Pitcairn Island in the Pacific
Sierra Leone Company founded

1791
Canada Act creates Upper (Ontario) and Lower Canada (Quebec), each
    with a Governor and an elected assembly
Slave rebellion in the French colony of St Domingue

1792
Bill to abolish slave trade within four years passes in the House of Commons,
    defeated in House of Lords
Baptist Missionary Society founded

1793
Lord Cornwallis' Permanent Settlement of the Bengal Revenues
French Revolutionary War (until 1802)
Lord Macartney's embassy to China
Tobago regained from the French
Upper Canada passes an anti-slavery law

1794
Secretary of State for War given responsibility for colonies
Seychelles captured from the French; administered as a dependency of
    Mauritius
French National Convention abolishes slavery without compensation
First Christian church built in New South Wales
Britain briefly recaptures Guadeloupe

1795
Non-denominational London Missionary Society founded
Warren Hastings acquitted
Second Maroon War, Jamaica
Trincomalee and Cape Colony captured from Dutch
Mungo Park's first expedition to trace the course of the Niger

1796
Scottish Missionary Society founded
East India Company takes parts of Ceylon from the Dutch
Andaman Islands penal colony abandoned
Penang becomes a penal colony

1797
London Missionary Society sends an expedition to Tahiti
Trinidad wrested from Spanish control
St Lucia, Martinique, Tobago taken from the French
Malacca and Dutch Guiana captured from the Dutch
Merino sheep introduced in New South Wales

1798
Rebellion in Ireland
Napoleon conquers Egypt
British establish control of Belize

1799
Defeat of Tipu Sultan at Seringapatam, India
Church Missionary Society founded as Society for Missions in Africa and
    the East

1800
Province Wellesley acquired, Malay Peninsula
British drive French out of Malta

1801
Annexation of the Carnatic, India
Act of Union joins Ireland to UK
Creation of Colonial Department within Department of War and Colonies
    (transferred from Home Department)
Ceylon declared a Crown Colony
First settlement of Newcastle in northern New South Wales
Peace of Amiens returns Cape Colony, Malacca and Guiana to Dutch; and
    St Lucia, Martinique, Tobago and Gorée to French

1802
Slavery re-introduced in French colonies by Napoleon
College of Fort William, Calcutta founded (East India Company)

1803
Napoleonic War (until 1815)
St Lucia, Demerara and Surinam captured
Dominica formally recognised as British
First European settlement of Van Diemen's Land, Australia
Tobago and Trinidad ceded to Britain
Marathas defeated at battle of Assaye, India
Denmark halts slave trade
East India Company leases St Helena to the Crown for the internment of
    Napoleon

1804
British and Foreign Bible Society founded
St Domingue becomes independent as Haiti
Penang becomes a presidency of India

1805
Bligh mutiny, New South Wales
Mungo Park's second expedition to trace the course of the Niger
Haileybury College founded to train East India Company officials

1806
Foreign Slave Trade Act
British re-occupy Cape of Good Hope
British occupy Buenos Aires
French concede Dominica to British
British settlers at the Cape forbidden to own slaves

1807
Abolition of slave trade in British Empire
Heligoland and Malacca seized from Dutch
Society for the Abolition of the Slave Trade becomes the African Institution

1808
Sierra Leone becomes a Crown Colony
Capture of Moluccas from the Dutch

1809
British drive French out of Ionian Islands
Labrador administratively attached to Newfoundland

1810

British capture Java, Mauritius, Martinique, Guadeloupe, Seychelles and
 Réunion

1811

Java seized from Dutch; Thomas Stamford Raffles appointed Governor
Seychelles administered from Mauritius (until 1888)
Import of slaves to Bengal prohibited

1812

War with USA over border with Canada (until 1814)

1813

Wesleyan Methodist Missionary Society founded
East India Company Charter Act opens India trade and allows missionaries
 into India
Import of slaves to Bombay and Madras prohibited

1814

Formal British annexation of Cape of Good Hope
Ghurka War in Nepal (until 1816)
Annexation of Dutch colonies of Berbice, Demerara and Essequibo
Malta annexed
Treaty with Iran promising protection from Russia
First English missionaries arrive in New Zealand
British persuade European powers to declare the slave trade repugnant at
 Congress of Vienna
Dutch abolish slave trade
Thomas Middleton (1769–1822) appointed first Bishop of Calcutta
British add Corfu to their Ionian islands possessions

1815

Java returned to Dutch and Réunion to French
Treaty of Vienna guarantees Britain possession of Ceylon, St Lucia, Trinidad,
 Tobago, British Guiana, Berbice, Demerara and Essequibo
European powers agree to outlaw slave trade
British occupy Ascension Island, administered by the Admiralty Office
 until 1922
All of Ceylon brought under British control
Ionian Islands become a British Protectorate
Napoleon exiled to St Helena
Penal colony established on Mauritius

1816
Maratha War, India (until 1818)
Bathurst (Banjul Island, The Gambia) establishes a base (garrison) for Anti-Slavery (West Africa) Squadron
British resident appointed to Nepal
Slave revolt in Barbados
Annexation of Tristan da Cunha (South Atlantic)
Guadeloupe returned to France

1817
Creation of post of Secretary of State for Colonies
War against Xhosa, South Africa (until 1819)

1818
Final defeat of Maratha Confederation, India

1819
Thomas Raffles establishes a trading station at Singapore
Britain lays claim to British Antarctic Territory
Foundation of Albany Colony in eastern Cape

1821
Bathurst (Banjul Island, The Gambia) and Gold Coast placed under Crown rule, administered from Sierra Leone
Greek War of Independence (until 1829)
Royal Asiatic Society founded
Coasts of Africa surveyed by W. F. Owen
Guatemala claims right to control Belize
Hudson's Bay Company claims west coast of Canada as New Caledonia

1822
First Britons cross the Sahara
Source of Niger River established by A. G. Laing
Liberia established for freed slaves by American Colonisation Society
Brazil becomes independent of Portugal

1823
Act creates a nominated Council in New South Wales, limiting power of governor
African Institute replaced by Society for the Amelioration and Gradual Abolition of Slavery
Slave revolt in Demerara
Monroe Doctrine prevents further colonisation in the Americas

1824

Anglo-Dutch Treaty divides Malay archipelago into two spheres of influence; Bencoolen ceded to Dutch in exchange for Malacca

First Anglo-Burmese War

Britain recognises independent republics in Latin America

First Queensland settlement at Moreton Bay, Australia

First bishoprics in Barbados and Jamaica established

First British settlement of Natal

Army mutiny in Barrackpur, India

1825

Anguilla, St Kitts and Nevis linked for colonial administration

Tasmania (Van Diemen's Land) becomes a separate colony

John Clunies Ross visits the Cocos Islands for the first time

1826

Creation of Straits Settlements colony (Penang, Province Wellesley, Malacca and Singapore), administered until 1867 by Government of Bengal

Treaty of Yandabo ends first Anglo-Burmese War, giving Assam, Arakan and Tenasserim to British

British win trading concessions in Siam

Confederation of Canada

First European settlement of Western Australia

Penal colony established at Brisbane

New Zealand Company founded

Rejection by British government of a request to make Tahiti a Protectorate

1827

John Clunies Ross returns to the Cocos Islands to settle with his family

1828

Appointment of a Select Committee on Canada

Cape Khoikhoi confirmed as a free people by ordinance, South Africa

1829

Entire continent of Australia declared British

Swan River colony established in western Australia

Edward Gibbon Wakefield's *Letter from Sydney* published, laying out his vision for free settlement

1830

Extension of territory inland from Gold Coast (Africa) declared a Protectorate

France occupies Algeria

Wakefield founds Colonization Society

Mysore added to British holdings in India
Royal Geographical Society founded
'Black Line', Tasmania

1831
Berbice, Demerara and Essequibo joined as colony of British Guiana
Baptist War (slave revolt) in Jamaica, Barbados and other Caribbean islands
State-assisted migration to Australia begins

1832
First resident appointed for New Zealand
Falkland Islands declared a Crown Colony
Newfoundland granted a Representative Assembly

1833
Emancipation Act abolishes slavery in British Empire from 1 August 1834
East India Company loses China trade monopoly
Import of Nepalese slaves to India prohibited

1834
Introduction of large-scale indentured labour to the Caribbean
War against Xhosa in Cape Colony (until 1835) ends slavery
St Helena becomes a Crown Colony rather than an East India Company
  possession
First European settlement of Victoria at Port Philip
South Australia established by Act of Parliament

1835
United Presbyterian Church of Scotland Mission Society founded
Boers at Cape Colony begin 'Great Trek' to settle further north on the
  Orange River

1836
First settlers arrive in South Australia
'Black Act' whereby Europeans outside Calcutta subject to East India
  Company courts in civil cases
William Broughton (1788–1853) becomes first Bishop of Australia
First colonial railway in British Empire opens east of Montreal
Singapore replaces Penang as capital of Straits Settlements

1837
Rebellions in Upper and Lower Canada over subjugation of legislative
  assembly to governor and council
New Zealand Association founded, later becomes New Zealand Land
  Company

1838

Abolition of slave apprenticeships

Crown rule established on Pitcairn Islands

Anglo-Ottoman commercial convention (Balta Liman)

Establishment of Boer republic in South Africa

British government again rejects a request to make Tahiti a Protectorate

1839

Aden seized by East India Company, administered by Government of Bombay

Indentured labour from India prohibited

Lord Durham's *Report on the Affairs of North America*

First Opium War prompted by confiscation by Chinese government of colonial-grown opium

Incorporation of New Zealand Company

Boers in South Africa found Orange Free State and the Transvaal

Grand Trunk road linking Calcutta and Delhi, Calcutta and Bombay, Bombay and Agra begun: completed 1840

British invade Afghanistan to prevent Russian advance towards India's north-west frontier

African Civilization Society founded to establish model settlements in Africa

1840

Transportation to New South Wales ended

First free settlers arrive in Queensland

Treaty of Waitangi in which Māori chiefs acknowledge Queen Victoria's sovereignty in return for guaranteed ownership of lands; New Zealand becomes a Protectorate

Colonial Land and Emigration Commission appointed as sub-department of Colonial Office

1841

British Consul established at Zanzibar (administered until 1873 by Government of Bombay)

Sultan of Brunei appoints James Brooke Rajah of Sarawak

Union of Upper and Lower Canada

Failed Niger experiment (backed by African Civilization Society): Thomas Fowell Buxton's attempt to legitimise Niger commerce to replace slave trade

First Bishop of New Zealand appointed

Establishment of Colonial Bishoprics Council

1842

Treaty of Nanking ends Opium War, cedes Hong Kong to Britain and opens five treaty ports in China to foreign trade

Intervention at Montevideo to protect it from Argentinian dictator

James Brooke installed as Rajah of Sarawak
British troops attacked, and retreat from Afghanistan
New South Wales granted representative government

1843
Hong Kong becomes a Crown Colony
Annexation of Natal, South Africa
Annexation of Sind, India
Legal support for slavery in India withdrawn
The Gambia becomes a Crown Colony

1844
Indentured labour from India re-authorised
Gold Coast comes under direct British rule
Invention of Morse telegraph
Army mutiny in Northwest Provinces, India

1845
Natal declared a dependency of the Cape
Sikh Wars begin (until 1846)
Britain purchases Danish East Indies
New Zealand Wars begin (until 1872)

1846
Western USA/British North America set at 49th parallel
Responsible government granted to Nova Scotia
Lower Canada renamed Canada East
Irish famine begins
Labuan acquired from the Sultan of Brunei

1847
Establishment of colony of British Kaffraria
Sweden abolishes slave trade

1848
Canada attains responsible government
Annexation of Orange River Sovereignty, South Africa
Labuan becomes a Crown colony
First settlement at Dunedin and Christchurch on South Island of New
    Zealand
France and Denmark abolish slavery
Second Sikh War, India

1849
Indentured labour from India again suspended
Annexation of the Punjab following Sikh Wars; Army mutiny in the
    Punjab
Repeal of Navigation Acts
Vancouver Island becomes a Crown Colony
David Livingstone crosses Kalahari desert
Bight of Biafra Protectorate established

1850
Australian Colonies Government Act extends charter for responsible self-
    government to Victoria, South Australia and Van Diemen's Land
War breaks out again at the Cape
Western Australia begins transporting convicts
Britain purchases Danish Gold Coast

1851
Indentured labour from India resumed
Colony of Victoria, Australia, separated from New South Wales
Prince Edward Island attains responsible government
Discovery of gold in New South Wales and Victoria
Dissolution of New Zealand Land Company
Second Anglo-Burmese War (until 1852)
Basuto War (until 1853)
Slave trade ends in Brazil
Lagos Protectorate established

1852
New Zealand Constitution Act gives self-government to New Zealand
Sand River convention recognises Boer independence in Transvaal
Second Burmese War brings Pegu into British territory and annexes Lower
    Burma as British territory
Bight of Benin Protectorate established

1853
Transportation to eastern Australia ends
David Livingstone traverses Africa
First railway track built in Bombay
Telegraph reaches India
Last East India Company charter renewal
Nagpur annexed by East India Company

1854
Creation of Colonial Office as a stand-alone department
Bloemfontein Convention grants Orange Free State full sovereignty

Representative government established in Cape Colony
New Brunswick and Newfoundland granted responsible self-government
First telegraph line, from Calcutta to Agra, opened in India

1855
Responsible self-government granted to New South Wales, South Australia
and Victoria as well as Newfoundland
Windward Islands Crown Colony established (consisting of St Lucia, St
Vincent, Grenadines, Grenada, and French Martinique)
Britain and Afghanistan declare war on Persia (until 1857)

1856
Responsible self-government granted to New Zealand and Van Diemen's Land
Annexation of Oudh, India
Second Opium War, after China seizes a British ship
Secret ballot introduced in Victoria and South Australia
Responsible replaces representative self-government in New South Wales
Separation of Natal and Cape; Natal becomes a Crown Colony
Van Diemen's Land renamed Tasmania

1857
Indian Mutiny (until 1858)
Lieutenant Speke reaches Uganda
Canton occupied by Anglo-French forces
Cocos (Keeling) Islands in Indian Ocean annexed

1858
East India Company abolished
Act for the Better Government of India establishes India Office as formal
branch of British government
Queen Victoria's Proclamation promises to respect ancient rights in India
Foundation of colony of British Columbia
Second Opium War ends; Treaty of Tientsin
Penal colony established at Port Blair, Andaman Islands

1859
Queensland separated from New South Wales; acquires responsible
self-government
Britain concedes the right of Canada to determine own tariff policy
Indian Civil Procedure Code ratified
Cayman Islands become a Crown Colony

1860
Māori Wars (until 1863)
Universities Mission to Central Africa founded

British troops burn Imperial Summer Palace at Beijing
Acquisition of Kowloon and Stonecutters Island extend territory of Hong Kong
Convention of Peking gives Europeans greater rights in China
Indian Penal Code ratified
Slave ownership prohibited in India

1861

Indian Councils Act gives Indians advisory representation on presidency legislative councils
Formal annexation of Lagos as a separate colony
Bights of Biafra and Benin united as a single Protectorate
First English cricket teams visit Australia
Bahrain (Persian Gulf) becomes a Protectorate
Gold discovered in New Zealand
South Australia grants women the vote in local elections

1862

British representative established at Mandalay
China Inland Mission founded
Female Middle-Class Emigration Society founded
British Honduras (Belize) formally colonised, administered from Jamaica until 1884
Annexation of Lower Burma (Pegu, Arakan and Tenasserim)

1863

Foundation of international settlement at Shanghai
Dutch abolish slavery
Third New Zealand (Māori) War (until 1864)

1864

First black Anglican bishop appointed to Sierra Leone: Samuel Adjayi Crowther
Border territory in Bhutan seized
Ionian Islands ceded to Greece
First discussions of federation in Canada held on Prince Edward Island

1865

Colonial Laws Validity Act gives Westminster right to invalidate colonial laws which run counter to British statute law
Morant Bay uprising, Jamaica
Thirteenth Amendment abolishes slavery in US
Capital of New Zealand moved from Auckland to Wellington
Trade treaties open Japan to merchants

1866
Colonies of British Columbia and Vancouver Island united
British Kaffraria incorporated into Cape Colony
Canadian federation plan presented to British government
Dadabhoi Naoroji founds East India Association in London
Jamaica becomes a Crown Colony
Fenian attack on Canadian border

1867
Straits Settlements become a Crown Colony
British North America Act federates the Dominion of Canada
Canada East reverts to the name Quebec
Newfoundland chooses not to join Canada
Māori given four seats on New Zealand's general assembly
Diamonds discovered on the Orange River, South Africa
Discovery of gold in New Zealand
Fenian agitation in Britain for Irish independence
Transportation of convicts to Western Australia ends

1868
Foundation of Royal Colonial Institute
Aboriginal cricket team tour England
Basutoland becomes a Protectorate
End of transportation to Western Australia
Abyssinia Expedition

1869
Opening of the Suez Canal
Discovery of gold at the Transvaal
Hudson Bay Company lands pass to Crown
Britain acquires Nicobar Islands from the Danes
First Aboriginal Protection Act in Australia (Victoria)

1870
Province of Manitoba established
Alberta becomes part of Northwest Territories, no longer controlled by
    Hudson's Bay Company
Western Australia acquires representative government
Home Government Association founded to press for self-government in
    Ireland

1871
Annexation of Griqualand West
British Columbia becomes a Canadian province
Basutoland transferred to Cape Colony

Leeward Islands Federation established (consisting of Dominica, Antigua,
St Christopher, Nevis, Montserrat, British Virgin Islands)
Anglo-Dutch treaty recognises Sumatra as Dutch

1872
Responsible self-government granted to Cape Colony
First Māori appointed to New Zealand's Upper House
Sir Bartle Frere signs anti-slavery treaty with Sultan of Zanzibar
Andaman and Nicobar Islands linked administratively
Lord Mayo, governor-general of India, murdered at Port Blair, Andaman
Islands

1873
Aden Protectorate formed
Prince Edward Island becomes part of Dominion of Canada
Spain abolishes slavery in Puerto Rico

1874
Treaty of Pangkor: sultans of protected Malay States accept British Residents
Fiji becomes a Crown Colony
Gold Coast becomes a Crown Colony

1875
Purchase of Khedive of Egypt's shares in Suez Canal by Disraeli

1876
Empress of India Act
Canadian Trans-Pacific Railway completed
Perim and Sokotra (offshore islands close to Aden) become a British protect-
orate as part of Aden
Death of Truganini
Central African Trading Company
North and South Islands of New Zealand united as a single colony

1877
British re-annex the Transvaal
North Borneo ceded to British by Sultan of Brunei

1878
British Protectorate, Walvis Bay, South-West Africa
Cyprus placed under British administration, leased from Sultan of Turkey
Cocoa production introduced to Gold Coast
Congress of Berlin called to avert a European war over disintegration of
Ottoman empire

1879
Irish Land War (until 1882)
Anglo-Zulu War; Zululand becomes a protectorate
Anglo-French control over Egyptian finances after mutiny of Egyptian army
Treaty of friendship with Tonga
Canada imposes protectionist tariffs on British goods
Central African Trading Company becomes United African Company
Second Anglo-Afghan War after British Resident in Kabul murdered
New Zealand introduces manhood suffrage

1880
First Anglo-Boer War (until 1881)
Britain authorised by new ruler, Abdurrahman, to supervise Afghanistan's
    foreign relations while leaving internal affairs alone
First refrigerated meat from Australia arrives in Britain

1881
Battle of Majuba Hill – British defeat by Boers, re-taking Transvaal
Pretoria Convention recognises self-government for Transvaal, Britain
    retaining nominal control over foreign relations
Royal Charter granted to British North Borneo Company
Urabi revolt, Egypt
The Mahdi (Muhammad Ahmad ibn Abdullah) gains power in Sudan; revolt
    against Anglo-Egyptian forces

1882
Occupation of Egypt
Emirs of Bahrain enter into treaties of protection with British
First cargo of frozen meat leaves New Zealand for England

1883
Ilbert Bill, India
Queensland attempts to annex eastern New Guinea
Discussions on federating Australia begin
Basutoland's administration returned to London under a High Commissioner

1884
Mahdist regime, Sudan (until 1898); expelled British
British Somaliland (on the Red Sea, across from the Gulf of Aden) becomes
    a British Suzerainty, administered from India until 1898
Papua (New Guinea) becomes a British Protectorate
Bechuanaland returned to British protection
Berlin Conference establishes rules for African partition – imperial power
    had to substantiate territorial claims by demonstrating "effective
    administration."

Foundation of Imperial Federation League
British Honduras becomes a separate colony
Walvis Bay annexed to Cape Colony
Treaties with Niger chiefs signed

1885
Formation of Indian National Congress
General Gordon killed at Khartoum
Anglo-Egyptian forces withdraw from the Sudan
Niger Districts (Oil River) and Bechuanaland Protectorates established
Third Anglo-Burmese War precipitated by Burmese king's confiscation of
    property of Bombay-Burma Company: Upper Burma annexed
Establishment of Colonial Defence Committee
Canadian Pacific Railway reaches Vancouver
Grenada becomes part of the Windward Islands Colony

1886
Gold discovered at Witwatersrand, Orange Free State
Charter granted to Royal Niger Company
Anglo-German Agreement on East Africa and on Western Pacific
Colonial and Indian Exhibition staged in London
Spain abolishes slavery in Cuba
Gilbert and Ellice Islands become British
Home Rule Bill for Ireland defeated in House of Commons
Queen Victoria grants the Cocos (Keeling) Islands to the Clunies Ross family
    in perpetuity
Burma becomes a province of British India

1887
Colonial and Imperial Conferences founded in London
Informal Anglo-Russian division of Persia into spheres of interest
Anglo-French Pacific condominium over New Hebrides
Maldive Islands (Indian Ocean) become a Protectorate, administered
    from Ceylon
Treaties of protection with Arab Trucial States
Administration of New Guinea transferred to Queensland government
Annexation of Zululand
Cecil Rhodes founds British South Africa Company

1888
British Residency established at Pahang
Protectorates established at North Borneo, Sarawak and Brunei, Cook
    Islands
Charter granted to Imperial British East Africa Company
The Gambia re-established as a Crown Colony

Trinidad and Tobago governments united as a Crown Colony
Slavery abolished in Brazil
British New Guinea becomes a Crown Colony
Territorial legislature established for Alberta
Christmas Island, Indian Ocean, annexed by British; administered by
    Singapore until 1958
British Somaliland Protectorate established

1889
Anglo-French agreement on Gold and Ivory Coasts, Senegal and The Gambia
Charter granted to British South Africa Company
Second Berlin Conference agrees spheres of influence in Pacific: Samoa
    Agreement

1890
Anglo-German Heligoland-Zanzibar Treaty resolves East African disputes;
    Zanzibar declared a British Protectorate; Heligoland Islands ceded to
    Germany
Anglo-French agreement defines their Niger territories
Labuan incorporated into North Borneo
Joint Protectorate between British and Transvaal over Swaziland
British East Africa Company signs treaty with kingdom of Buganda
Western Australia granted responsible self-government

1891
Anglo-Italian Red Sea agreements
Anglo-Dutch Treaty defining Borneo territories
Anglo-Portuguese agreement over East and Central Africa
British Central African Protectorate created
Foundation of United Empire Trade League
Northern Zambesia (Northern Rhodesia) allocated to British South Africa
    Company
Niger Districts Protectorate becomes Oil Rivers Protectorate

1892
Protectorate established at Gilbert and Ellice Islands
Indian Councils Act increased Indian representation at central and
    provincial level
Buganda declared a Protectorate
Dadabhai Naoroji elected Liberal MP for Central Finsbury constituency,
    London

1893
Natal granted responsible government
British Protectorate established over southern Solomon Islands

Home Rule Bill defeated in House of Lords
New Zealand women win right to vote
Oil Rivers Protectorate becomes Niger Coast Protectorate; Yoruba added
  to territory

1894

Uganda (East Africa) declared a British Protectorate
Foundation of British Empire League
First English cricket teams visit South Africa
Anglo-Japanese Treaty of Commerce and Navigation
Additional territory added to The Gambia as a Protectorate
Women granted vote in South Australia
Swaziland becomes a Protectorate of the Transvaal

1895

Jameson Raid, Transvaal
Anglo-Ashanti War (until 1896) – British overrun Ashanti and annex as far
  as Gold Coast
Kenya added to East African Protectorate
Collapse of Imperial British East Africa Company
Part of Bechuanaland transferred to Cape Colony; remainder becomes a
  Protectorate

1896

Anglo-French agreement guaranteed independence of Siam
Federated Malay States (Perak, Selangor, Negri Sembilan, Pahang)
  established as a Protectorate
Asante Confederation agreed to Protectorate status
Inland territory of Sierra Leone becomes a Protectorate
Further protectorates in Buganda region added
Shona uprising against British, Rhodesia
Italian army defeated at Adowa, Abyssinia

1897

First English cricket teams visit West Indies
Zululand annexed to Natal
Aborigines' Rights Protection Society formed at Gold Coast
Second Colonial Conference held
Benin becomes part of Niger Coast Protectorate

1898

Sierra Leone Hut Tax rebellion (until 1901)
Anglo-Egyptian administration (Condominium) established in the Sudan
  after its reconquest at Battle of Omdurman
Anglo-French boundary agreement, Niger territories

Leasing of New Territories as part of Hong Kong

Wei Hai Wei in north China leased to British

Anglo-German agreement on future of Portuguese colonies (Britain would get Mozambique; Germany Angola)

Anglo-French Fashoda Crisis (Sudan) – confrontation with French on Upper Nile

Legislative Council established, Southern Rhodesia

American annexation of Hawaii and Sandwich Islands

Administration of British Somaliland passes from India to Foreign Office

Pitcairn Island settlers given legal protection under the Fiji High Commissioner

1899

Bloemfontein Conference failure leads to Boer War (until 1902)

Anglo-French convention resolves dispute over the Sudan

Samoa divided between Britain, Germany and USA

Acquisition of Solomon Islands and Tonga

Withdrawal of Royal Niger Company charter; establishment of separate Southern and Northern Nigerian Protectorates

Arab emirates sign treaties of protection for Kuwait

Transvaal and Orange Free State form an alliance

New Zealand restricts non-white immigration

1900

European states co-operate to suppress Chinese national rebellion (Boxer Rising)

Crown rule replaces company rule in Niger Protectorate; becomes two Protectorates of Southern Nigeria and Northern Nigeria

Annexation of Orange Free State and Transvaal

Ruler of Tonga places himself under British protection

Britain acquires Ghana after Fourth Ashanti War

Northern and Southern Rhodesia established as Protectorates

Buganda Agreement guaranteeing African land rights

Niue (South Pacific) becomes a British Protectorate

1901

Australia acquires a national constitution and becomes a federation: Commonwealth of Australia

Australia restricts non-white immigration

Annexation of Asante (west Africa) as a Crown Colony

Cook Islands annexed to New Zealand

Empire Day established in Canada (24 May, Queen's birthday)

Ugandan railway completed

Niue annexed to New Zealand

1902

Boer War ends; Treaty of Vereeniging (Transvaal and Orange Free State forced into the Empire)

Anglo-Japanese Alliance against Russia (until 1923)

Formation of Committee of Imperial Defence

Pacific Cable completes all-British global telegraph system

Preferential tariffs agreed with Canada, Australia and New Zealand

First English cricket teams visit New Zealand

Eastern province of Uganda transferred to East African Protectorate

Colonists' Association formed in East African Protectorate (white settlers)

Administration of New Guinea assigned to Australia

Seychelles become a Crown Colony

1903

Cocos Islands become a Protectorate of Singapore

1904

Anglo-French entente (*entente cordiale*) recognising respective interests in Egypt and Morocco

Gandhi founds his first newspaper, *Indian Opinion*

Central African Protectorate transferred from Foreign Office to Colonial Office jurisdiction

1905

British guarantee of Afghanistan independence

Partition of Bengal against Indian desires

British Somaliland administration moves to Colonial Office

Uganda transferred from Foreign Office to Colonial Office jurisdiction, becoming a Crown Colony

Empire Day established in Australia

Saskatchewan and Alberta become Canadian provinces

1906

Formation of Muslim League in India

Tripartite Pact (Britain, France, Italy) agreeing status of Abyssinia

Autonomy restored to Transvaal and Orange Free State

Zulu rebellion in Natal (until 1908)

Legislative Council established in Kenya

British New Guinea transferred to Australian control

Joint French-British control established over New Hebrides

North Borneo becomes a Crown Colony

Britain assumes sole control of Swaziland protectorate

Brunei acquires a British Resident

Anglo-French Condominium of the New Hebrides (Vanuatu) formed

1907

Dominion Division established at Colonial Office when New Zealand, Canada, Newfoundland and Australia declared Dominions

Confirmation of Siamese independence by Britain and France

Anglo-Russian entente on Tibet, Afghanistan and Persia

Central African Protectorate renamed Nyasaland

Responsible government granted to Orange Free State and Transvaal

First Imperial Conference

1908

Removal of protective tariff on Caribbean sugar

British control of South Georgia and South Sandwich Islands as Falkland Island Dependencies

1909

Anglo-Siamese Treaty: Unfederated Malay States (Kelantan, Trengganu, Kedah, Perlis) placed under British protection

Anglo-Persian Oil Company founded

Indian Councils Act: Morley-Minto reforms allowing directly elected Indian legislators to propose resolutions and initiate debate on legislative matters

Creation of Imperial Cricket Conference

British and Foreign Anti-Slavery Society changes its name to Anti-Slavery and Aborigines Protection Society

Canberra established as the new capital of Australia

1910

Creation of Union of South Africa (Cape Colony, Orange Free State, Natal, Transvaal)

Empire Day established in New Zealand and South Africa

1911

First Imperial Conference held in London

First Indian cricket team tours England (other than a Parsi team which had toured in 1884)

Treaty with ruler of Bhutan guaranteed internal autonomy in exchange for British control of foreign policy

Delhi Durbar marks coronation of George V

Seat of government in India moved from Calcutta to Delhi

Rhodesia divided into Northern and Southern Rhodesia

1912

Third Home Rule Bill passes

Foundation of South African Native National Congress

Establishment of Afrikaaner National Party by James Hertzog

Reunification of Presidency of Bengal

1913
South African Natives Land Act creates rural reserves for Africans
Women's campaign against pass laws, South Africa
South Africa restricts non-white immigration
Norfolk Island becomes an Australian dependency

1914
Irish Home Rule implementation delayed by outbreak of First World War
Unification of Northern and Southern Nigeria Protectorates; Lagos included
    as its capital
Egypt becomes a Protectorate
Cyprus becomes a colony when Turkey declares war on Britain
Occupation of Togoland and Cameroons
First African National Congress delegates arrive in London to protest Native
    Lands Act
British acquire responsibility for Johore (Malaya)

1915
Gilbert and Ellice Islands become a Crown Colony

1916
Easter Rising, Ireland
Lucknow Pact reunites Indian National Congress and Muslim League
Arab revolt against Ottoman empire
British occupation of Palestine (including Jerusalem) and Syria
Qatar enters treaties of protection with British
Secret Sykes-Picot Treaty between France and Britain
Empire Day established in Britain
Kamaran Islands (close to Aden) become part of British protectorate of Aden

1917
Indian indentured labour ended
Imperial War Conference and Cabinet established
Balfour Declaration commits Britain to a national Jewish homeland
Britain acquires Palestine from Turkey
Rioting in Quebec in response to conscription
Montagu Declaration promises eventual Indian self-governance
Claim to British Antarctic Territory defined
Newfoundland granted Dominion status

1918
Montagu-Chelmsford Report on Indian self-governance
Kingdom of Sikkim's autonomy (Tibet) returned under British protection
Foundation of National Congress of British West Africa by J. E. Casely
    Hayford

1919

Amritsar massacre, India

Rowlatt Acts, India, extend wartime restrictions on civil liberties into peace years

Anglo-Irish War (until 1921)

Government of India (Montagu-Chelmsford) Act permits partial self-government

Treaty of Versailles creates League of Nations and establishes mandate system

Britain acquires part of German Cameroon (incorporated into Niger Protectorate) and some of Togoland

German colony around Walvis Bay becomes part of South Africa mandate

Tanganyika (German East Africa) becomes a British mandate

British invasion in Afghanistan to quell unrest

Jamaican women win the vote

1920

East Africa Protectorate renamed Kenya and becomes a Crown Colony

National Congress of British West Africa

British mandate in Iraq, Transjordan and Palestine

Kikuyu Association founded in Kenya

Australia acquires Nauru (South Pacific) under League of Nations mandate

1921

Afghanistani independence won

Malta granted a legislature

Control of Palestine passes from Foreign Office to Colonial Office

Chamber of Princes established in India as a consultative body

1922

Founding of Irish Free State as a Dominion

Declaration of Egyptian independence (Britain retains control of Suez Canal)

Frederick Lugard's *The Dual Mandate* published, advocating indirect rule in Africa

Violence at Chauri Chaura leads Gandhi to suspend his non-co-operation campaign

Chanak crisis when Britain on verge of war with Turkey is refused aid by Dominion countries

Ascension Island brought under Colonial Office

League of Nations approves British mandate in Palestine and Egypt, French mandate in Syria and Lebanon

White Rhodesians reject merger with South Africa

Revolt in Iraq (from 1920) establishes a monarchy and a treaty of alliance with Britain

1923
Britain recognises rights of Dominions to freedom in treaty-making
Southern Rhodesia granted responsible self-government after opting not to join the South African Union
Devonshire White Paper declares Kenya "primarily an African territory"
Colonial Office acquires responsibility for Northern Rhodesia
Creation of Arab kingdom of Transjordan
Antarctic (Ross Dependency) placed under New Zealand jurisdiction
Chinese settlers excluded from Canada

1924
Crown rule replaces Company rule in Northern Zambesia
Northern Rhodesia becomes a Crown Colony
British South Africa Company surrenders its sovereign rights to the British government
St Lucia granted representative government

1925
Dominions Office separated from Colonial Office
Cyprus becomes a Crown Colony
South African Native National Congress changes its name to African National Congress

1926
Dominions now known as Commonwealth
Balfour Report defines dominion status as autonomous communities within the empire
African National Congress adopts tactics of passive resistance

1927
Simon Commission established to consider the political status of India
Federal Parliament of Australia moves from Melbourne to Canberra

1928
Donoughmore report proposes right to vote to be given to all men over 21 and all women over 30 in Ceylon

1929
Arab revolts against Jewish immigration to Palestine
Colonial Development Act

1930
Anglo-Iraqi Treaty
Gandhi's Salt March to Dandi
Wei Hai Wei returned to China

1931

Statute of Westminster granted Dominions full independence, dissolving the Colonial Laws Validity Act (1865)

Ceylon granted partial self-government

1932

Ottawa Conference establishes Imperial Preference tariff system for first time since 1846

Gandhi imprisoned and Indian National Congress banned

Formal independence of Iraq

1934

Treaty of Sana'a; Yemen becomes last territorial acquisition of British Empire

Newfoundland returned to colonial rule under a board of nominated commissioners

Establishment of Australian Antarctic Territory

1935

Government of India Act gives responsible self-government to Indian provinces and promises eventual self-government for India

1936

Anglo-Egyptian Treaty recognises Egyptian sovereignty

Arab rebellion in Palestine

1937

Irgun (Jewish Activist group) begins terrorist campaigns against Arabs in Palestine

Separate government for Burma created

Irish Free State becomes Eire

Aden becomes a British Crown Colony

Peel report proposes partition of Palestine into Jewish and Arab zones

1938

Moyne Commission proposes social, economic and governance reforms for Caribbean

Tristan da Cunha Islands become a dependency of St Helena

1939

Congress boycotts provincial governments after India forced into Second World War

1940

Colonial Development and Welfare Act

Jinnah's Lahore Resolution calling for creation of separate Muslim state of Pakistan

Change in definition of Commonwealth to permit republics to remain members
Italian occupation of British Somaliland
Dominica transferred from Leeward Islands Colony to Windward Islands Colony

1941

Atlantic Charter between US and UK
Invasion of Iran (with Soviets) to drive out Germans
Restoration of Ethiopian independence
Japanese occupation of Indochina
Britain occupies Iraq until 1947
New Zealand establishes a national health service
Restriction of Jewish immigration into Palestine

1942

Quit India movement
Occupation of Singapore, Hong Kong, Burma, Malaya, Sarawak, North Borneo, Andaman and Nicobar Islands, Solomon Islands and Gilbert and Ellice Islands by Japanese; bombing of Christmas and Cocos Islands

1943

Colonial Secretary's pledge that Britain would 'guide colonial people along the road to self-government within the British Empire'

1944

Universal suffrage introduced in Jamaica; formation of semi-responsible government headed by Alexander Bustamente
New constitutions in Trinidad and British Guiana

1945

Ceylon acquires responsible self-government
Colonial Development and Welfare Act
Singapore, Burma, Malaya, Hong Kong recovered
Anti-Slavery and Aborigines Protection Society changes its name to Anti-Slavery Society for the Protection of Human Rights

1946

UN Trusteeship Council acquires functions of League of Nations Mandate Commission
South Africa refuses to recognise UN jurisdiction in Namibia
Crown rule replaces Brooke dynasty in Sarawak
North Borneo becomes a Crown Colony
Transjordan gains independence
Irgun bombs the King David Hotel in Jerusalem

1947
Partition of India and Pakistan
Dominions Office renamed Commonwealth Relations Office
Palestine question referred by British to UN
Aung Sen and other politicians in Burma assassinated
Malta granted self-government
Nauru transferred to UN trusteeship
Nicobar and Andaman Islands passed to newly independent India

1948
Declaration of State of Israel; Britain withdraws from Palestine, surrendering
  mandate: first Arab-Israeli War
British Commonwealth becomes plain Commonwealth; abandonment of
  term 'Dominions'
Burma and Ceylon gain independence; Burma opts not to join Commonwealth
Creation of Federation of Malaya; state of emergency declared in Malaya
Assassination of Gandhi
Apartheid begins in South Africa when National Party comes to power
Gold Coast riots (starting in Accra and spreading)
British Nationality Act – first time UK citizenship defined
Maldives granted self-government

1949
British monarch appointed Head of the Commonwealth
Eire becomes a republic and leaves the Commonwealth
Newfoundland and Labrador become part of Canada
Nyasaland famine
Kwame Nkrumah founds Convention People's Party, Gold Coast
Papua and New Guinea united under Australian control
Transjordan changes its name to Jordan

1950
Colombo conference: plan to stimulate economic growth in India, Pakistan,
  Ceylon, Malaya and British North Borneo
India and Pakistan become republics within the Commonwealth
Virgin Islands granted representative government
Mau Mau banned in Kenya

1951
ANZUS Pact, Britain excluded

1952
King Farouk of Egypt deposed in a military coup by Gamal Abdel Nasser
State of emergency declared in Kenya as Mau Mau rebellion grows

1953
Federation of northern and southern Rhodesia and Nyasaland as Central African Federation

1954
Anglo-Egyptian agreement to withdraw British forces from Canal Zone
Algerian war of independence
Anti-colonial disturbances in Cyprus
Eastern, Western and Northern Nigeria federated as Nigeria

1955
Britain's last annexation: island of Rockall, north Atlantic
Cocos Islands placed under Australian sovereignty

1956
Suez crisis; establishment of Egypt as a republic
Morocco and Tunis become independent of France
Republic of Sudan proclaimed
French 'loi cadre' allows diverse development in colonies
Antigua leaves Leeward Islands Federation and becomes a Crown Colony
Eastern and Western Nigeria receive internal self-government

1957
Gold Coast becomes independent as Ghana, the first African colony to win independence
Malaya becomes independent
Defence White Paper proposes end of national service in Britain

1958
Coup in Iraq and establishment of an Islamic Republic
Empire Day becomes Commonwealth Day
British West Indies Federation formed
Antigua and Barbuda become an associated state of UK
Sovereignty over Christmas Island transferred from Singapore to Australia

1959
Declaration of state of emergency in Nyasaland
Federation of Arab Emirates of the South
Antarctic Treaty lays down regulations for activities in Antarctica
Cayman Islands become separate colony
Northern Nigeria given internal self-government

1960
Nigeria becomes independent
Cyprus gains independence

Belgium grants independence to Congo
British Somaliland gains independence
Sudan gains independence
UN General Assembly passes Resolution 1514: Declaration on the Granting
    of Independence to Colonial Countries and People
Lancaster House conference recommends majority rule for Kenya
State of emergency in Kenya lifted
Montserrat acquires partially elected executive and legislative councils

1961

Sierra Leone and Tanzania (Tanganyika until 1964) gain independence
South Africa withdraws from Commonwealth over objections about apart-
    heid from new member nations
India occupies and takes over Goa
Kuwait gains independence
Cameroons gain independence
Barbados and British Guiana granted internal self-government
Bechuanaland acquires an elected legislature and an executive council

1962

Western Samoa gains independence
Uganda gains independence
Trinidad and Tobago and Jamaica gain independence
First barriers to Commonwealth citizens entry to UK established
Britain declares a British Antarctic Territory
British West Indies Federation dissolved

1963

Kenya granted internal self-government in June; independence in December
Zanzibar granted internal self-government, and then full independence
Federation of Malaysia (Malaya, Sarawak, North Borneo [now called
    Sabah]) formed
Aden joins South Arabian Federation
Central African Federation dissolved
Nigeria becomes a republic

1964

Nyasaland (Malawi) and Northern Rhodesia (Zambia) become independent
Malta gains independence
Tanganyika unites with Zanzibar and becomes Tanzania
Bahamas and British Honduras granted internal self-government
Self-government introduced in Gibraltar
Kenya becomes a republic
Zanzibar Revolution overthrows Sultan of Zanzibar

1965

Southern Rhodesia's Unilateral Declaration of Independence

The Gambia gains independence

Cook Islands become independent

Singapore secedes from Federation of Malaysia as an independent republic

Chagos Islands placed under direct British administration as British Indian
    Ocean Territory

Anglo-French Pacific condominium over New Hebrides

Maldive Islands gain independence

Establishment of Commonwealth Secretariat

Aden emergency: British troops attacked by Egypt-backed Front for the
    Liberation of Occupied South Yemen

1966

Guyana (British Guiana) and Barbados become independent

Lesotho (formerly Basutoland) and Botswana (formerly Bechuanaland) gain
    independence

1967

British withdraw from Aden; collapse of South Arabian Federation; estab-
    lishment of Republic of South Yemen

Leeward Islands and Windward Islands gain internal self-government

Anguilla declares unilateral independence from Leeward Islands Federation

Virgin Islands confirmed as British colonial dependency

Kingdom of Buganda abolished

Gibraltar referendum overwhelmingly votes to stay British

Swaziland granted internal self-government

Biafra secedes from Nigeria

1968

Foreign and Commonwealth Office replaces old separate structures

Mauritius, Swaziland and Nauru gain independence

British troops begin withdrawing from Persian Gulf and Singapore

Bermuda gains internal self-government

Nauru gains independence

1969

Anguilla brought back under direct British administration as a dependency

Libya demands withdrawal of British troops

St Vincent acquires internal self-government

1970

Fiji and Tonga become independent

New Zealand High Commissioner installed as Governor of Pitcairn Island

Biafra rejoins Nigeria

1971
Bahrain and Qatar gain full independence
Arab Trucial States gain independence as United Arab Emirates
East Pakistan secedes to form Bangladesh

1972
Ceylon becomes Sri Lanka
Simla Agreement offering interim partition of Kashmir rejected by separatists
Cayman Islands become a British Dependent Territory

1973
Bahamas gain independence
Turks and Caicos Islands become a separate colony
British Honduras changes its name to Belize
Papua New Guinea granted self-government

1974
Grenada gains independence
Niue gains internal self-government
Coup in Cyprus leads to Turkish military presence in north

1975
Portuguese Africa gains independence: Angola, Guinea-Bissau and Mozambique
Indonesia occupies East Timor
Papua New Guinea gains full independence
Ellice Islands become independent as Tuvalu
Seychelles granted internal self-government

1976
British Indian Ocean Territory islands (except Chagos, retained by British)
    returned to Seychelles
Solomon Islands granted internal self-government

1978
Dominica gains independence
Solomon Islands gain full independence
Sierra Leone becomes a one-party state
Northern Territory (Australia) becomes self-governing
Seychelles gain full independence

1979
Lancaster House conference on Southern Rhodesia
Kiribati (Gilbert Islands) gains independence
St Lucia gains independence
St Vincent and the Grenadines gain full independence

1980

Vanuatu (New Hebrides) and Zimbabwe (Southern Rhodesia) become independent

Anguilla Act formalises Anguilla as a British dependency

1981

Antigua and Barbuda, and Belize, win independence

British Nationality Act: 14 remaining Crown Colonies renamed British Dependent Territories; British overseas citizens and citizens of British Dependent Territories denied right to live in Britain

1982

Argentinian invasion of Falkland Islands leads to Falklands War

Canada Act granting complete and independent sovereignty, opposed by Quebec

1983

Brunei becomes an independent state

St Kitts and Nevis gain independence

American invasion of Grenada

1984

Anglo-Chinese agreement to restore Hong Kong to China in 1997

Cocos Islanders vote for integration with Australia

1987

Meech Lake Accord attempts to pacify Quebec's opposition to Canadian Constitution; rejected by Newfoundland and Manitoba

1990

South-West Africa Protectorate and mandate become independent as Namibia

1992

Charlottetown Accord tries once more to unify Canadian opinion; rejected in a national referendum

1994

South Africa rejoins Commonwealth; abolition of apartheid

1995

Bermudans reject independence in a referendum

1997

Hong Kong returned to China

2009

Legal action begins in the High Court by Mau Mau survivors

2010

Litigation launched in the European Court of Human Rights by former inhabitants of the Chagos Islands

2013

British government agreed to pay £19.9 million in compensation for abuse to over 5,000 Mau Mau claimants

2015

Successful protests for the removal of the Cecil Rhodes statue at the University of Cape Town

2016

UK Referendum on leaving European Union narrowly votes to leave

2018

Second Kenya Emergency Group Litigation dismissed in court

Index

Aboriginals 48–51, 52, 55, 60, 99, 113, 124–5, 128, 129, 133, 142, 155, 157, 201, 237, 242, 245, 250
Acadia 25, 214, 215, 217, 219
Adams, Grantley 174
Aden 65, 88, 127, 177, 200, 232, 238, 239, 246, 249, 253, 254
Afghanistan 80, 94, 95, 166, 232, 233, 235, 239, 244, 245, 247
Africa x, 13, 15, 16, 17, 21, 24, 26, 31, 40, 45, 60, 63, 77, 83, 85, 86, 88, 91–3, 96, 98, 109, 110, 111, 113, 114, 115, 118, 125, 126, 127, 131, 132, 133, 135, 136, 140, 143, 146, 149, 151, 152, 158, 174, 176–7, 181, 185, 187–9, 191, 196, 197–8, 200, 203, 207, 217, 218, 224, 229, 230, 232, 234, 239, 243, 247, 248, 252, 255; east 23, 93, 96, 109, 114, 125, 126, 128, 133, 137, 177, 191, 195, 240, 241, 242, 244, 247; north 23, 27, 59, 83, 89, 90; south 58–9, 60, 85, 87, 92, 93, 97, 106–7, 108, 109, 123, 124, 125, 126, 127, 130, 131, 133, 145, 149, 153, 164, 166, 174, 176, 194–5, 196, 229, 230, 232, 233, 237, 242, 245, 246, 247, 248, 250, 251, 253, 256; west 13, 15, 16, 59, 91, 92, 129, 137, 153, 176, 187, 188, 215, 217, 221, 229, 243, 246, 247
Africanisation 131, 203, 206
African National Congress 176, 246, 248
agriculture 15, 17, 18, 24, 31–2, 34, 48, 51, 54, 55, 56, 58, 68, 71, 74, 80, 97, 126, 128, 132–3, 151, 152, 189
Ahmad, ibn Fumo Bakari 96

Algeria 199, 230, 252
America 4, 5, 6, 9, 10, 13–28, 31–41, 43, 45, 46, 48, 55, 57, 60, 64, 68, 69, 85, 87, 91, 102, 104, 113, 117–8, 127, 129, 140, 143, 150, 185, 196, 212, 215, 217, 218, 219, 220, 222, 223, 224, 233, 237 *see also* USA
American aid to Britain 186, 187, 189, 194, 196, 209
American Revolution 6, 24, 27, 32, 34, 45, 222
Ambedkar, B. R. 183
Amin, Idi 203
Andaman Islands 45, 64, 88, 122, 145, 225, 226, 235, 238, 250, 251
anti-colonialism *see* nationalism
Antigua 20, 215, 217, 238, 252, 256
Argentina 59, 89, 98, 208, 222
Arthur, George 49
Ashanti 88, 114, 242, 243
asiento 25, 213, 219
Attlee, Clement 196
Australia 9, 34, 43, 45–52, 53–5, 56, 60, 74, 83, 87, 97, 98, 108, 110, 113, 124–5, 126, 127, 128, 129, 130, 132, 135, 140, 145, 149, 155, 157, 158, 164, 165, 190, 194, 195, 197, 201, 202, 225, 227, 230, 231, 234, 235, 236, 237, 239, 241, 242, 243, 244, 245, 246, 247, 248, 249, 251, 252, 255, 256

Baartman, Sara 149
Baden-Powell, Agnes 112
Baden-Powell, Robert 104, 112
Bahamas 200, 215, 216, 219, 220, 224, 253, 255
Bahrain 89, 236, 239, 255
Baker, Herbert 124

Balfour Declaration 175, 199, 246
Banks, Joseph 15
Barbados 16, 20, 24, 87, 215, 217, 229, 230, 231, 253, 254
Bayly, Christopher 86, 164
Belgium 96, 187, 253
Belize *see* British Honduras
Bengal 37, 65, 66, 67, 68, 69, 70, 71, 77, 144, 215, 219, 221, 222, 225, 228, 230, 244, 245
Bentinck, William 72, 76, 147
Berlin Conference 96, 238, 239, 241
Bevin, Ernest 196, 198
Bismarck, Otto von 96
Blyden, Edward 176
Boer War *see* South African War
Bose, Subhas Chandra 173
Brazil 18, 89, 229, 234, 241
British Columbia 110, 235, 237
British Commonwealth 43, 168, 187, 190, 194, 195–6, 204, 243, 248, 250, 251, 252, 253, 254, 256
British Guiana 89, 176, 216, 228, 231, 250, 253, 254
British Honduras 89, 224, 236, 240, 253, 255
British Indian Ocean Territory i, 200–1, 254, 255, 257
Brockway, Fenner 180
Bronte, Charlotte 119
Brooke, James 86, 232, 233
Buganda 177, 241, 242, 243, 254
Burma 64, 71, 77, 83, 88, 126, 178, 179, 180, 181, 196, 230, 234, 236, 240, 249, 250, 251
Butler R. A. B. 203
Buxton, Thomas Fowell 60, 113

Canada 15, 23, 24, 31, 38, 40–1, 60, 74, 86, 87, 97, 99, 108, 110, 118, 124, 129, 130, 135, 145, 155, 165, 168, 174, 190, 195, 201, 214, 217, 222, 224, 225, 228, 229, 230, 231, 232, 233, 235, 236, 237, 238, 239, 243, 244, 245, 248, 251, 256
Canning Charles Lord 79
Cape Colony 58, 87, 92, 106, 123, 226, 231, 235, 237, 238, 240, 242, 245
Casement, Roger 166
Castle, Barbara 180
Central African Protectorate 93, 226, 241, 244, 245

Ceylon 57, 64, 71, 93, 126, 134, 166, 179, 190, 226, 228, 240, 248, 249, 250, 251, 255
Chagos Islands *see* British Indian Ocean Territory
Chamberlain, Joseph 97, 117
children 19, 20, 47, 79, 99, 102, 104, 109–10, 111, 112, 119, 125, 134, 140, 142–3, 144, 145, 149, 150, 151, 152, 155, 157, 182
China 55, 64–5, 66, 72, 74–6, 85, 144, 212, 221, 225, 231, 232, 235, 236, 243, 248, 256, 257
Churchill, Winston 173, 174
civilising mission 85, 104, 108, 191
class 9–10, 34, 53–4, 55, 68, 80, 88, 109, 110–11, 113–4, 116, 141, 143, 154, 170, 172, 174, 181, 183
Clive, Robert 66, 67, 68, 221, 222, 223
Cobden, Richard 179
Codrington, Christopher 21
Cold War 177, 180, 186–7, 188, 193
Colenso, J.W. 136
collaboration 9, 70, 109, 113–4, 123–4, 143
Colley, Linda 4
colonial development 97–9, 114–5, 126, 132, 188–9, 198, 206, 248, 249, 250
colonial exploration 1, 15, 43–5, 54, 92, 153–4, 212, 213, 214
colonial men 125–6, 140–1, 144–5, 146–8
commerce 4, 10, 26–7, 32–5, 40, 44–5, 55, 64–7, 75–6, 85, 89, 92, 104, 105, 129
Commonwealth *see* British Commonwealth
concubinage 145, 147, 150–1
Congo 188, 253
convicts 16, 45–8, 50, 64, 111, 140, 145–6, 234, 237; women 47–8, 145–6
Cook Islands 240, 243, 254
Cook, James 43–5, 55, 222, 223
Cornwallis, Charles Lord 6, 39, 68, 69, 224, 225
cotton 15, 24, 33, 90, 97, 98, 128, 189
Cromer, Evelyn Baring Lord 91, 164
Cromwell, Oliver 16, 216
Curzon, George Lord 127, 164
Cyprus 90, 191, 196, 197, 198, 199, 207, 238, 246, 248, 252, 255
Czechoslovakia 180

Dalhousie, James Lord 76, 77
Darien expedition 7, 218, 219
Darwin, Charles 22
decolonisation 112, 162, 181, 183, 185–209
Demerara 20, 227, 228, 229, 231
Denmark, abolition of slavery in 22, 227, 233
Dickens, Charles 119
disease 16–17, 31, 48–9, 109–10, 125, 127, 128, 131, 133–4, 147–8, 149–50
Disraeli, Benjamin 75, 90, 238
Dominica 27, 38, 200, 221, 222, 227, 238, 250, 255
Dominions *see* British Commonwealth
Durham, John Lord 86
Dyer, Reginald 171–2

East India Company 37, 57, 63–81, 108, 123, 134, 179, 213, 215, 216, 217, 218, 219, 222, 224, 226, 227, 228, 231, 232, 234, 235
Edison, Thomas Alva 151
education 2, 9, 70, 72, 99, 113, 118, 119, 122, 134–5, 155, 157, 177, 187, 198, 202
Egypt 77, 85, 89–91, 113, 128, 129, 151, 166, 179, 196, 199, 200, 226, 238, 246, 249, 252, 254; nationalism in 91, 164, 174, 193–4, 239, 244, 247, 251
Ethiopia 77, 93, 250
European Economic Union (European Union) i, 187
Eyre, Edward 95, 171

Falkland Islands xiii, 59, 207–8, 222, 223, 231, 245, 256
Fiji 88, 97, 130, 131, 132, 133, 200, 206, 238, 243, 255
First World War 80, 155, 162, 164–5, 170, 176, 178, 185, 190, 191, 197, 198, 199, 246
Flinders, Matthew 54
France 2, 4, 5–6, 27, 38–40, 41, 59, 96, 97, 112, 165, 174, 187–8, 215, 219, 220, 222, 223, 229, 230, 233, 245, 252; alliances with 93, 193–4, 217, 244, 246
Freud, Sigmund 142

Gallagher, John 84–5
Gambia, The 91, 213, 224, 229, 233, 240, 241, 242, 254

Gandhi, Mohandas 171, 172, 183, 244, 247, 248, 249, 251
Garvey, Marcus 176
Gaulle, Charles de 187
gender 111–2, 140–59, 204; and work 126, 127, 151–3
Germany 34, 93, 96, 97, 162, 166, 185, 191, 241, 243
Gibraltar 25, 27, 39, 59, 219, 253, 254
gold 55, 56, 58, 87, 92, 97, 106, 108, 124, 126, 127, 130, 131, 164, 234, 236, 237, 240
Gold Coast 13, 91, 117, 177, 188, 196, 214, 229, 230, 233, 234, 238, 241, 242, 251, 252; Ghana 188, 193, 243, 252
Gordon, General Charles George 93, 240
government: colonial 35, 41, 45, 52, 57–8, 60, 63–4, 68–9, 72, 76–7, 79, 85–6, 88, 92, 109, 123, 125; representative self-government 35, 41, 86, 235, 237, 249, 252, 253, 254, 255; responsible self-government 40, 43, 52–3, 58, 86–8, 123, 166, 171, 235, 238, 241, 245, 247, 248, 249, 250, 251
Grant, Charles 60
Greece 59, 90, 236
Grenada 20, 27, 39, 221, 222, 223, 224, 235, 240, 255, 256
Griffin, Lepel 103
Griqualand West 92, 237
Gun, Ma 127

Hailey, Malcolm Lord 198
Haiti *see* St Domingue
Hastings, Warren 68–9, 74, 224, 225, 226
Hawkins, John 21
Hemming, Augustus 117
Hobson, J. A. 179
Holland 34, 45, 57–8, 64, 96, 214, 216, 217, 218, 219, 222, 226, 227, 228, 230, 236, 238, 241
Hong Kong 74–6, 83, 85, 88, 93, 97, 114, 115, 129, 133, 151, 179, 232, 233, 236, 243, 250, 256, 257
Hungary 180

indentured labour 10, 15–16, 19, 31, 34, 53, 54, 55, 58, 71, 106, 108, 110, 130–1, 133, 140, 145, 153, 206, 231, 232, 233, 234, 246

India ix, x, 5, 11, 24, 27, 37, 55, 57, 58, 63–81, 83, 85, 88, 89, 90, 92, 93, 95, 97, 98, 102, 104, 105, 108, 109, 110, 111–12, 113–4, 115, 116, 118, 123, 124, 125, 127, 128, 129, 130, 131, 132, 133, 134–5, 137, 140, 141, 143, 144, 145, 147, 150, 151, 152, 155–7, 158, 164, 165, 166, 169–73, 178, 179, 180, 182, 183, 188, 190, 191, 192, 196, 197, 198, 199, 204, 207, 213, 214, 216, 221, 222, 223, 224, 226, 227, 228, 229, 230, 231, 232, 233, 234, 235, 236, 238, 239, 240, 241, 243, 244, 245, 246, 247, 248, 249, 250, 251, 253; All-India Muslim League 170; Indian National Army 173; Indian National Congress 170, 171, 172–3, 181, 191, 240, 246, 249; partition of 157, 173, 191, 192, 199, 206, 251
indirect rule 93, 113, 123, 247
Indochina 199, 250
informal empire 85, 89
internal colonialism 1–11
Ionian Islands 27, 59, 227, 228, 236
Iran 192–3, 200, 228, 250
Iraq 166, 175, 191, 193, 196, 199–200, 206, 247, 248, 249, 250, 252
Ireland x, xiv, 1–11, 25, 28, 34, 37, 53, 88, 115, 127, 165, 168, 173, 179–80, 185, 196, 201, 202, 206, 219, 220, 226, 237, 240; Easter Rising 165–6, 173, 246; famine, 53, 88, 233
Irish Free State 168, 173, 247, 249
Israel 191, 193, 199, 206, 251
Italy 97, 162, 244

Jamaica 17, 18, 20, 23, 95, 102, 123, 124, 135, 136, 171, 205, 212, 216, 217, 218, 220, 221, 222, 226, 230, 231, 236, 237, 247, 250, 253
Japan 173, 178–9, 236, 242, 250; invasion of British colonies 179, 188, 190, 191, 250
Jardine, William 75
Java 57, 64, 66, 228
Jefferson, Thomas 19
Jordan 193, 200, 247, 248, 250, 251

Kaffraria 92, 233, 237
Kashmir 79, 191, 206, 255
Kenya 109, 110, 126, 128, 129, 130, 131, 164, 174, 176–7, 177, 189, 194, 196, 199, 203, 206, 242, 244, 247, 248, 253, 257; emergency 115, 180, 207, 251, 253; Mau Mau i, 158, 207, 251, 257
Kenyatta, Jomo 174
Kidd, Colin 2
Kingsley, Charles 153
Kingsley, Mary 153
Kipling, Rudyard 144
Knox John 3
Knox, Robert 9
Krivine, J.D. 190
Kruger, Paul 164
Kuwait 89, 200, 243, 253

Lagos 91, 198, 234, 236, 246
landscape, effect of colonialism on 56–7, 124, 128, 132–3
language 3, 9, 21, 50, 63, 69–70, 72, 102, 134–5, 136
Lawson, Philip 72
League of Nations 162, 191, 199, 247, 250
Lebanon 191, 247
Lennox-Boyd, Alan 198
Lessing, Doris 173
Lewin, Jane 53
Linnaeus, Carl 149
Livingstone, David 92, 234
Long, Edward 149
Lugard, Frederick 93, 113, 247
Lutyens, Edwin 124

Macaulay, Thomas 72, 113
MacCarthy, Charles 135
Macnamara, T. J. 154
Madras 65, 69, 80, 158, 215, 220, 224, 228
Malay area 57, 64, 83, 88, 93, 114, 123, 140, 164, 178, 198, 200, 213, 224, 226, 230, 238, 242, 245
Malaya 98, 125, 128, 131, 188, 194, 195, 196, 199, 207, 246, 250, 251, 252
Malaysia x, 181, 206, 207, 253, 254
Malta 59, 64, 190, 226, 228, 247, 251, 253
Malvinas *see* Falkland Islands
Mamdani, Mahmood 202
Mansfield, W. R. 116
Māori 55–6, 94, 123, 124, 236
Maroons 17, 220, 226

marriage 7, 8, 48, 51, 52, 71, 72–3, 108, 111, 119, 122, 131, 141, 142–3, 144, 145, 147, 150–1, 157, 182, 204, 220
martial races 80, 146
Mauritius 23, 45, 57, 64, 66, 88, 97, 130, 131, 200, 225, 228, 254
medicine 111, 115, 133–4, 141, 205
Melanesia 55
Melbourne, William Lamb Lord 123
mercantilism 4, 25–7, 28, 33, 34, 36, 38, 64, 71, 115
Mercer, W. H. 88
Milner, Alfred 104, 106, 131, 164
migration 10, 16, 32–3, 108–9, 113, 124, 128, 130, 174, 175, 199, 206, 248; African 15–17, 20, 31, 34, 174, 199, 201; female 53, 145–6, 236; hostile environment policy 204–5; Irish 2, 9, 10, 34, 88; restrictions on 130, 201–5, 243, 246, 250; sponsored 53, 58–9, 231, 232; to America 9, 31, 32–3, 34; to Australia 45–6, 53–4, 67, 145, 197, 231; white 16, 31, 33, 41, 58–9, 118, 201, 206
Mir Jafar, Syed 66, 221
missionaries 21, 56, 71, 73, 76, 99, 109, 110, 117–9, 134, 135–6, 137, 143, 154–5, 158, 171, 225, 226, 228
Montagu, Edwin 171
Montagu, Mary Wortley 159
Montesquieu, Charles, Baron de 21
Mountbatten, Louis Lord 192
Muscat and Oman 89
Muslim League 170, 244, 246

Naidu, Sarojini 181
Naoroji, Dadabhai 153, 237, 241
Nasser, Gamal Abdel 193, 251
Natal 58, 136, 176, 230, 233, 235, 241, 242, 244, 245
nationalism xiv, 9, 131, 162–83, 186, 207; anti-colonial ix, 80, 111, 123, 128, 131, 162–83, 185, 186, 188, 190, 194–5, 199, 200, 201, 207; women and 181–2
native Americans 31–3, 35, 40, 104, 113, 218
Nehru, Jawaharlal ix
Newfoundland 31, 212, 213, 214, 219, 220, 227, 231, 235, 237, 245, 246, 249, 251, 256
New Guinea 96, 155, 159, 239, 240, 241, 244, 251, 255

New Holland *see* Australia
New South Wales 46, 47, 48, 52, 53, 55, 56, 127, 225, 226, 227, 229, 232, 233, 234, 235
New Zealand 43, 53, 54, 55–6, 60, 83, 87, 94, 97, 98, 99, 110, 123, 124, 129, 130, 140, 158, 165, 194, 202, 222, 223, 228, 230, 231, 232, 233, 234, 235, 236, 237, 238, 239, 242, 243, 244, 245, 248, 250, 255
Ngidi, William 136
Niger Districts Protectorate 93, 241
Nigeria 176, 177, 193, 204, 206, 243, 246, 252, 253, 254, 255
Nkrumah, Kwame 188, 251
North Borneo 88, 92, 238, 239, 240, 241, 244, 250, 251, 253
North, Frederick Lord 39, 68
Northern Territory 155, 255
Northern Zambesia 93, 241, 248
Nova Scotia 25, 40, 87, 214, 215, 216, 217, 219, 222, 233

O'Dwyer, Reginald 171
Opium Wars 64–5, 74–6, 232, 235
Orange River 58, 106, 231, 233, 237
Orwell, George 179
Ottoman Empire 74, 89–90, 95, 159, 174, 185, 191, 197, 232, 238, 246

Pakistan 79, 95, 173, 191, 192, 196, 204, 206, 249, 251, 255
Palestine 158, 174–5, 190–1, 199, 246, 247, 248, 249, 250, 251
Pan-African Congresses 177
Papua New Guinea *see* New Guinea
Parnell, Anna 181
pass laws 17, 125, 131, 246
penal colonies 45–8, 64, 111, 130, 224, 225, 226, 228, 230, 235
Penang 45, 57, 224, 226, 227, 230, 231
Perak 114, 115, 242; Perak War 93, 114
Perham, Margery 146
Permanent Settlement 68, 77, 225
petroleum oil 89, 91, 97, 192–3, 199, 200, 245
Phalke, D. G. 170
Philippines 98, 186, 222
Pitt, William 3, 69, 224
Plassey, Battle of 66, 67, 221
police, colonial 96, 115
Porter, Bernard ix
Portugal 1, 18, 64, 89, 93, 185, 214, 229, 241, 243, 255

Powell, Enoch 204
Prince Edward Island 27, 87, 222, 234, 236, 238
prostitution 125, 142, 152; military 147–8
Punjab 76, 77, 234
Purim 88

Quebec 27, 28, 38, 41, 44, 215, 221, 222, 223, 225, 237, 246, 256
Queensland 51, 52, 55, 96, 130, 131, 230, 232, 235, 239, 240

race and labour 15–16, 55, 125–6
racial difference 16, 88, 99, 110, 111–3, 156–7
racial mixing 155–7
racial segregation 108, 110, 116, 124–5, 129
Raffles, Thomas Stamford 57, 228, 229
railways 76, 80, 89, 98, 114, 126, 128, 130, 231, 234, 238, 240, 243
religion 2–4, 33, 73, 117–9, 127, 135–6; Catholicism 2–4, 5, 8, 28, 33, 34, 38, 40–1, 168, 215, 219, 220, 223
resistance to colonialism 36–40, 92–5, 162–83, 185, 188–9, 190–1, 192–5, 198–201
Rhodes, Cecil 104, 106, 108, 164, 240, 257
Rhodesia 108, 109, 110, 177, 242, 245; Northern 108, 177, 188, 241, 242, 243, 245, 248, 252, 253; Southern 108, 129, 152, 155, 189, 194–5, 196, 243, 245, 248, 252, 254, 256
Robinson, George 49–50
Robinson, Ronald 84–5
Roy, Ram Mohan 72
Russia 80, 90, 95, 174, 228, 232, 240, 244, 245 *see also* USSR
Rye, Maria 53

St Domingue 18, 23, 185, 225, 227
St Vincent 27, 39, 221, 222, 223, 224, 235, 254, 256
Samoa 146, 241, 243, 253
Samoei, Koitalel 177
Sarawak 86, 93, 125, 232, 233, 240, 250, 254
science, colonial 43–4, 112, 113, 115
Scotland xiv, 1–11, 34, 128, 218, 219, 231; Jacobite rebellions 5, 7
Scott, Michael G. 180

Second World War x, 174, 179, 185, 186, 188, 189, 201, 208, 249
Seeley, John 83
Seligman, C. G. 136
settler colonialism 31–5, 40–1, 46–7, 51–5, 58–9, 60, 65, 69, 86–7, 97, 98–9, 104, 108, 109, 110–1, 117–8, 123, 125, 128, 129, 130, 134, 140, 141, 145, 154, 158, 165–8, 172, 174–5, 177, 181, 189, 194, 196–7, 201, 204, 215, 216, 227, 231, 232, 243, 244
Seven Years' War 4, 27, 34, 35, 36, 38, 221, 222
sex 20, 125–6, 140–59; age of consent 144, 150, 182; homosexuality, fears of 147; sexual primitivism 142–4, 148–9; sex ratios 33, 48, 53, 71, 109, 131, 140, 145, 159; vulnerability of women 20, 131, 141, 155–8
Seychelles 64, 88, 225, 228, 244, 255
Shah Alam 67
Shanghai 115, 236
Shaw, George Bernard 179
Siam *see* Thailand
Sierra Leone 24, 40, 59, 91, 135, 177, 225, 227, 229, 236, 242, 253, 255
Singapore 45, 57, 64, 85, 88, 97, 113, 115, 124, 152, 178, 179, 198, 229, 230, 231, 241, 244, 250, 252, 254
slavery 13–28, 38, 57, 87, 91, 108, 125, 130, 227, 233; abolition of 21–4, 40, 51, 60, 71, 91, 123, 124, 130, 135, 154, 225, 227, 228, 229, 231, 232, 233, 235, 236, 238, 240, 241; anti-slavery 21–3, 28, 59, 91, 118, 130, 225, 229, 238, 245, 250; characteristics of Atlantic 13–15; profit from 24–5; revolts against 17, 18, 20–1, 23, 108; ships 16–17, 25, 26
Smith, Adam 21, 28
Smith, Ian 194
Smuts, Jan 166
Socorro 88
Somaliland 92, 166, 177, 239, 241, 243, 244, 250, 253
Somersett, James 22
South African War 77, 164, 243, 244
South Australia 48, 52, 54, 127, 231, 234, 235, 236, 242
Spain 1, 2, 5, 7, 18, 25, 27, 39, 40, 59, 185, 213, 216, 217, 219, 220, 223, 224, 225, 238, 240

Speke, John H. 92, 235
Stanbrook, Ivor 204
Stanley, Henry Morton 119
Steckel, Richard 20
Strachey, John 108
Straits Settlements 57, 93, 113, 125, 183, 230, 231, 237
Sudan 90, 92, 93, 118, 206, 239, 240, 242, 243, 252, 253
Suez Canal 90, 95, 97, 174, 175, 193, 198, 237, 238, 247
Suez crisis 193–4, 195, 199, 200, 252
sugar 15, 18–19, 20, 23, 24–5, 33, 35, 36–7, 40, 55, 64, 87, 97, 115, 128, 130, 132, 220, 222, 245
Sumatra 57, 66, 218, 238
superiority, British sense of xiv, 76, 104–8, 112–3, 141, 143
Swan River Colony *see* Western Australia
Switzerland 34
Syria 90, 175, 191, 246, 247

Tahiti 45, 222, 226, 230, 232
Tanganyika 93, 247, 253
Tasmania 46, 47, 48, 49, 50, 52, 54, 227, 230, 231, 234, 235
taxation 35, 36–7, 65, 68, 71, 76–7, 80, 128, 131, 132, 170, 177, 242
tea 37–8, 66, 71, 74, 76, 97, 151, 223; Boston Tea Party 37, 223
technology 95, 97–8, 114–5, 186, 189
terra nullius 51, 129
Thailand 57, 89, 230, 242, 245
Thakombau 88
Thatcher, Margaret xiii, 204, 208
Thuku, Harry 174
Tobago 20, 27, 212, 221, 222, 224, 225, 226, 227, 228, 241, 253
Tone, Wolfe 2, 6
trade 4–6, 7, 10, 13–28, 32–3, 35–7, 38–9, 40, 41, 57, 63–4, 65–6, 69, 71–2, 74–6, 80, 85, 87, 89–90, 93, 96–8, 129, 187, 214, 215, 216, 218, 219, 220, 221, 228, 231, 232, 236; free trade 23, 25, 28, 40, 64, 71–2, 73, 75, 84, 89, 90, 97, 179, 187
transportation 16, 45–8, 50, 54, 64, 130, 132, 220, 232, 234, 237
Transvaal 58, 92, 106, 130, 131, 164, 232, 234, 237, 238, 239, 241, 242, 243, 244, 245
treaty ports 86, 115, 118, 232

Trinidad 20, 24, 115, 226, 227, 228, 241, 250, 253
Turkey 74, 96, 166, 173, 193, 200, 238, 246, 247, 255
Turks and Caicos Islands 218, 222, 255

ud-Daulah, Siraj 66, 221
Uganda 92, 128, 131, 188, 202, 203, 206, 235, 242, 243, 244, 253
United Nations 188, 192, 194, 195, 199, 201, 204
United Soviet Socialist Republics (USSR) 180, 186–7, 188, 192, 193, 194, 196, 198, 199, 250
United States of America (USA) xii, 20, 22, 40, 87, 89, 96, 97, 109, 168, 176, 177, 186, 187, 190, 192, 193–4, 200–1, 202

Van Diemen's Land *see* Tasmania
Victoria (Australia) 51, 52, 231, 234, 235, 237
Vidyasagar, Ishwar Chandra 72
violence xi, xiv, 20–1, 27, 35, 49, 77–9, 93, 112, 126–7, 130, 140, 143, 157–8, 170, 176–7, 190–1, 194–5, 196–7, 199–200, 203, 206, 207, 247; Arab-Jewish 175, 199, 205; communal 127, 172–3, 183, 192, 206; towards Native Americans 33, 35
voting rights 3, 10, 48, 56, 122–3, 158, 174, 179, 236, 239, 242, 247, 248, 250

Wakefield, Edward Gibbon 54, 55, 230
Wales 1–11
Wallis, Samuel 45
Ward, J. Langfield 51
Wedgwood, Josiah 22
Western Australia 48, 54, 87, 230, 234, 237, 241
Wesley, John 118
West Indies x, 13, 15–16, 17, 18–19, 20, 23, 24–5, 27, 33, 35, 36, 38, 40, 60, 110, 113, 115, 118, 127, 130, 131, 133, 135, 150, 151, 174, 191, 195, 200, 214, 215, 216, 217, 218, 242, 252, 253
Wilberforce, William 21
Wilde, Oscar 147
Williams, Eric 36
Wilson, Harold 194–5
Woolf, Leonard 179

women: activism among 22, 153, 158–9, 181–2; and reproduction 19–20, 47–8, 149, 154, 181; and work 125–6, 151–3; British 71, 144–5, 145, 152, 155–7; circumcision of 143, 159; defining civilisation 145–6; female infanticide 143, 144; in slavery, 19–20; unsuitability for empire 140–1, 146

Yemen 200, 249, 254

Zanzibar 93, 232, 238, 241, 253
Zimbabwe 108, 195, 206, 256